Doomsday Has Been Cancelled

Doomsday

THE FUTURE
Earth-life reaches ever out,
sundark streaming by,
as consciousness dawns.

Has Been Cancelled

J. Peter Vajk

PEACE PRESS
1978

Peace Press
3828 Willat Avenue
Culver City, California 90230

Printed in the United States of America
by Peace Press.

Library of Congress Cataloging in Publication Data

Vajk, J   Peter, 1942-
  Doomsday has been cancelled.

  Includes bibliographical references and index.
  Twenty-first century—Forecasts. 2. Technology
and civilization. 3. Civilization, Modern—1050-
I. Title.
CB161.V35   909.83   78-62300
ISBN 0-915238-24-1

9 8 7 6 5 4 3 2

To Helen, my companion on the journey
through the now into the future,
for our children who will play
in the worlds we build.

CREDITS

COVER: Painting by Don Davis, the Earth viewed from geosyncronous orbit in about 2025 A.D. The enormous Solar Power Satellites in the foreground beam clean, inexpensive energy to all parts of the planet, lighting up cities and industries throughout the formerly underdeveloped countries. Skilled hard hat workers in the foreground carry out routine maintenance work on the Solar Power Satellites, communication satellites, and other industrial installations in space.

ILLUSTRATIONS: The Frontispiece is a painted Egyptian clay figure from the Nagadah I culture, mid-fourth millennium B.C. The chapter opening inset is from a design for a 17th century English "knot" or pattern garden. Both are courtesy of the California Academy of Sciences. The photographs on pages 170 and 178 are by Bob Fitch. The photographs on pages 48, 172, 188 and 208 are by Art Rogers from Point Reyes Nation — A Family Album. The California Academy of Sciences provided the illustrations on pages 40 and 224. The remaining illustrations are from the National Aeronautics and Space Administration of the U.S. Government.

Book design by Robert P.J. Cooney

Table of Contents

Foreword

On a bright Sunday morning in 1977, R. Buckminster Fuller and I shared the guest spots on a TV talk show in Boston, Massachusetts. Though I can't recall the details of our conversation, I remember him poking fun at me, an astronaut, for being a terrestrial chauvinist because I used terms such as up and down in describing my experiences in spaceflight. For Bucky, with his cosmic orientation, the terms in and out are more appropriate to our true responsibility, the universe.

During a break in the show, Bucky scratched a poem for me on a scrap of paper I had with me. I have it still . . .

> Environment to each must be
>   "All that is, excepting me."
> Universe in turn must be
>   "All that is including me."
> The only difference between environment
>   and universe is me . . .
> The observer, doer, thinker, lover, enjoyer.

I have reflected many times on this poem and its grand implications. It enlarges the scale of what I had learned on my flight on Apollo 9, i.e., what I thought was my environment is too small. And to the extent that one accepts responsibility for one's effects on the environment, Bucky's poem calls for the same "infinite responsibility" acknowledged by the Zen Buddhist. To be aware is to be responsible.

In this universe it is I, you, we, in whom this awareness resides. Observing, doing, thinking, loving and enjoying, we are the consciousness of the universe. Who we are we do not fully understand, but we sense that we are more than merely a simple collection of individuals.

But where are we going? Where is the evolution of consciousness leading us as our awareness of the universe and ourselves enlarges? Are we acting out some inexorable apocalyptic logic shaped by the structure of nature, leading to doom and extinction? Or is there a future of diverse and humane possibilities which we create by shaping our attitudes, our tools, and our actions in affirmative directions?

Doomsday Has Been Cancelled

Peter Vajk argues strongly for this latter view. Doomsday is a cliché whose purveyors have spread a gospel of despair based upon acceptance of all problems and rejection of all solutions. This is not only a terribly selective view of life, but one in which there is no room for hope, imagination, creativity, or expanded awareness. It's as if one inherited a beautiful garden and then devoted one's full attention to pulling the weeds and casting out the bugs only to be left with a plot of stunted and wilted vegetables. The reversal of this negative mindset is what Mr. Vajk proposes in this book; a world in which the creative energies of humanity are focused on the flowers and vegetables, not the weeds and bugs.

In 1975, Peter Vajk analyzed the M.I.T. "world dynamics" computer models developed in conjunction with the Club of Rome's *Limits to Growth* report. Not surprisingly, he found that the emerging scenarios depended strongly on both the input assumptions and conditions and on the absence of future innovation and creativity. To dramatize the significance of these factors, Mr. Vajk explored the influence on the various scenarios of the concepts of space colonization and the availability of extraterrestrial resources (concepts developed and popularized by Dr. Gerard K. O'Neill of Princeton University). Instead of choking on pollution and running out of food and other resources in the early 21st Century, the new results showed a continuing rise in the global quality of life and a decrease in environmental degradation. The key to a positive future for humanity is the recognition that the world is not trapped in a gigantic zero-sum game. At least we have the option now to open the physical system we have been nurtured in and admit larger possibilities for the future than have ever been possible in the past.

How? By accepting our responsibility to emerge from the womb of earth into the larger and seemingly hostile environment of the universe. At least that part of the universe which is our neighborhood, the solar system.

And is this idle romance? Escapism? Cowboy mentality? Hardly! Communication, weather and environmental monitoring satellites have already changed our relationships to one another and to the earth, in profound and irreversible ways. We riders on the earth together, to paraphrase Archibald MacLeish, know now that we are truly brothers and sisters. We know also, from countless clear images from space, that we and the planet on which we live are one interdependent life system, sensitive to misunderstanding and abuse.

And in the future? Surely a vision through a glass darkly. Even with the limited vision of a cosmic infant, we can see possibilities of preserving the unique environment of our home planet by removing some of our more toxic wastes, and waste-producing activities from the terrestrial biosphere while gaining access to the continuous and virtually limitless flow of solar energy streaming past the earth. The panoply of extraterrestrial resources is not limited to non-substances such as solar radiation, pure vacuum and

Foreword

weightlessness, but also includes the whole gamut of mineral resources of which the moon, the asteroids and other extraterrestrial bodies are composed. Today we gouge these same resources from the earth and mold them into countless products to meet the necessities and desires of humanity. But the physical and psychic price of this earthbound activity continues to rise as the concept of equal rights to material goods and increasing population clash with finite resource stocks and a growing desire to maintain a life-enhancing environment.

The choice, then, is to open the future to new and exciting possibilities for human development or to reject the cosmic invitation and suffer the increasing agonies of the zero-sum game. As Peter Vajk argues so well in this book, the quality of our thoughts and actions in choosing and creating our future will determine the course of evolution, as life begins to emerge from the comfortable environment of earth into the uncertain but beckoning environment of the universe.

RUSSELL L. SCHWEICKART
Astronaut

Preface

During the 1960s and the 1970s, it has been very fashionable among intellectual circles to proclaim the imminent end of civilization as we know it. A variety of popular books bearing such ominous titles as *Silent Spring*, *The Population Bomb*, *The Limits to Growth*, *Famine 1975*, and *The Coming Dark Age* have portrayed a dismal future of dwindling energy and mineral resources, ever-wider starvation, accelerating environmental degradation, and more stringent social controls, while rivalries between nations become more strident, with more and more countries armed with nuclear weapons.

Such scenarios make great headlines, but little fanfare greets the good news which can also be found in abundance, if we listen to softer voices and read deeper than the headlines. Western society has been immersed in a prevailing mood of despair and futility, and it has been very easy to believe the voices of the headlines proclaiming that we are all doomed, perhaps even in the short run.

I must confess that I used to have a blind and naive technological optimism. It seemed clear to me that, although the problems plastered across the headlines were probably real enough, we would find appropriate means to cope with these difficulties, and we would continue to keep at least our heads above water. But it was far more comfortable not to think about these matters very much, keeping my head in the sand in the secure posture of the frightened ostrich.

During the winter of 1973-74, as we waited in long queues for gasoline for our automobiles, because of the OPEC boycott on petroleum exports to the United States and Europe, the voices of the doomsday prophets sounded more convincing. Perhaps civilization had indeed peaked; as petroleum and other resources became progressively depleted, we might find ourselves sliding down into the caves once more. My confidence was shaken.

In September of that year everything turned upside down once more in the space of one week, when I read three magazines: the September 1974 issue of *Scientific American*; the fiftieth anniversary issue of *Saturday Review* (August 24, 1974); and the September 1974 issue of the professional journal *Physics Today*. The *Scientific American* issue was devoted to population growth and related issues, while the *Saturday Review* issue attempted to envision life in the year 2024.

The vision of the future portrayed in these two magazines was bleak and forbidding; the world of 2024 seemed horribly grim, rigid, and joyless. Scarcity would have become the rule rather than the exception. Society would very likely be severely regimented or, at best, highly over-regulated. These articles left little hope that the later years of my life would be to my liking, and the prospects for my children seemed worse still.

But the third magazine I read that week contained a revolutionary article by Dr. Gerard K. O'Neill, a physics professor at Princeton University. From my own graduate school career in the physics department at Princeton, I knew that O'Neill was sensible and respectable, so I could accept his ideas at face value. In that article, O'Neill sketched out a radically different future for humanity. We are not constrained, O'Neill argued, to the surface of the planet Earth. If we choose to do so, we have the technological know-how to build Earth-like habitats in space *before the year 2000*. With virtually unlimited solar energy available in space, we eventually could build countless new settlements in space, with the total land area ultimately available *many thousands of times* greater than the total surface area of the entire planet Earth.*

In O'Neill's vision of the future, the privately owned house with its own garden need not vanish from human memory; symphony orchestras, opera companies, and cinema theaters need not be shut down due to shortages of energy and materials; travel by airplane need not be restricted to emergency or official uses only; and it would be possible for me and my family to choose whatever lifestyles we preferred, without having to fend off a starving world determined to enforce other standards.

My earlier confidence about the future was restored. Armed with this radically optimistic vision of the future, I began to read more and more about the difficulties and problems underlying the prophecies of doom. Reading much of the doomsday literature, carefully for the first time, I was horrified to discover how very reasonable and persuasive these gloomy visions would seem, if the reader overlooked the tacit assumption in all of them that the future of humanity is necessarily restricted to this tiny speck in the cosmos which we call Earth.

Further reading and searching has brought me, gradually, to yet greater optimism about the future: it seems to me that we are in the midst of a transformation, a major evolutionary step, a quantum leap into the new possibilities and opportunities. Even without new lands in space, we have far more reason for hope than for despair. From a purely materialistic point of view, the climb into space is not a prerequisite for the kind of open-ended future I desire for myself and my family. Humanity and industrialized

*The story of how O'Neill came to his advocacy of a major drive into space is described in his book *The High Frontier: Human Colonies in Space*, (New York: William Morrow, 1977).

Preface

civilization can indeed survive without space colonization, indefinitely far into the future. The human habitation of space responds to certain, deep drives and needs within ourselves, and is so complementary to other elements of the transformation underway that it would be injurious to our spirit to shrink away from the challenge.

My optimism about the future comes from several considerations besides the possibilities of space. Working with the ideas of space colonization and its implications for the socioeconomic system, I soon realized that I was becoming involved in something far more profound than advocating a specific space program: I was involved in nothing less than the *conscious and deliberate creation of the future*. More and more it became clear to me that the creation of the future is in the hands of those who can clearly identify their own values, conceive goals which embody those values, and devote their best efforts toward achieving those goals. Part of the transformation in which we are presently engaged involves a growing number of individuals seeking to identify and elaborate their own values and goals; I find this to be a source of optimism.

Reexamining the doomsday authors, I saw again and again how the underlying assumptions, especially those unstated or hidden, even from the authors themselves, determined the conclusions they reached. On a deeper level, the idea slowly dawned on me that the gap between the technological optimists and the neo-Malthusians seldom lay in disagreements about the facts themselves, but rather in their unspoken assumptions about reality itself and their own values. Because of profound differences in metaphysical (even religious) viewpoints, proponents of either position differ on which facts are relevant to any given issue.

This book is a journey of exploration to discover some of the barely visible quantum leaps all around us, many of them unheralded by the news media. A multitude of new options is emerging, brought about through new human capabilities, or through the more effective development of human potentialities as latent and marvelous as are the butterfly's wings in the awkward caterpillar. *We have abundant cause for hope, in ever-multiplying directions, most of it little-noticed, but nonetheless, vibrant and dynamic.*

The facts alone, as I suggested above, are insufficient: the hidden assumptions which limit our worldview must be laid bare and examined carefully. I believe a pattern will emerge from this journey of exploration, forming the metaphysical foundations for an ever more humane and positive future of widening options, a manifestation of modern hope for humanity as it is transformed into a solar species.

The cumulative effect of these new discoveries, new perspectives, and new options go beyond postponing doomsday: doomsday has in fact already been cancelled.

Archimedes, in his study of simple machines such as levers and pulleys, said more than twenty-two centuries ago, "Give me a place to stand and I will move the Earth." Today, the torrent of ideas about space industrialization and space colonization, triggered by O'Neill's article four years ago, provides a new perspective for thinking about the future. This book represents an attempt to consider the future prospects for humanity and civilization from the vantage point of the post-terrestrial society. This new perspective, by changing the ways in which we think about the world and about the future, will indeed move the Earth and the heavens, too.

For centuries, the future has had a recognizable, but sometimes unconscious constituency. The overwhelming majority of those who had been concerned with the shape of times to come have been parents. Others similarly concerned have included religious visionaries and speculative philosophers. Now the constituency for the future is awakening, it is becoming aware of itself and beginning to articulate its concerns. *In the present age, we are all becoming parents to the infant human race, on the verge of climbing out of its planetary crib and standing up in the cosmos, free, confident, playful, and joyful.*

Philosophers, poets, and biologists have offered many different images of the human animal in an attempt to capture the essence of what humans are:

Man, the Fire Maker.
Man, the Maker and User of Tools.
Man, the Laughing Animal.
Man, the Thinker.
Man, the Language Maker.

In the present age, sometimes confusing and frightening, at other times thrilling and challenging, I suggest a more relevant and inclusive image is emerging more and more clearly:

Man and Woman, the Future Makers; they are, really, the subject of this book.

Walnut Creek, California
September 1978

Acknowledgments

I am deeply indebted to Barbara Marx Hubbard and John J. Whiteside, cofounders of The Committee for the Future, who suggested the theme of this book and commented extensively on the manuscript. (Barbara's autobiography, *The Hunger of Eve: A Woman's Odyssey Into the Future*, Stackpole Books, Harrisburg, 1976, tells the story of The Committee for the Future.)

I am most grateful for the hospitality of David K. Hall, Robert J. Gelinas, and Ralph C. Sklarew who made the facilities of Science Applications, Inc., in Pleasanton, California, available to me while writing this book. They have offered valuable suggestions on the manuscipt, as have many other friends, too numerous to list here; to all of them I am indebted.

Dorothy Schuler, my editor at Peace Press, deserves special thanks, for her guidance and patience through the final revisions of the manuscript, during a frantic and hectic few months.

Johan Kooy of the California Academy of Sciences and Sandee Henry of NASA were especially helpful in the location of illustrations.

Finally, none of this would have been possible without the love and friendship of my wife, Helen. Some of the insights which I consider to be most important in this work came from her incisive and perceptive criticisms of the manuscript, fragment by fragment, reflecting her wisdom as a woman, a physician, a wife, and a mother.

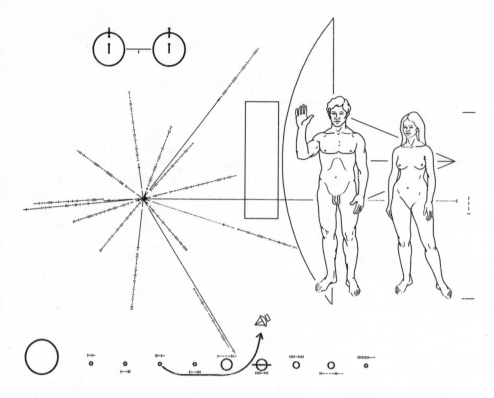

Plaque aboard the Pioneer 10 spacecraft.

I.

The Future is Made, Not Born

*First photograph of the Earth
and Moon together, with the Earth in the
foreground. Taken by Voyager I
at a distance of over 7 million miles, 1978.*

1. Images of the Future

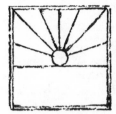 What will our daily lives be like in the future? Will humanity and the biosphere of Earth survive for another century? Will our descendants bless us or curse us for the decisions we make? Will the world fifty years from today be as different from our world as ours is different from the world of fifty years ago when Lindbergh had just crossed the Atlantic Ocean?

Speculation about the future, once largely confined to the science fiction pulp magazines, has become respectable even in the bastions of the academic world and the government agency. Books dealing with the shape of the future have captured the public imagination, and such titles as *Future Shock, Small is Beautiful,* and *The Limits to Growth* have become household phrases for many. Most thinking and speculating about the future has been characterized by a deep and dark current of pessimism, even despair. Several best sellers in this genre have argued that, even if we should somehow escape a nuclear holocaust, we are doomed to extinction by starvation, overpopulation, exhaustion of natural resources, or the cumulative poisoning of the biosphere by our industrial wastes and agricultural pesticides.

Many of these serious studies of the future have called for sweeping changes in our social, political, and economic systems if we are to hope for the survival of civilization. Some have been totalitarian proposals, prescribing mandatory ceilings on energy and raw materials consumption, compulsory sterilization for couples who have had two children, and abolition of economic growth by government fiat. Humanitarian groups have been denounced for aggravating the population problem by their work to relieve human misery, whether by providing food for the starving, medical care for the sick, immunizations for children, or public education in hygienic measures. We are told that immediate implementation of severe measures is absolutely necessary, if we are not to be reduced to a meager diet of soybeans and algae within our lifetime.

The future, seen through such perspectives, looks bleak and desperate — especially when so many have their fingers poised on the nuclear trigger. Negative views make good newspaper headlines, but headlines can never tell the whole story. The real world is full of new discoveries, new ideas, and new insights, springing up in laboratories and homes, in universities and industries and government offices. These breakthroughs provide abundant

3

reason for hope and offer a realistic basis for building a constructive and positive future for ourselves and our descendants. My aim in this book is to uncover some of these discoveries, and to present some insights and perspectives which show that we can create the kind of future we choose, individually and collectively. The future can be joyful, dynamic, and increasingly free; it need not be bleak, austere, and repressive.

Suppose I were attempting to explain my daily life today to a time-traveler from a century ago. Clothing styles have changed continually throughout history, so I would have to explain very little about the differences between my hypothetical visitor's apparel and my own. But the contents of my pockets, the artifacts most used in my daily life, would require a great deal of elaborate explanation. A typical middle-class resident of the United States in the latter part of the 1970s might carry most of the following items in his pockets or in her purse:

- car keys, house keys, office keys, bicycle padlock keys
- coins, bills, postage stamps, checkbook, plastic credit cards, magnetically encoded commuter tickets for the regional rapid transit system, a wallet made of synthetic materials
- a driver's license, a Social Security registration card, insurance cards, membership cards for a variety of social and leisure-time interest clubs, a CB license, photographs of family and friends
- ball point pens, mechanical pencils, perhaps a digital watch or a pocket calculator
- chewing gum or candy, aspirin or antacid tablets, a comb, lipstick and face powder, handkerchiefs or a pack of paper tissues, perhaps a pack of cigarettes and a lighter

With few exceptions these items would be foreign to a visitor from a century ago, and an attempt to explain any of them solely in terms of new technological discoveries, current social trends, or international political arrangements would be hopelessly inadequate.

Suppose my visitor asked for an explanation of a plastic credit card issued by a gasoline company. Certainly he would ask about the material from which it is made, and I would begin by discussing the technological aspects of synthetic materials made from petroleum, coal, and wood pulp. I would have to tell my visitor about the use of the card for purchasing fuel for automobiles, private airplanes, and pleasure boats. Explanations of the economic affluence which has lead to so much leisure time and discretionary income would be necessary, as well as a discussion of the social changes, in this century, triggered by the private automobile.

The mysterious pattern of raised bumps and dots on the credit card would lead into a discussion of the use of electronic computers for commercial billing and accounting, for banking, and for scientific research, with another lengthy detour into electronic technology. The concept of *consumer credit*, based on future income rather than present assets, would seem strange, perhaps even degenerate, carrying the discussion into the changing public attitudes on the morality of labor, thrift, and instant gratification. Returning to the subject of petroleum, as a chemical feedstock and as a convenient fuel, would lead inevitably to explanations of the present international political scene and international trade, which is on a scale far surpassing the wildest imaginations of a century ago. Explanations of what we, today, take for granted would continue far into the night.

To survey our prospects for the future, on Earth, in outer space, and in inner space, we must range far and wide, across the spectrum of human affairs, to recognize that we have the power to choose and build a positive future of unlimited potential. Some readers may consider some of my omissions serious or my discussion of some topics too shallow. The choice of materials included reflects my personal interests and taste, my ignorance, and the inevitable limitations of time, as well as my judgment of the range of topics which must be included to present my case. Much of the discussion will necessarily be speculative, since the broader issues cannot be proven or disproven on mathematical or scientific grounds.

The reality we experience is strongly shaped by our mental images and maps of the world. Language, a process of symbol manipulation within our minds, constitutes a large part of our mental constructs about reality and its everyday aspects — time, space, matter — and we all interpret the world in terms of these mental images. We have all toyed with these mental constructs, at last occasionally, but we leave their systematic examination and manipulation to professional philosophers and theologians, dismissing our interest in such matters as irrelevant, childish, or unscientific. Since we think so rarely about these matters, we are startled when we encounter concrete examples of the profound impact such mental images of reality have on everything we do and experience.

In his *Critique of Pure Reason*, Immanuel Kant observed that our perceptions of space, matter, and most other elements of the objective world of modern science, have been built upon indirect sensory impressions. Only our perception of the passage of time is directly and innately experienced. Yet our mental constructs about time, derived from our direct experience of the passage of time, can have profound effects on the reality we perceive and the reality we create. Since these effects are very important, but somewhat subtle, I would like to give some examples of how our mental maps of space affect reality.

One of my hobbies is piloting small airplanes. A few years ago, I was returning to California from a conference in Dallas, Texas, with two passengers in a four-seater, single-engine plane. I had charted a nearly direct course to Albuquerque, New Mexico, our first refueling stop. As weather conditions were excellent, it was very easy to navigate. I held a heading and checked our position every fifteen or twenty minutes against the map, as we crossed the level terrain of West Texas, neatly laid out in square sections one mile on each edge. As far as the eye could see, the checkerboard pattern continued uninterruptedly except for occasional towns, a few riverbeds, and a handful of major highways or railroads traversing the landscape diagonally. Some of the square sections were irrigated and green, but most were muddy yellow, brown, or almost black rangeland.

As we all know, political boundaries are artificial. Rain, sunshine, and wildlife will blithely ignore the arbitrarily chosen boundary line between Texas and New Mexico. It was astonishing, then, for us to recognize one of the north-south lines of the checkerboard as the actual boundary between the two states without looking at the map. It was as if two quilts of different patterns had been sewn together. On the New Mexico side of the line, instead of one square out of six or seven being green, nearly half the squares were green. This discontinuity is highly visible and it is real — the result of our mental invention of boundary. The laws and regulations, governing the use and pricing of water for irrigation, are different in each state, producing this inadvertent, but dramatic, alteration of reality.

More subtle examples of differing mental images of the same reality can be found in cross-cultural contexts. Himalayan mountain expeditions owe their successes in assaulting the great peaks to the Sherpas, the native guides who farm the high valleys of the Himalayan foothills. Yet their conception of space is very different from that of the Westerners they have guided. The modern Western mind thinks of space in terms of three dimensions of linear extension — length, width, and height — and attempts to place every object or geographical location into a consistent map. For the Sherpa, each peak is part of the daily landscape and has a name associated with its distinctive shape. When a Sherpa visits other villages, some at great distances from home, he or she learns the shapes and names of the peaks visible from those villages. The Sherpa does not naturally connect the north face of Mount Everest, for example, with its south face, and each face has a different name. But the Sherpa willingly accepts the two faces as parts of the same mountain when the correlating similarities are pointed out by Westerners.

Is the Sherpa conception of space wrong? It is just as firmly rooted in personal experience as our Western conception. The world of the Sherpa is a network of lineal paths he or she (or a parent or a friend) has walked, including the various panoramas visible along each of these paths. This lineal, network view of the world is entirely sufficient for the Sherpa way of life. Fitting all of these paths and panoramas together into a consistent two or three-dimensional Cartesian map would provide no practical benefit, nor would it satisfy any of the Sherpa's necessities better than the network view of reality. Detailed instructions can be given to explain how to get from a given village to some other village, by a narrative description of the path taken, with frequent references to prominent features of the panoramas along the way. But in the modern Western world, such a mental model of space would be hopelessly inadequate: without our three-dimensional Cartesian map, navigation of airplanes would be possible only on clear, sunny days. Armed only with the Sherpa's networks, it would be very difficult to find one's way around Manhattan without memorizing every prominent building or landmark along each of the avenues and most of the crosstown streets.

Different mental images of time exist also among various cultures. The predominant Western view of time is a lineal model, with past, present, and future moments perceived as beads on a string. The conjugation of verbs in most Indo-European languages reflects this mental image. Common figures of speech reinforce this casual image, and we can ensnare ourselves in logical traps by the implicit metaphors we use in our relation to time. In English, for example, we picture ourselves as voyagers in an externally determined landscape, speaking of the *past* as that which has been *passed* as we journey along. We talk unthinkingly about the future that lies *before* us and about the past that lies *behind* us. Such idioms suggest an inevitability and an immutability about the future which are contradictory to the notions of free will and personal responsibility embodied in our legal, ethical, and religious codes.

Many of the Semitic languages use a very different metaphor when speaking of the past and the future. In these tongues the past lies *before* us, where we can see it clearly and examine it in its immutability, while the future lies *behind* us, where we cannot see it — where we then must tread carefully in a formless and unknown terrain.

The Hopi Indians of the American Southwest have a different mental image of time, having no words for *past, present,* or *future*. The entire language is verb-oriented rather than noun-oriented, using nouns to denote only really enduring things. The Hopi conjugation of verbs has only two tenses: the *manifested,* corresponding, more or less, to our past and present tenses, and the *manifesting*, corresponding to our present and future tenses. This grammar, firmly rooted in the passage of time at the present moment, is very similar to the Semitic metaphor. What is past or present can be seen clearly — it has been manifested. What is beginning to happen now, or can be expected to happen, is just coming into view from behind us, manifesting itself at the edge of our experience in the present instant.

These different conceptions of time, when brought to bear on Western society, reveal some little-noticed but pervasive effects. A job applicant is invariably asked, "What work have you done? What work are you doing now?" The answers to these questions are usually taken to define who and what the applicant *is*. Who or what the applicant *is becoming*, in terms of learning new skills and developing new goals, is almost never asked, except perhaps as a polite aside. Yet our personal goals and aspirations are as essentially a part of our selves as our accomplishments.

For the Hopi, the world is, in a very real sense, timeless. *Timelessness* does not imply the absence of aspirations and goals, but rather a lack of anxiety and impatience about the rate of attainment of those goals as measured by a clock or a calendar. Such an existentialist immersion in the present moment, paradoxically, is much more future-oriented than is the standard Western view of time.[1] While the Hopi world view is admirable and we can learn a great deal from it, it is not adequate for dealing with the complexities of the interdependent, modern world, or for charting the future; nor is the Western lineal model adequate.

In primitive societies the future is hardly an identifiable concept, if social change is minimal over an individual's lifetime, even if the language has past, present, and future tenses. It is taken for granted that each individual experiences the progression of growing up, mating, child-rearing, growing old, and dying. But individuals in such societies can seldom think about the future as something which can be planned or altered. The future is an external given, with little to distinguish it from past or present except memorable external events beyond our control, such as major floods, epidemics, or famines. Some memorable events, such as skirmishes with neighboring tribes, may appear to be controllable to an outsider's eyes; but controllability may be more illusory than real, since events are often triggered inexorably by external events or may be mandated by ritualistic function.

As societies become more complex, with greater division of labor, with increasing diversification of occupations and social roles, the individual can begin to think about his or her personal future. "What will I be when I grow up? Whom will I marry? Will I be rich?" These questions can only become

---

[1]Some branches of modern theoretical physics suggest similar insights. Einstein's theory of general relativity is a mathematical description of the behavior of gravitation. As such, it can be used to describe the large scale evolution of the universe, which is the subject of cosmology. One of the most profound and fruitful insights in cosmology and general relativity theory has been the recognition that the entire history of the cosmos (past and future) can be computed from the configuration of the universe at a single instant, provided that we understand *configuration* to mean not only the geometry of space and the distribution of matter and energy in space, but also the state of motion (the rate of change) of the matter, the energy, and the geometry. In other words, a complete description of what the universe *is* at any instant necessarily includes information about what the universe *is becoming*. General relativity, however, is not a complete theory since it does not include quantum mechanical effects, which make it impossible to predict detailed behavior at the microscopic level. On the galactic scale, these effects do not change the behavior of gravitating bodies, so that these insights still apply.

meaningful when real choices become available within the society, even if society as a whole remains unchanging for generations.

In the modern world society itself can change radically in a very short time. Many American military pilots, who were imprisoned in North Vietnam for periods of up to eight years, had severe difficulties adjusting to the profound social changes in the United States — changes from which they had been totally isolated. Despite the evidence of rapidly accelerating change all around us, we are still unaccustomed to the idea that tomorrow will not be just like today. When changes nonetheless intrude on our static world view, we suffer *future shock*.

We are now confronted with a radical idea to which we are as unaccustomed as our remote ancestors would have been. The future is not a fixed landscape; the future is not rigidly and inexorably determined by external forces. *We ourselves determine, not only the course of our lives, but also the very context of our lives.*

Because of the high degree of interdependence in the world today, we can no longer think about our personal futures without considering changes in society as a whole. We cannot think about how to ensure a high quality of life for ourselves and our families, separate from the rest of the world. We are compelled to become concerned with the quality of life throughout society and throughout the world. The design of the future has become everyone's business.

Multiple exposure of the 1970
solar eclipse from beginning to end
as it passed over the TIROS tracking antennae at
Wallops Island, Virginia.

2. Quality of Life and Our Goals for the Future

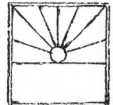 The phrase "quality of life" has come into vogue in recent years as a shorthand expression for the common features underlying people's satisfactions, goals, and aspirations. Although everyone seems to have very strong ideas about what it means personally, few can agree on how to define it universally. Most people will agree that quality of life does not include disease, hunger, pain, fear, grinding poverty, or enslavement. But negative definitions are incomplete and can lead to very strange distortions. Such a purely negative definition of quality of life belies a mindset that considers the external world intrinsically hostile.[1]

The Western world has been highly successful in eliminating disease, hunger, povery, and slavery by pursuing affluence. Yet the arrival of affluence for the majority has not automatically provided high levels of quality of life. Indeed, we in the Western nations suffer from a widespread mood of discontent and dissatisfaction, occasionally even despair. Is our despair the result of too much emphasis on eliminating poverty without simultaneously seeking something positive? To be sure, no one was ever ennobled by being constrained against his or her will to live in abject poverty (or, for that matter, in ostentatious opulence). Some of those whom we most admire, such as Francis of Assisi, have deliberately chosen to turn away from wealth, in favor of a life of austerity. It might seem, at first glance, that we admire such people for their acceptance of poverty and rejection of affluence; but these are negatives. What we really admire in Francis of Assisi is the positive element—love and generosity—which motivated his unconventional behavior.

I do not mean to suggest that we can become content by abandoning our negative goals in favor of total dedication to purely positive goals, but rather

[1]George B. Leonard, *The Transformation: A Guide to the Inevitable Changes in Humankind*, (New York: Delacorte Press, 1972). Leonard describes how such attitudes led to the extremes of Victorian prudery and repression in the United States in the latter part of the nineteeth century, and to the prevalent myth that real men never cry. In the 1830s Dr. Sylvester Graham began teaching that our survival depends on the greatest possible acuity of our five senses, to warn us of external dangers. Any sensations from within ourselves would only distract attention from external attacks, and should thus be considered symptoms of illness or dysfunction. He eventually advocated a bland vegetarian diet. He invented Graham flour and Graham crackers, nutritious foods which would produce a minimum of internal sensation. Needless to say, emotional reactions and sexual feelings were vehemently condemned.

that both types of goals are necessary if we are to achieve a higher quality of life. While we work to reduce suffering; to eliminate disease, starvation, and privation; and to abolish industrial pollution and nuclear terror; we also need to cultivate a deeper knowledge of ourselves, to share more intimate acquaintance with our neighbors, and to develop greater communion and harmony with the rest of nature. Without positive goals, total success in achieving our negative goals would turn to dry ashes in the mouth. The need for positive goals accounts for the rising interest in the United States and other Western countries in Eastern religious movements such as Zen Buddhism, Transcendental Meditation, Sufism, Taoism, and Krishna Consciousness.

A great deal has been written about the differences between Eastern and Western philosophies and religions. Eastern thought is generally inwardly directed and contemplative, considering the spiritual realm more "real" than the material, and viewing time and the universe as cyclical. Western thought, on the other hand, tends to be outwardly directed and active, more interested in the material realm than the spiritual, with a linear, progressive view of time and reality. Basically the East-West differences are contrary reactions to the problem of dealing with pain and suffering in daily life.

The Eastern response to this problem is a deliberate, mental act of withdrawal: if you believe that the material world is illusory and of little importance, it is much easier to deal with personal tribulations. Through many centuries of elaboration, in a variety of Eastern religious movements, this approach leads to strong emphasis on positive spiritual goals (which many disillusioned Westerners find so attractive today). Because Eastern philosophies seem indifferent to pain and suffering, many Westerners have concluded erroneously that Eastern societies have little regard for individual human lives. The East has come to accept pain, suffering, and evil as intrinsic parts of reality, along with pleasure, joy, and good: the Yin and Yang are inseparable.

The West, on the other hand, with its wellsprings in Greek philosophy and the Judaic and Christian traditions, sees pain (that could be avoided), suffering (that could be assuaged), and evil (that could be destroyed) as intolerable. The response to these negative conditions has been personal or social action, using all the available, material resources at hand. When material resources were inadequate, various spiritual resources may also have been used. If pain and suffering are inescapable, they can be endured; sometimes great things can be accomplished in spite of them, but never because of them. Deliberate action to eliminate disease, reduce suffering, or curb social injustice, has generally been foreign to Eastern thought.

For the Christian philosopher or theologian, the existence of evil and suffering creates a paradox: how can a just and merciful Creator condone pain, evil, and the suffering of innocents, when the Creator is absolved of responsibility for creating evil in the first place? As Teilhard de Chardin has observed, this paradox has no rational answer. In the still of the night, the believer can only fall back on his or her faith in some higher meaning or purpose. Meanwhile, it is the obligation of the believer to continue to feed the hungry, clothe the naked, and comfort the suffering, while striving always toward the ultimate positive goal: to know, love, and serve the Creator.

Following the Age of Enlightenment, the Industrial Revolution, and the spread of secularism throughout most of the Western world, the positive goals of the religious traditions are forgotten, but the negative goals remain with us. The major emphasis of domestic policy in the United States for the last half century, for example, has focussed on the reduction of unemployment, with secondary attention to control of inflation and elimination of discrimination.

In the Eastern civilizations, on the other hand, such social evils as corruption in government and business, caste systems, and widespread famine (despite the availability of food reserves) continue to be accepted and tolerated, because of the philosophical basis which has ignored the negative goals with which the West has been so successful. It is no accident that reformers such as Mahatma Gandhi were educated in the West. The Eastern beneficiary of medical treament is profoundly grateful for it, of course, having no more love of pain than any Westerner. The lack of negative goals in Eastern societies is just as deadly as the lack of positive goals in the West. Japan's current environmental problems provide a case in point:

> . . . in premodern times, harmony with nature meant an acceptance of the cycles of nature — their malevolent as well as beneficent manifestations. The Japanese conceived of man and nature as interacting within a single unified sphere in which man lived in awe of natural powers. This sense of harmony thus entailed a degree of resignation and endurance: One had to wait for natural disasters to eventually subside and beneficent conditions to return. Human examination and domination of nature via modern science were conceptual imports that were introduced along with Western technology. In the process of modernization, nature was secularized, but the sense of harmony in the form of resignation to the caprices of nature still persists.[2]

If the future is to have a higher quality of life for everyone, then we must include both types of goals in our approach to the future. The elimination of pain, suffering, and evil and the postponement of death are valid, negative

[2]Norie Huddle, Michael Reich and Nahum Stiskin, *Island of Dreams: Environmental Crisis in Japan*, (Tokyo and New York: Autumn Press, 1975), pp. 268-9.

goals, but they must be complemented with positive goals (such as personal satisfaction, development, and creativity) that are in greater harmony with our neighbors and the rest of nature. Peace is far more than the absence of war; health is more than the absence of disease; and a longer lifespan is worthless without personal purpose and fulfillment.

Each one of us has radically different ideas about the positive elements which constitute quality of life for us. For an academic scholar a high quality of life may mean a salary sufficient to pay for housing, food, clothing, and some transportation; but, most of all, it means the freedom to pursue the intellectual life, with free-wheeling discussion, at the cutting edge of knowledge, lasting far into the night, with brilliant colleagues. For a Cockney housewife it may mean a modest, tidy little house in the mews with a neighbor dropping in for a cup of tea and a chat every morning. For an ardent nature lover, it may mean the opportunity to make frequent and lengthy backpacking trips into the remote wilderness areas alone or with a few friends.

Historically, it has been far more difficult to agree on positive goals for society as a whole, than it has been to find consensus on negative goals. It seems that the only positive goal wide enough to embrace a diversity of personal aspirations is the maximization of opportunities for individuals and groups to choose their own value systems and to implement their own lifestyles. (Any society, of course, must impose certain minimal restraints to discourage activities which demonstrably harm others.) No narrower goal for society is likely to enjoy more than temporary success.

A common, positive goal, such as the one above, is far more than a call for a "do-your-own-thing" ethic; it is a call for deliberate cooperative efforts to build a social, philosophical, economic, legal, and technological context in which the widest variety of personal goals — both yours and mine — can be fostered and respected. Such a context is the necessary precondition for a truly humane future.

3. Technology and Quality

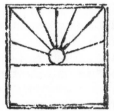Despite much-vaunted successes in raising the material standard of living, Western civilization has shown signs of weakness and faltering confidence during the 1960s and 1970s. Many blame this sense of alienation on technology and science and denounce science, technology, and rationalism as intrinsically evil forces, profoundly destructive to both the natural environment and the human soul. But few who proclaim these views ask the deeper question: whether such an antithesis is inevitable.

Why do so many of the products of technology seem so lifeless and ugly? Why does our highly developed industrial system produce so much plastic junk, marketed with such ruthless vigor against our very wishes and our better judgment? These questions, which lie at the very crux of our malaise about the future, are the subject of a remarkable book with the peculiar title, *Zen and the Art of Motorcycle Maintenance: An Inquiry Into Values*, by Robert M. Pirsig.[1] I will summarize the principal points, because of their relevance to thinking about the future, with an earnest recommendation that you read Pirsig's book carefully and introspectively.

I should first explain that *Zen and the Art of Motorcycle Maintenance* is really two books interwoven into one. The "outer" book is an account of a cross-country motorcycle trip by Pirsig and his son. On the first half of the trip they are accompanied by two friends whose attitudes toward the maintenance of their motorcycle are, at first, unfathomable to Pirsig. Pirsig maintains his motorcycle meticulously, but he cannot convince his friends that it is in their interest to take care of their cycle in the same manner. The "inner" book is a kind of Chautauqua, a travelling lecture series on ideas and philosophy, which is triggered in part by the events and conversations of the outer book. I am concerned mainly with the inner book.

Why, Pirsig wonders, do his friends "freak out" at the idea of doing their own maintenance instead of hiring a mechanic to do it for them, even if the mechanic is likely to be inept and indifferent? Why, when they have trouble starting the engine at high altitude, do they keep trying randomly at this or that combination of throttle and choke settings, getting more and more angry, cursing and swearing at the motorcycle when it still does not

[1]Robert M. Pirsig, *Zen and the Art of Motorcycle Maintenance: An Inquiry Into Values*, (New York: Bantam Books, 1974).

start, instead of trying to analyze the difficulty dispassionately?

Pirsig identifies two fundamentally different ways of looking at the world: *romantic* and *classic*. The romantic or "hip" view is based upon the immediate, artistic appearance of things, focusing on feelings and intuition. The classic or "square" view of reality is based upon a rational analysis and scientific understanding, focusing on the underlying function and form, cause and effect, parts and relationships.

Pirsig's friends are thorough romantics. Motorcycle riding provides them with a sensory experience and allows them to quickly and easily get out of the city to "groove on nature," (in the slang of the 1960s). But when the motorcycle malfunctions, the classic face of reality suddenly intrudes on their romantic view and they feel understandably and personally threatened. They can no longer look solely at the motorcycle's external appearance; they are confronted by the hierarchy of classical ideas implicit in the parts and relationships, the forms and functions of the motorcycle subsystems. Given their romantic orientation, they feel profoundly uncomfortable with the processes of deductive and inductive logic, which they need, to find their way through the hierarchy of ideas, to trouble-shoot the cycle. The confrontation between the two views of reality is what brings Pirsig's friends to their profound hatred of technology, and they come to perceive dimly some blind, mechanical, inhuman, and evil force lying at the very roots of technology and science.

Conversely, many people whose basic view of reality is classical (engineers and scientists often fall into this group) are angered by abstract art — which cannot be understood in classical terms. "But what is that supposed to be a picture of? What does it mean?" Their own view of reality is threatened by abstract art, and as a result, they hate it as fiercely as the most rabid antitechnological hippie detests electrical appliances.

Most people are not fully in one camp or the other; they compartmentalize their everyday experience classically and romantically. Several years ago two computer programmer friends and I (all three of us pilots) invited an astrophysicist friend (a non-pilot) to join us for a sightseeing flight over the Sierra Nevada mountains in a single-engine, four-seater airplane. Our friend was deeply impressed by the magnificent perspectives accessible from the air.

On the return leg of the flight, across the flat and monotonous Central Valley of California, my computer programmer friends, who were then working toward their instrument pilot ratings, decided to practice radio navigation techniques. The astrophysicist expressed contempt for this activity. Learning to fly so you could go sightseeing made sense to him, but flying on instruments with radio navigation and complex, communications procedures (with air traffic controllers on the ground) seemed to be an infantile preoccupation "with more dials and knobs to twiddle." The two pilot friends, of course, were totally oblivious to the physical dials and knobs; their attention was riveted to the ideas of the plane's position, altitude, airspeed, pitch, bank, heading, and rate of climb or descent. The astrophysicist was, in his professional life, as totally classical in his mindset as he was romantic about flying.

The epitome of the classical approach to reality is the scientific method, which has been so successful and so central to Western civilization for the last two or three centuries. In essence, the scientific method is a six-step process for approaching the truth. First, I must carefully define the problem, solely in terms of what I already know for certain: *The motorcycle will not start. Why not?* Second, I must formulate one or more hypotheses: *Perhaps the gas tank is empty. Perhaps the trouble is in the electrical system.* Third, I must design suitable experiments to test each hypothesis: *Try rocking the motorcycle from side to side.* Fourth, I must deduce what result I should obtain from the experiment, if the hypothesis being tested is (or is not) true: *If the gas tank is empty, I won't hear gasoline sloshing back and forth when I rock the cycle.* Fifth, I must carry out the experiment, carefully noting the results: *I could hear gasoline sloshing in the tank.* Sixth, I must draw conclusions from the comparison of the expected results with the results actually observed: *The gas tank is not empty; in fact, based on previous experiences, it sounds about half full.* I must then repeat the entire process until I have found a hypothesis which does not contradict anything I already know for certain, and which does explain as much of what I wanted to know as it is possible to learn at the present time.[2]

The scientific method itself is impossible to justify on purely rational grounds. The method tells me nothing about how to invent hypotheses; it tells me nothing about how to determine which hypothesis is most likely to lead to useful results. Yet, somehow, I must choose between the countless hypotheses which I can invent at each step; otherwise, I cannot make any progress. These key elements of the scientific method remain outside the structure of rational thought.

On what basis are hypotheses evaluated? The mature, experienced scientist develops an intuitive feel for higher quality hypotheses, without being able to define just what he or she means by *quality*. Pirsig then takes up the question: "What is *Quality*?" Presented with a group of artifacts, or with a collection of literary works, almost everyone can recognize which ones are superior and which are not. Although we can recognize it, Quality is undefinable in classical understanding. Pirsig shows that the essence of *squareness* is the inability to see Quality before it has been intellectually defined; the

---

[2]The reader may find this description of the scientific method disconcerting, since I have not described it in the more usual impersonal language: "First, the problem must be defined solely in terms of what is known for certain . . . .." Describing the scientific method in the passive voice creates the illusion of objectivity by concealing the essential role of the scientist in the process.

very process of defining it destroys the perception of Quality, by chopping it up into words.

Is Quality subjective or objective? Is it in the mind or in the external, material world? Pirsig rejects this apparent dilemma (it is easy enough to show that neither pole fits) and recognizes that the mind/matter duality is an artificial construct. Quality lies neither in the subjective nor in the objective world, but rather in the relationship between the two. If I let my hand get too close to the fire so that my fingers get burned, I react in a preintellectual manner, with a yell and a jerk, which removes my hand from an environment of poor Quality. Then the intellectual, classical mode takes over, analyzes the situation, and proceeds to form mental constructs such as *hot, fire, pain,* and *fingers*.

> In our highly complex organic state we advanced organisms respond to our environment with an invention of many marvelous analogues. We invent earth and heavens, trees, stones, and oceans, gods, music, arts, language, philosophy, engineering, civilization and science. We call these analogues reality. And they *are* reality . . . Quality is the continuing stimulus which our environment puts upon us to create the world in which we live. All of it. Every last bit of it.[3]

From the stimulus of Quality in the experiential confrontation between ourselves and our environment, we deduce the existence of subject and object. The summer I turned six my parents had the old coal furnace in our home replaced with an oil burner. The morning the oil tank was to be buried in our back yard, my brother and I were playing a kind of hide-and-seek around it on the front lawn. The tank was cylindrical, about four feet in diameter, and perhaps ten feet long. We chased each other around it, erratically reversing direction, to scare each other. When I caught sight of my brother's head sticking out above the tank, I could tell which way he was going, and I really surprised him. In that instant, in that moment of high Quality, I realized that my ambush had succeeded because my body was smaller than the oil tank; my physical size was a property, not of the "me" who was enjoying the game, but of a thing, my body, somehow attached to "me." For many days, I was entranced by the discovery of subject and object.

The Eastern religions place great emphasis on the Sanskrit doctrine of *Tat tvam asi* ("Thou art that"). To be enlightened is to exist without the division between what you think you are and what you think you perceive. It is because Quality resides in the moment of vision, before intellectualization can take place, that the classic, intellectual view of reality cannot grasp Quality or define it. In this perspective, Eastern mystical ideas, which Lao Tzu described 2,400 years ago in the *Tao*, and which Gautama Buddha

[3]Pirsig, *Zen and Motorcycle Maintenance*, p. 245.

taught at about the same time, become comprehensible to the Western mind.

Why do we all have different ideas about Quality? Why can't we agree on what constitutes *quality of life*? Because each of us has had different experiences in life, each of us has created different analogues of reality, different mental constructs about the way the world functions — different ideas about what constitutes quality of life.

Did Western civilization ever have a preintellectual, direct awareness of Quality? Pirsig's search to understand how and why Western thought came to place objectivity and rationalism above values, above Quality, leads back to the Greeks. Every course in the history of science traces the origins of Western science and technology to the pre-Socratic, Ionian philosophers: beginning with Thales; continuing through Anaximenes, Heraclitus, Anaxagoras, Pythagorus, and Parmenides; until Socrates, Plato, and Aristotle refined the methods of dialectical inquiry. The common theme among pre-Socratic philosophers was their conscious search for permanence and imperishability in human affairs—a search directed, for the first time, in the realm of human thought (rather than in the arena of the mythical gods). These philosophers may be conveniently lumped together as Cosmologists, searching for a universal, *Immortal Principle*.

Parmenides was the first to suggest that the Immortal Principle was separate from appearance or opinion:

> . . . the importance of this separation and its effect on subsequent history cannot be overstated. It's here that the classic mind, for the first time, took leave of its romantic origins and said, 'The Good and the True are not necessarily the same,' and goes its separate way.[4]

Socrates and Plato settled finally on the idea of *Truth* as the Immortal Principle, and waged a bitter war against the Sophists, who they considered decadent:

> . . . Truth. Knowledge. That which is independent of what anyone thinks about it. The ideal for which Socrates died. The ideal that Greece alone possesses for the first time in the history of the world. It is still a very fragile thing. It can disappear completely . . .
>
> The results of Socrates' martyrdom and Plato's unexcelled prose that followed are nothing less than the whole world of Western man as we know it. If the idea of truth had been allowed to die unrediscovered by the Renaissance it's unlikely that we would be much beyond the level of prehistoric man today. The ideas of science and technology . . . are dead-centered on it.[5]

[4]Pirsig, *Zen and Motorcycle Maintenance*, p. 366.
[5]Pirsig, *Zen and Motorcycle Maintenance*, p. 368.

Doomsday Has Been Cancelled

My own course on the history of science said as much; we followed the corpus of Greek knowledge to the library of Alexandria, into the hands of Islamic scholars, and rediscovered it, centuries later, in the Renaissance. But Pirsig goes back to see what the "decadent" Sophists had been teaching. These teachers of "wisdom" centered on the beliefs of people rather than on abstract principles, and sought to improve people. They held that "man is the measure of all things;" that there are no absolute principles or absolute truths. It is no wonder that Plato held them in such scorn. The outcome of this war between the Sophists and the Cosmologists is that Western thought has lost sight of the central teaching of the Sophists: *aretê* (a word which has been translated incorrectly as virtue but is closer to excellence, Quality, the *Tao*).

The Homeric, pre-Socratic hero was motivated by a duty toward self, a reaching for excellence. He was not a specialist: everything he attempted he did well. He measured personal excellence by the improvement of humanity (incarnate in him). This is exemplified beautifully in the *Iliad*, when the Trojan prince, Hector, bids farewell to his wife and son, just prior to leaving for his fatal battle with Achilles:

> . . . when he had kissed his dear son and dandled him in his arms, he prayed to Zeus and to the other Gods: Zeus and ye other Gods, grant that this my son may be, as I am, most glorious among the Trojans and a man of might, and greatly rule in Ilion. And may they say, as he returns from war, 'He is far better than his father.'

What the Sophists taught as the absolute, Lao Tzu and Gautama Buddha were teaching at the same time; before the dialectic of Socrates, Plato, and Aristotle divided reality into subject and object, mind and matter, form and substance. Plato encapsulated *aretê*, the very stimulus which prompts us to create our mental analogues, and degraded it into a mere analogue. A permanent and fixed Idea of Good ranked high in the Platonic scheme of things, just below Truth. Aristotle subsequently proceeded to demote it a few steps further in his "true" order of things. Pirsig's analysis (highly condensed here) seems to me to be a major contribution to understanding our present difficulties and anxieties.

The Judaic and Christian traditions, the other wellsprings of Western civilization, also had a pervading consciousness of Quality. In the Genesis account of Creation, at the end of a day's work, "God saw that it was Good." God did not see Creation as rational or cost-effective—but Good. The Old Testament indicates the same measure of excellence as the Homeric hero, with the same phrasing, when Elijah flees into the desert to escape from the impious king who seeks to kill him. Elijah had worked long and arduously, but not successfully, to bring the people of Israel back to their God:

20

Technology and Quality

> And he went forward one day's journey into the desert. And when he was there, and sat under a juniper tree, he requested for his soul that he might die, and said: It is enough for me, Lord, take away my soul: for I am no better than my fathers. (I Kings 19:4)

In the Age of Enlightenment, Aristotelian rationalism cast out the entire religious tradition of Western civilization as mere superstition, and the West relegated all sense of Quality to a private matter of individual conscience. Thus Western civilization has arrived at the point where we so blithely do what seems expedient or reasonable with so little concern for what is Good. The social sciences today strive so hard for value-free methodologies, even while theoretical physicists tend, more and more, to make conscious value judgments of tentative new theories on the nonrational bases of mathematical elegance and simplicity.[6] We teach our children the proverb, "Anything worth doing is worth doing well," but we seldom apply it consciously in our daily work.

Technology and science are not to blame for the ugliness and the disamenities of life in the industrialized United States, any more than the constitutional form of government. When Thomas Jefferson wrote, "The price of liberty is eternal vigilance," he was not suggesting that we adopt an attitude of perpetual paranoia toward the rest of the world. He was reminding us that liberty is not an object but a relationship; that government is a set of structured interactions; and that relationships among living things are, themselves, living things which must be cared for.

Technology, likewise, is not an object or the sum total of all our marvelous gadgetry. It is a relationship between our minds and the world around us; the health and vitality of this human activity needs care just as much as any other relationship. If we do not care about a relationship, if we lose sight of Quality in a relationship, whether it be marriage, school, or government, then the relationship sickens, and the end result is broken homes, functional illiteracy, or perennial political scandal.

Rather than condemning and abandoning technology and science, we need to reconsider our attitudes toward them. We must begin, again, to care about the quality of that relationship with the universe which is technology. To hate the products of technology, to despise the technologists who created them — especially when products break down and need repair, as they will do, from time to time — is a form of not caring. The result is a predictable deterioration of quality of life.

We can recapture what was lost, in the philosophical war more than two thousand years ago, and further trampled in the facile fads of the Age of Enlightenment two centuries ago. We can recapture quality of life without

[6]Fritjof Capra, *The Tao of Physics*, (New York: Bantam Books, 1976). This book gives insight into the aesthetic elements involved in modern theoretical physics.

throwing away what Western civilization has gained in its refusal to tolerate pain and evil. We must recognize that classical understanding and romantic understanding are each incomplete. We must expand our use of both modes of perception, in all aspects of life and work, for they are complementary aspects of Quality, which is reality itself, the *Tao* and Buddha-consciousness.

4. A Positive Vision of the Future

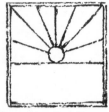 Because of the extent to which our behavior reflects our assumptions and our modes of thinking, a future of high quality of life depends on high quality visions of the future. "Where there is no vision, the people perish." (Proverbs 29:8). This is not an endorsement of the Pollyanna school of thought, which suggests that seeing only the good will automatically bring about only good results. Quality can come from only quality efforts, motivated by quality goals.

If I am determined to have a beautiful garden, with a multitude of flowers and fruits, filled with songbirds and butterflies, how shall I achieve my goal? I do not want my garden to be full of thorns and crabgrass, crawling with snails and slugs; but if I devote most of my energy to preventing all the negatives, I will clearly fail in obtaining my garden of delights. I will, instead, have a desert, with all the weeds and pests exterminated, but nothing beautiful will be growing there. I can have my garden only if I put most of my effort into planting and nurturing the plants I desire.

A society is very much like a human individual: no human being can mature into a healthy, creative, and happy adult, if, as a child he or she was criticized constantly, repressed in aspirations, and lectured repeatedly on delinquencies, and warned of an end in jail or on the gallows.

The founding fathers of the United States succeeded in creating a better future for themselves and their children. Despite their wide and profound knowledge of history, and the many failures of the past, they had a clear, positive vision of the future they wished to create. In a letter to his wife, Abigail, in 1780, John Adams eloquently described the goal which motivated his arduous efforts for the new nation:

> I must study politics and war, that my sons may have liberty to study mathematics and philosophy, geography, natural history, and naval architecture, navigation, commerce, and agriculture, in order to give their children a right to study painting, poetry, music, architecture, statuary, tapestry, and porcelain.[1]

In our concern and preoccupation with negative goals, we seem, sometimes, to have forgotten that one of the "inalienable rights" of the Declaration of

[1]Charles Francis Adams, ed., *Letters of John Adams Addressed to His Wife*, Vol. 2, (1841), Letter 78.

Doomsday Has Been Cancelled

Independence, finally adopted by the Continental Congress, was "the pursuit of happiness."

Too much attention to future perils and forecasts of doom will guarantee a barren and desolate future of increasing violence, frustration, and self-hatred. Since we create our individual and collective futures, we must develop — and keep in mind — our joyous visions of desirable futures, as guides for planting the seeds of new worlds.

5. Predicaments and Potentialities

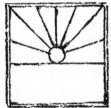 How can it be realistic or responsible to advocate a future in which everyone is free to pursue his or her own vision of quality of life, when we are beset on all sides by the "hard realities" of global poverty, famine, environmental despoliation, and expanding population? If millions of people on this planet are undernourished or even starving today, how can we ever feed everyone, when there may be twice as many mouths to feed in fewer than forty years? How can we provide a decent standard of living for everyone, when six percent of the world's population, living in the United States and Canada, consume more than thirty percent of the world's annual production of fossil fuels? How are we to avoid nuclear holocaust, when the gap between rich and poor nations grows wider every year, and more and more of the poorest nations acquire the capability of building nuclear weapons? Don't such trends necessarily imply that we must all compromise our personal visions of quality of life if we are to survive at all?

Such arguments have been raised with increasing frequency in the 1960s and 1970s, and many doomsday prophecies have been seemingly well documented. Most of the pessimistic forecasts tell us that the future will be very bleak, unless we curtail our options drastically — all in the name of quality of life. Narrowing our choices, however, inevitably means a decrease in quality of life for everyone, since no one else can decide for you what quality of life means to you.

The prophets of doom, for the most part, seem very grim, because their attention has been focussed exclusively on negative predicaments, resulting in an inability to see the potentialities becoming manifest in the world today. Reading modern doomsday literature, it is easy to be swept away by the persuasive reasonableness of the arguments; but the tunnel vision becomes obvious if one looks for it.

Perhaps the most famous prediction of disasters resulting from population growth, the 1798 treatise of Thomas Robert Malthus, entitled *An Essay on the Principle of Population as it affects the Future Improvement of Society, with remarks on the Speculations of Mr. Godwin, M. Condorcet, and Other Writers*, provides a clear example of one-sided, tunnel vision. Malthus argues, in this first edition, that the reproductive capacity of human beings must always greatly exceed our capacity to produce enough food for everyone. Population growth according to Malthus, is restricted either by misery (malnutri-

25

tion and starvation), or by vice (sexual gratification outside of normal conjugal relations).

While the essay totals some 50,000 words (about two-thirds the length of this book), the essence of Malthus' argument is contained in a scant, two pages, which juxtapose two propositions. First, given sufficient food and material resources, the number of people could double every twenty-five years or less. (At that time the United States had the most rapid rate of population growth known to Malthus, corresponding to a doubling of population every twenty-five years). Second, the amount of food produced can grow, at best, arithmetically.

Since Malthus' conclusions concerning our dismal prospects for the future depend equally on both of these propositions, it would be reasonable to expect that he would devote about equal discussion to each of these propositions. Yet the bulk of the essay discusses the contemporary sociological factors (including misery and vice) affecting the fertility patterns of civilized countries. The entire discussion of food production can be quoted verbatim here:

> Let us now take any spot on earth, this Island [Great Britain] for instance, and see in what ratio the subsistence it affords can be supposed to increase. We will begin with it under its present state of civilization.
>
> If I allow that by the best possible policy, by breaking up more land and by great encouragements to agriculture, the produce of this Island may be doubled in the first twenty-five years, I think it will be allowing as much as any person can well demand.
>
> In the next twenty-five years, it is impossible to suppose that the produce could be quadrupled. It would be contrary to all our knowledge of the quality of land. The very utmost that we can conceive, is, that the increase in the second twenty-five years might equal the present produce. Let us then take this for our rule, though certainly far beyond the truth, and allow that by great exertion, the whole produce of the Island might be increased every twenty-five years, by a quantity of subsistence equal to what it at present produces. The most enthusiastic speculator cannot suppose a greater increase than this. In a few centuries it would make every acre of land in the Island like a garden.
>
> Yet this ratio of increase is evidently arithmetical. It may be fairly said, therefore, that the means of subsistence increase in an arithmetical ratio . . .
>
> But to make the argument more general and less interrupted by the partial views of emigration, let us take the whole earth, instead of one spot, and suppose that the restraints to population were universally removed. If the subsistence for man that the earth afforded was to be increased every twenty-five years by a quantity equal to what the whole world at present produces, this would allow the power of production in the earth to be absolutely unlimited, and its ratio of increase much greater than we can conceive that any possible exertions of mankind could make it.

Predicaments and Potentialities

> Taking the population of the world at any number, a thousand millions, for instance, the human species would increase in the ratio of — 1, 2, 4, 8, 16, 32, 64, 128, 256, 512, &c. and subsistence as — 1, 2, 3, 4, 5, 6, 7, 8, 9, 10, &c. In two centuries and a quarter, the population would be to the means of subsistence as 512 to 10: in three centuries as 4,096 to 13, and in two thousand years the difference would be almost incalculable, though the produce in that time would have increased to an immense extent.
>
> No limits whatever are placed to the productions of the earth; they may increase for ever and be greater than any assignable quantity; yet still the power of population being a power of a superior order, the increase of the human species can only be kept commensurate to the increase of the means of subsistence by the operation of the strong law of necessity acting as a check upon the greater power.

Nowhere else in the entire essay is there any further discussion of food production; the argument depends entirely on Malthus' assertion that the rate of increase in food production must be very limited — an assertion made without any supporting evidence. (Incidentally, between 1950 and 1975, the world population doubled, food production more than doubled).

At the very least, we should expect some careful consideration of the following questions:

- What fraction of available arable land was already under cultivation?
- What fraction of the labor force was already employed in agriculture?
- How much could the yield per acre be increased by more labor?
- Assuming productivity per acre must remain constant, what fraction of the labor force would be required to increase total cultivated land by 3% a year to keep in step with population growth?
- If a 100% increase in the labor force during the first twenty-five-year period can be conceded to achieve a 100% increase in food production, why should a 100% increase in the labor force during the twelfth, twenty-five year period result in only an 8.3% increase in food production, as Malthus asserts?

We can easily excuse Malthus for failing to ask how rapidly, newer agricultural technologies could increase productivity (the Industrial Revolution had barely begun at that time); but all of the above questions are simply dismissed before they can be asked, by Malthus' sweeping assertion of pessimism.

Contemporary critics attacked Malthus on philosophical, sociological, and moral grounds, but they did not raise the above issues. Five years later he published a revised and expanded version, entitled *An Essay on the*

Doomsday Has Been Cancelled

Principle of Population, or A View of its Past and Present Effects on Human Happiness; with an Inquiry into Our Prospects Respecting the Future Removal or Mitigation of the Evils Which It Occasions. In this second edition Malthus sharply reversed his views on the possibilities of checking population growth. Whereas in the first edition he had admitted only misery and vice as checks on population growth, he now acknowledged moral restraint, that is, "restraint from marriage which is not followed by irregular gratifications" or by the use of "improper arts."[1] Although this second edition and the subsequent, five minor revisions are about three times longer than the first edition, Malthus adds nothing more to the discussion of food production.

Much of the present doomsday literature, if considered carefully and skeptically, clearly contains the same kind of argument by assertion — a blind spot resulting from too great a fascination with a particular predicament. It is intellectually indefensible to assert an impossibility, without a detailed consideration of what could actually be done, if we were willing to do it. Even then, limitation of what we find possible must always be qualified by recognition of our present ignorance, ignorance which may be overcome at any moment, often unexpectedly. While some of the predicaments we face may seem awesome, our potentialities for satisfactorily dealing with them are far greater — if we are only willing to use what we already know, in cooperation with each other.

---

[1]Malthus was an ordained clergyman of the Church of England and would have been appalled by present-day "Malthusianism" with its promotion of artificial contraception, sterilization, and abortion.

28

*Abou Simbel Rock Temple
of Ramses II, Egypt.*

6. Consciousness Dawning

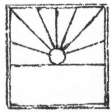 Before discussing some of the specific, new options for the future of humanity on the Earth and in space, I want to set the stage by sketching, in broad outline, the main features of our home planet and its evolutionary history. When people today talk about "the environment," they usually mean the biosphere, the life-zone of the Earth and all the life forms inhabiting the Earth. In 1968 the Apollo 8 astronauts brought back the first photographs of the entire planet Earth, viewed from the distance of the Moon. These photographs provided convincing, visual proof that the Earth is finite. A deeper and perhaps more important perception also resulted from seeing these photographs, an insight which verges on the mystical and religious: the biosphere of Earth is unique and sacred; it maintains a precarious foothold in a bleak, desolate, and otherwise lifeless corner of the universe, by only its global interdependence and symbiosis.

What is the extent of the planet and its biosphere? The visible Earth is about 12,750 kilometers (7,960 miles) in diameter, with a total mass of 6×10^{24} kilograms (13.2×10^{24} pounds), and an average density nearly 5.5 times that of water. At the present moment in the Earth's geological history, the oceans cover about seven-tenths of the surface area to an average depth of 4 kilometers (2.5 miles). The mass of water in the oceans accounts for about one part in four thousand of the total mass of the Earth. Enveloping the planet is the protective blanket, the atmosphere, with a total mass slightly less than one-millionth of the total planet.

Because of turbulent mixing processes, the composition of the Earth's atmosphere, except for water vapor, is essentially the same from sea level up to about one hundred kilometers altitude, consisting roughly of 21% oxygen, 78% nitrogen, nearly 1% argon, and small fractions of a percent of carbon dioxide, hydrogen, neon, and helium, in that order. The density of the atmosphere falls off roughly exponentially with altitude, decreasing by half every 6 kilometers (18,000 feet) or so. If the density were constant instead, and at a uniform temperature, such as we experience at sea level, the thickness of the atmosphere would be only about eight kilometers (five miles), and the upper 1,300 meters (4,000 feet) of Mount Everest would be exposed to the vacuum of outer space (as would be the tips of two or three hundred other peaks).

The atmosphere has no clearcut upper boundary, but we can form some

31

notion of its extent. Note that the lifetime of a modest-sized, artificial satellite, at an altitude of one hundred kilometers is measured in terms of tens of months before the orbit decays, due to atmospheric drag, while a similar satellite at 500 kilometers altitude has a lifetime measured in tens of years. This thick blanket of air moderates day-night temperature changes, protects the biosphere from excess amounts of cosmic radiation and solar ultraviolet light, and minimizes the potential hazards of meteorites.

The geomagnetic field, which originates deep within the core of the planet, extends outward to distances several times the diameter of the solid planet, while the gravitational attraction of the total mass of the Earth extends — at least in principle — throughout the universe.

So far the picture seems very static. But every feature mentioned above changes with time, albeit the time scales, characterizing dramatic changes, are very different for various features. The processes of plate tectonics, which depend on slow circulation of the Earth's mantle, have timescales of a half to two or three billion years, resulting in the slow wandering of continents about the surface, and the creation and destruction of the ocean floors themselves. Possibly related to these same processes in the interior of the Earth, the geomagnetic field completely reverses polarity at variable intervals, sometimes as short as 10,000 years. Cold surface waters sink to the ocean floors, languishing in the darkness for ten or twenty millenia, before rising to the surface somewhere else.

Locally, the atmosphere exhibits the formation and dissipation of weather fronts and tropical storms, in periods ranging from a few days to about two weeks. Global changes in precipitation patterns and mean temperatures occur over decades or centuries. The extreme changes of ice age glaciations require tens of millenia, accompanied by significant changes in the ratio of land area to ocean area, as sea level changes in response to the advance or retreat of the ice caps. Because of tidal friction, even the rotation rate of the Earth on its axis changes: the length of the day is now a fraction of a percent longer than it was when dinosaurs roamed the Earth.

Not even the mass of the Earth has remained constant. Meteorites and cosmic rays continually add matter, while atoms and molecules of gas boil off the upper atmosphere, to escape permanently, at rates which depend on the mean temperature of the atmosphere: the intensity of cosmic radiation falling on the atmosphere, the strength of the geomagnetic field, and the level of sunspot activity. Even the chemical composition of the atmosphere has undergone radical changes.

Now let's look at the extent of the biosphere itself. Tiny spiders, riding atmospheric currents on little silk streamers they have spun, to get a ride, have been detected at altitudes of five kilometers, while the timber line sometimes extends up to about five kilometers.

Burrowing animals, ranging from termites to rodents, penetrate a few meters, or even a few tens of meters, into the soil, as do the roots of many plants. A host of different species of insects, fishes, and newts have been discovered in the waters of caves one to two kilometers deep. In the oceans photosynthesis occurs only in the uppermost one hundred meters or so; for sunlight cannot penetrate below that depth in sufficient quantities to support even the most efficient algae. A wide assortment of animals live at greater depths, commuting to near-surface layers each night to graze in these rich pastures, and retreating into the darkness of the depths during the daytime. Yet another assortment of animals live perpetually in the abyss down to about six kilometers below the surface. Their food chains, often rather complex, begin with organic debris, steadily raining down from the upper layers.

In a different dimension, life forms span the temperature extremes of the planet from certain primitive one-celled plants, living in hot sulfurous springs at 104° C (219°F), to penguins, hatching their eggs in the Antarctic night at temperatures of -60°C (-80°F) or less.

While water is essential for all terrestrial lifeforms, algae have been found in the most dehydrated environments on Earth, in such hot deserts as the Negev and the Sinai, and in the ice-free, dry valleys of Victoria Land, Antarctica, at latitude 77° S. In both extremes, these microorganisms have colonized the microscopic air spaces a few millimeters below the surface of exposed porous rocks. Protected from the dessicating macroenvironment outside, by windborne dust lodged in the surface pores of the rocks, these algae are presumed, in times of extreme aridity, to enter a cryptobiotic state, resuming normal metabolism, when moisture, in the form of dew or melting snow, seeps into the network or pores.

The habitable biosphere is a thin layer extending from a few kilometers below mean, sea level to a few kilometers above, forming a shell whose thickness is perhaps two-thousandths of the radius of Earth.

Now I would like to point out some milestones in the evolution of the biosphere. Present astrophysical thinking holds that the planets of the solar system condensed out of the same cloud, of galactic gas and dust, as the Sun some five or six billion years ago. That cloud contained what is called the "mean cosmic abundance of elements," part of it in the form of "prebiotic" molecules such as carbon monoxide, carbon dioxide, methane, ammonia, various oxides of nitrogen, hydrogen sulfide, nitric acid, and formaldehyde, all of which have been detected in the interstellar medium.

Once the initially chaotic conditions here on Earth subsided, and once the early period of heavy meteor bombardment (which formed most of the craters seen on the Moon) ended, the first steps toward the emergence of life took place (by processes which have been simulated in the laboratory). The prebiotic substances, dissolved in the newly-condensed ocean waters of Earth, could interact with solar, ultraviolet light, lightning discharges, hot springs, and the tides and waves. After a surprisingly short time, much more complex organic molecules were synthesized. These included a wide variety of amino acids (the building blocks for proteins) and nucleic acids (the "alphabet" in which the genetic code is written in DNA molecules).

After unknown eons, by processes which are still poorly understood, the first unicellular organisms emerged, no later than 3.4 billion years ago, perhaps as little as one hundred million years after the formaton of the oceans. These first creatures were very simple types, biologists now call prokaryotic microbes, microbes with little if any internal structure. These simple organisms used the more complex organic compounds available in the environment for food, metabolizing these substances back into the simple prebiotic molecules.

During the next few billion years, these simple lifeforms explored various niches available in the almost barren, inorganic environment. But the total biomass of the planet was tightly constrained by the rate at which, in certain limited places, such as tidepools, the highly inefficient abiotic processes could resynthesize the complex organic substances needed for food. Thus the biosphere was very limited in extent and very vulnerable. In fact, life on this planet could have been completely exterminated and started anew several times during that period.

About two billion years ago, a new class of prokaryotic microbe emerged, the blue-green algae, and the entire planet was remade. The blue-green algae discovered a way to side-step the limits to growth, implicit in dependence on the inefficient abiotic processes, for resynthesis of the complex organic molecules. Armed with chlorophyll, the blue-green algae reached outside the existing system — to use sunlight directly — performing the necessary synthesis of foodstuffs, for the entire biosphere, with far greater efficiency. The biosphere could begin to exploit the vast resources of prebiotic molecules, not only in special, limited places at the edge of the ocean where abiotic processes provided food, but everywhere on the planet.

The way was open for life to expand from the littoral zones, to colonize the fertile medium of the open oceans with a primeval plankton. The physical atmosphere was also drastically altered over the next 1.4 billion years, by the accumulation of free oxygen, a waste product of photosynthesis. This build-up of the oxygen level probably exterminated a wide variety of anaerobic microbes, which could not adapt to such anaerobic niches as remained available.

Sometime later, perhaps as little as one billion years ago, more complex forms of unicellular organisms arose, by the symbiosis of various types of prokaryotic microbes, to form the modern eukaryotic cells found in all multicellular animals and in fungi. Organelles of the modern cells, such as the mitochondria, the cilia and flagella, and the nucleated cell body, are now believed to be the descendants of these original prokaryotic symbionts.

Some blue-green algae also entered symbiotic unions with early eukaryotic cells, and evolved into the chloroplasts, found in the higher green plants today. Other blue-green algae found ways to develop communally into large, multicelled forms such as kelp.

With the development of advanced multicellular plants, 600 to 800 million years ago, life began to colonize the land as well, carpeting the rocky terrain with mosses and lichens. These accelerated the decomposition of rocks into small grains. Combining with bits of dead plant tissues, these fragments of rock formed the first true soils on Earth, and a new niche for microorganisms opened.

Multicelled animals could multiply and develop rapidly, once the oxygen level rose significantly and the eukaryotic cells advanced somewhat. The land was colonized first by various mollusks, annelid worms, and arthropods, perhaps 450 million years ago; the vertebrates emerged onto the land less than four hundred million years ago, and finally achieved complete terrestrial reproduction with the reptilian evolution of the amniotic egg, about three hundred million years ago.

The total biomass of the planet was enormously increased by the invention of chlorophyll, and the biosphere became far less vulnerable to total extinction. From here on, the picture of the evolutionary history of the biosphere has been clear for many years, through the work of paleontologists, geologists, and biochemists.[1]

The next major step in evolution happened in the last four million years or so in East Africa, when the genus *Homo* appeared, with *Homo sapiens* emerging perhaps one hundred thousand years ago. Four biological properties of our species are especially significant to the discussion of the future:

- Humans, along with the cetaceans (whales and dolphins), are the only animals which are perennially sexual — whose sexual behavior is not restricted to those times when the female is fertile. Ethnologists today are just beginning to unravel the profound effects this has had on the development of the social patterns of the human race.
- The synergisms in the evolution of the hand, the eye, and the brain have produced capabilities and adaptabilities in the species which are totally unprecedented in the evolutionary history of the planet.
- Measured in intrinsic metabolic terms, we are by far the longest lived vertebrates. Typical lifespans for all other vertebrate species are approximately one billion heartbeats, while our lifespan is four billion heartbeats.
- With the possible exceptions of the cetaceans and our close relatives

[1]*Scientific American*, September 1978, presents nine, highly readable and up-to-date articles on various aspects of the evolutionary history of the biosphere.

like the chimpanzee (to a very limited extent), humans represent the first appearance in the biosphere of self-awareness — the biosphere has woken up.

Since *Homo sapiens* first appeared, the species has successfully exploited most available environments, from the Arctic tundra to the South American rainforest. It seems that there is no intrinsic biological obstacle to the survival of *Homo sapiens*, as a distinct, identifiable species, for several million years. While concern for the welfare of humanity for the next generation, or the next one hundred years, is admirable and commendable, we need a larger perspective, with a time scale of thousands, if not millions, of years.

But won't our descendants, just a few hundred years from now, be so different in outlook that we cannot share their goals and aspirations? Hardly. We have no difficulty, whatsoever, in empathizing with the inhabitants of ancient Mesopotamia, Egypt, Palestine, China, or India, two or three thousand years ago, as revealed in writings of the times. Their personal concerns and emotional responses of love and anger, of mourning and hope, are perfectly understandable to us today, despite major cultural and technological differences. As long as our descendants are still the same biological species, we can empathize with them. They are unlikely to be alien to the qualities we consider human. The role defined for us by the hallmarks of our species compels us to adopt a much wider viewpoint, which is not a narrow, anthropocentric perspective. We need to create for ourselves a much wider viewpoint.

When photosynthesis appeared, the biosphere was born and began to arrange physical conditions on the planet to suit its needs. Some biologists — notably Dr. Lynn Margulis and Dr. James E. Lovelock — suggest we think of the biosphere as a single, living entity; they refer to this idea as the *Gaia Hypothesis*.

It appeared to us that the Earth's biosphere was able to control at least the temperature of the Earth's surface and the composition of the atmosphere. Prima facie, the atmosphere looked like a contrivance put together cooperatively by the totality of living systems to carry out certain necessary control functions. This led us to the formulation of the proposition that living matter, the air, the oceans, the land surface were parts of a giant system which was able to control temperature, the composition of the air and the sea, the pH of the soil and so on so as to be optimum for the survival of the biosphere. The system needed to exhibit the behavior of a single organism, even a living creature. One having such formidable powers deserved a name to match it; William Golding, the novelist, suggested Gaia—the name given by the ancient Greeks to their Earth goddess . . . .

Now for one more speculation. We are sure that man needs Gaia but could Gaia do without man? In man, Gaia has the equivalent of a central nervous system and an awareness of herself and the rest of the Universe. Through man she has a rudimentary capacity, capable of development, to anticipate and guard against threats to her existence. For example, man can command just about enough capacity to ward off a collision with a planetoid the size of Icarus. Can it then be that in the course of man's evolution within Gaia he has been acquiring the knowledge and skills necessary to ensure her survival?[2]

Lovelocks' and Upton's perspective suggests that the era in which the material world gropes blindly toward higher levels of organization, to break through into consciousness (as Teilhard de Chardin suggested), has come to an end. Henceforth the drive toward higher consciousness, and the transformation of more and more of the nonliving world into life and conscious life, will be consciously directed: we are the tools which the biosphere, having woken up, will use to shape its future. The future until now has been born of the laws of physics and thermodynamics, by the statistical selection of the most suitable variations produced by random shufflings of genetic materials. Now the future is being made—it is in the control of beings whom Gaia has endowed with awareness of their own personal mortality, beings who have progressed to recognition of Gaia's vulnerability as well.

As the present generation of humanity, we are participants in the magical moment when Gaia has looked, for the first time, in a mirror, beheld her own face, and suddenly become conscious, through us, of her existence and identity.

This evolutionary perspective is in opposition to the notion of humans conquering or subduing the forces of Nature. Instead, we are stewards who must nurture and care for what has been placed in our hands, to ensure our own survival and that of the biosphere. Instead of hubris, we are inspired to humility; we are called upon to accept our capabilities and the tasks to come, with dignity and grace.

Thinking of the biosphere as a single living organism is rich in meaning and insights, but it raises new questions as well. One of the classical defining properties of living things is the ability to reproduce; until now, the biosphere has not had the capacity to bring forth another biosphere. As we shall see later in this book, the capabilities with which we have been endowed have now developed to the point that within the next generation the biosphere may, in fact, reproduce itself off the surface of the planet, better ensuring the survival of humanity as well as of Gaian life itself. Besides stewards, we may also be destined to become midwives.

There is a sorrow in the recognition that the future will not be the same as the past, that we are at the helm and must assume responsibility for

[2]James Lovelock and Sydney Upton, "The Quest for Gaia," *New Scientist*, 6 February 1975.

navigating the course of Gaia's future (just as there is a sorrow in childbirth and an anxiety in adolescence). Much of the old and comfortable, the tried and true, is no longer valuable and must be left behind. We must emerge from the warmth, security, and limitations of the womb. There is no going back and it can be painful. Some wag recently wrote (with perhaps greater wisdom than he or she realized), "Nostalgia isn't what it used to be." We must go forward, with as much grace and humility as we can muster.

An analogy commonly used to illustrate the vastness of geological time scales, in comparison to human time scales, compresses the five billion years of the Earth's history into a single year; all of recorded human history, then, happens in the last five minutes before midnight on December 31. But the analogy, I would suggest, is somewhat misleading and conducive to pessimism; it suggests that we are rapidly approaching an imminent endpoint. If we take, instead, the past five billion years of the Earth's history, together with the ten billion years or so in the future that the Sun will last as a stable star, permitting the survival of the Earth as a planet; and if we compress that fifteen-billion-year span into a single day, then it is now eight o'clock in the morning, the biosphere has just woken up, and the real work day is beginning.

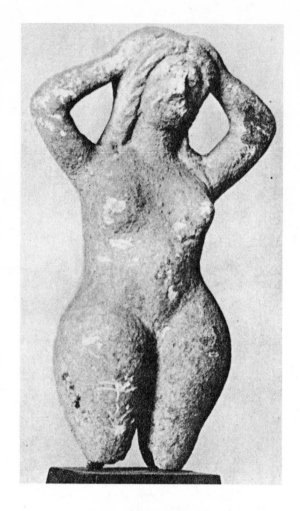

Gaia, the Earth, mother and nourisher of all things was the primal deity of the primitive Greeks.

II.
Of Wine,
Wealth, and War

Earth and the lunar surface
from Apollo 10, 1969.

7. The Elusive Boundary

 To make champagne, vintners begin with ripe grapes containing up to 24% sugar by weight. The grapes are crushed, and the fertile conditions of the mash stimulate the germination of fungal spores, always present on the skins of the grapes. The fungi multiply rapidly, feasting on the fruit sugars in the juicy pulp, and converting some of the sugar into alcohol, water, and carbon dioxide. After a brief period of fermentation in open vats, the pulp is strained out. The juices, innoculated with a prolific culture of fungi, are transferred to tightly sealed fermentation vats where the microbes continue to multiply gradually, converting more of the sugar into the metabolic waste products we desire. This stage lasts for several months.

The fermentation system is closed, and the accumulation of alcohol poisons the fungi at about the same time that the sugar content becomes sufficiently depleted to starve the microbes, and they all die. What is left behind is a brew containing 12-13% alcohol by volume, rich in dissolved carbon dioxide. The brew is allowed to age, permitting subtle, chemical processes to blend and mellow the trace, organic substances, which create the characteristic flavor and bouquet we associate with quality wines. The final product is filtered and bottled, under pressure, to prevent the escape of carbon dioxide, the release in bubbles which is the hallmark of champagne and related sparkling wines.

Although this process had been used for generations, we only began to understand it with Pasteur's discovery of the microbes involved, and it provides a classic example of the results of continuing growth in a closed system. In the end, resources are exhausted and life itself grinds to a halt.

In the twentieth century, the exploration of the far corners of the Earth by Westerners was completed. The North and South Poles had been reached, Mount Everest had been climbed, and the rivers of Africa, South America, and New Zealand had been explored and mapped. Notwithstanding the discoveries, in recent years, of two, small Stone Age tribes in the jungles of the Phillipines who have remained totally isolated since before the arrival of Europeans, no frontiers remain; and the human race appears to be living in a system as closed as a fermentation vat. Resources are available in abundance; but when they run out or when we have converted enough of them into pollutants, we too will starve to death while choking in our own wastes. This is the analogy suggested by the abundant doomsday literature, which warns that we are living in a closed system, and that we must adapt our behavior to the existing natural cycles of the biosphere, if we are to survive at all.

Is the system intrinsically closed, or do we only imagine it to be closed? In this part of the book I want to examine some of the differences between closed and open systems, and explore some of the ways in which the future we create will be affected by our views of the system as either open or closed.

In the English language, it is a compliment to describe a person as *open minded*, or to say that someone who is warm and friendly is *open*. In the first case, we praise a willingness or an eagerness to consider new ideas; in the second case, we mean that emotions and reactions are freely shared, without defensive barriers. People of either sort are described as alive in the fullest, human sense.

From our growing understanding of biochemistry and biophysics, we have begun to appreciate that every living thing, whether it is a single-celled microbe or the entire biosphere of Earth, is an open system. Unless a continual flow of energy and materials passes through the system, life will eventually cease, just as inevitably as the fungi, responsible for champagne, die in the sealed vat. It is a profound analogy to equate aliveness and openness.

The most obvious difference between an open system and a closed system is that a closed system has an impenetrable boundary. The concept of boundaries has provided rational analysis with one of its most powerful tools; but like any tool, if it is used carelessly, it can injure the user. The scientific method begins by defining the problem under consideration, by drawing a boundary between the particular object under scrutiny and the rest of the universe. To reduce the problem of understanding the structure of the DNA molecule to manageable proportions, we may, in the first approximation, ignore the commodity markets in Chicago and London and the flow patterns of the solar wind in the vicinity of Jupiter. We can make no progress at all in rational analysis, unless we narrow the scope of our attention, by deliberately drawing boundaries around the problem.

We forget, however, that in the process of rational analysis we draw another boundary as well: the division between subjective and objective. Perhaps because we have forgotten the artificial nature of this boundary, we, so often, equate the factual term *nonrational* (that which lies outside the scope of rational analysis) with the judgmental and pejorative *irrational*. Some of the most profound questions in modern, theoretical physics are centered on the issue of where to draw this boundary between experiment and experimenter, and when and if the two are separable from each other.

A conceptual boundary, drawn around a system to permit analysis, does not make the system closed. We must pay strict attention to the flows through the walls of the conceptual box, and we must remember that the box

44

is imaginary, a tool for analysis, and not reality itself. Detective mysteries provide instructive examples of how easy it is to forget that our mental analogues may be much more impenetrable than are real walls. The basic plot of the "closed room" mystery is that a murder victim is found inside a room which has been locked from inside. Everyone is baffled, until the ingenious detective recognizes that the walls are not as impermeable as everyone had assumed. It turns out, for example, that a door or window latch could be locked (as the murderer left), in such a way as to make it seem that it had been locked from within. Alternatively, an air duct or small window, too small for a normal adult to pass through, is large enough for an animal, or a circus midget. Perhaps the murderer, or the instrument of death, entered the room before the door was locked, leaving after the door had again been opened: after all, the room is closed only in space, not in time.

What about the biosphere itself? Prior to photosynthesis, most of the Earth was inaccessible to life, since all lifeforms depended on nonbiological processes for the synthesis of the complex, organic substances they used for food. The places where such processes took place, at sufficiently rapid rates to sustain life, were limited, and, in that sense, life on Earth was a closed system. But with photosynthesis the boundaries of the system were pushed open, to encompass the lowermost hundred kilometers or so of the atmosphere. Through the expanded outer boundary of the biosphere, a constant flow of energy, with sunlight flowing in and infrared (heat) radiation passing out, permits the biosphere to flourish.

The primary producers of the biosphere, the photosynthetic plants, are likewise flow-through systems. At the boundary in time when an individual plant begins its life as a spore, seed, or cutting, a small quantity of complex, organic molecules enter the space-time box, constituting the plant through its entire life. As the plant lives and grows, simple molecules of carbon dioxide, water, ammonium compounds, and other nutrients pass through the spacial boundaries of the box, together with the sunlight needed to accomplish the biochemical miracle of photosynthesis. Some complex molecules, such as the aromatic oils of floral fragrances and the genetic endowments of the next generation, pass outward through these same boundaries, together with such simple molecules as oxygen and water vapor, and with dissipated energy, in the form of infrared radiation. At the boundary in time when the individual plant dies, a large quantity of highly complex, organic molecules, making up the body of the plant, pass out into the environment to decompose.

The flows through the boundaries in time of an individual animal or nonphotosynthesizing plant (such as a fungus) are similar to those I just described. The flows through the boundaries of the individual creature are different, though. Sunlight flowing in is usually of little importance. The

45

flow of material into the box consists mostly of complex, organic molecules, in such highly organized forms as lettuce leaves, pieces of steak, or grape pulp, and some simpler molecules such as water and oxygen. What passes outward through these same boundaries, includes heat, simple molecules like water and carbon dioxide, and molecules of intermediate complexity, but in a very disorganized form in the wastes of the creature.

The diverse phenomena associated with living things can be viewed as *flows of entropy*, a thermodynamic concept closely related to the mathematical concept of disorder. Every living thing is a structure which acts to increase order within its spacial boundaries. Photosynethetic plants, and the biosphere as a whole, convert sunlight, a relatively ordered form of radiation, into infrared radiation, a less ordered form of radiant energy. The entropy of the energy flowing through the system is increased; this increase in entropy supports the decrease in the entropy of the matter flowing through the system, as the living system combines disorganized, simple molecules into highly organized, complex molecules like sugars, fats, proteins, and DNA molecules.

Animals and nonphotosynthesizing plants operate on the opposite flow, ingesting highly ordered materials, which are degraded into disorganized forms. The change in entropy provides the energy needed to rearrange some of the nutrients into tissue and to stimulate locomotion in animals.

The fabrication of human artifacts involves these same flows of entropy. Very highly organized forms of energy (electricity) are produced from less ordered energy (ancient sunshine), by the conversion of highly ordered forms of matter (fossil fuels) into disorganized matter (water vapor and carbon dioxide). The appropriate combination of highly ordered energy (electricity and flames) with disordered matter (low grade ore) results in the production of highly ordered material (pure aluminum ingots) and disorganized energy (waste heat).

To sustain life and its human extension, culture, it is thus necessary for the system to be open to flows of entropy in the forms of energy or matter or both. What determines the total biomass or the total economic wealth, then, is not the inventories of natural resources, but the structure and organization of the flows through the system. Looking for the boundaries or limits of the system, blinds us to the flows which are the very heart of any living system.

Perhaps we should not be surprised, then, that Western societies, which habitually have drawn conceptual boundaries through and around every system since Aristotle, persist in a conflict-oriented approach to problems which could, in principle, be dealt with much more effectively by mutual cooperation. If my mental image of the world includes a boundary encircling us and the resources we need for survival, and if I believe that boundary to be impenetrable and absolute, then I will start erecting compartment boundaries to seal off an adequate supply for myself and my family in order to ensure our survival. I will regard any encroachment on resources I have defined "mine" as a hostile act.

As the German philosopher, Arthur Schopenhauer, observed, "Every man takes the limits of his own vision for the limits of the world," and the results can be deadly. If we imagine the system in which we live to be closed, in that very instant we accept the rules of the "zero-sum game," with consequences I will address later. If, instead, we recognize the open-ended nature of the world, and we admit that "there are more things in heaven and earth . . . than are dreamt of in your philosophy," then it is not only sensible but possible to consider cooperation and mutual support. The attitudes of many non-Western cultures, which stress mutualism rather than confrontation, become as reasonable as they are humane and positive.

Bob Borello, Sheep Rancher,
Point Reyes, California, 1976.

8. The Roots of Economic Wealth

 What is the basis of economic wealth? Much of the history of Western civilization, as taught in our schools, could be interpreted as a succession of answers to this question. Feudalism was based on the idea that land itself was the basis of wealth. The rise of the craft guilds suggested that labor was wealth. The Industrial Revolution, based on entrepreneurs selling shares in new business ventures, brought about a reinterpretation of economics in terms of capital. The successes of fortunate inventors in the nineteenth century convinced many that technology was the true source of wealth in modern times. Political events since 1972 have brought vast sums of money into the coffers of the OPEC nations, creating a view that natural resources such as petroleum, bauxite, or phosphate are the ultimate basis of wealth, and reverting to a revised feudal theory of economics.

All of these answers are fragmentary at best. Land, labor, entrepreneurship and capital, technological innovations, material resources, and energy resources are all present in varying degrees in every economic system created by humans, from the hunter-gatherer economy of the Bush peoples in the Kalahari Desert to the very largest multinational conglomerates.

The two fundamental roots of wealth in all of these economic systems have been knowledge and cooperative efforts: knowledge of what is useful and needful, where things can be obtained, how they can be combined, who has essential skills, when to plant and harvest, why one source of materials or one method of production is preferable to another under some particular set of circumstances; cooperative effort to implement each stage in the production of wealth and to create the "marketplace" assumed in classical economic theory.

Overemphasis of any one of the visible factors of production results in lopsided conclusions. Some of the classical economists of the nineteenth century — Thomas Robert Malthus, David Ricardo, and John Stuart Mill, in particular — believed that economic growth would inevitably be limited by land and resources. In their view, the "marginal cost of extraction," the cost of developing one more acre of farmland or of mining one more ton of iron ore, would, inevitably, become greater. But the historical record strongly suggests that marginal costs can only rise, if knowledge itself becomes a finite or scarce resource, or if cooperation breaks down.

A detailed analysis of extractive industries (agriculture, mining, fishing, and forestry) showed that over the period from 1870-1957 (at least) the actual costs per unit of output in the United States declined steadily, when corrected for inflation, except in the forestry industries.[1] The authors of this study showed that the principal factors in the decline of both capital costs and labor costs were improvements in extractive technologies and new discoveries of mineral deposits.

Barnett and Morse also trace the historical development of the hypothesis of natural resource scarcity from the times of Malthus and Ricardo. During the period from 1890 to about 1920, the Progressive party in the United States was closely connected to the vigorous Conservationist movement which had been spearheaded by Theodore Roosevelt and Gifford Pinchot. The conservationists of that day correctly observed that some of the most scenic and spectacular wilderness areas in the country were in danger of exploitation in ways that would permanently deny their beauty to later generations. As a result of their efforts, vast tracts of public lands were added to the National Forest system and the National Parks system. But the Conservationists also accepted the scarcity doctrines of Malthus, Ricardo, and Mill. In their view, it was mandatory to conserve our legacy of raw materials, if any were to remain for the use of future generations. Iron ore, for example, was believed to be in danger of total exhaustion within a few decades. Today, despite dramatic growth in annual iron production, iron ore reserves are sufficient for at least several centuries.

The ideas of the Conservationist movement largely disappeared from the political scene in the United States as the Progressive party declined, and as euphoria in the 1920s swept the nation. Following World War II, however, both leisure time and disposable income increased enormously, leading to explosive growth in the use of the National Parks. The need for the allocation of additional wilderness lands for public recreation, and for better protection of existing preserves became widely recognized. Worldwide population trends were publicized and discussed, and as population growth rates in the late 1960s approached 2% a year for the world as a whole (higher than ever before), the earlier conservationist doctrines were revived, including the scarcity hypothesis.

Many environmentalists took the Apollo photographs of the Earth (viewed from the Moon) as graphic proof of the scarcity hypothesis: it seemed perfectly clear that "we have only the Earth," and the Earth is finite. The culmination of this viewpoint came in 1972 with the publication of *The Limits to Growth*, a popularly written report on a study undertaken by the Systems Dynamics Group at the Massachusetts Institute of Technology.[2]

[1]Harold J. Barnett and Chandler Morse, *Scarcity and Growth: The Economics of Natural Resource Availability*, (Baltimore: Resources for the Future, and Johns Hopkins University Press, 1963), Chapters nine and ten.

[2]D.H. Meadows, D.L. Meadows, J. Randers, and W.W. Behrens III, *The Limits to Growth*, (New York: Universe Books, 1972).

The Roots of Economic Wealth

Using a highly simplified model of the global socioeconomic system, the M.I.T. group carried out a number of computer calculations, which projected a massive collapse of the entire system early in the twenty-first century, with soaring death rates due to breakdown of the economy, ever-rising pollution, and famines. The computer model explicitly assumes that natural resources are becoming scarcer and much more expensive to obtain. The model tacitly assumes that the Earth is a closed system, and that throughout this century and the next, the only material and energy resources available for human use will be those of the planet Earth.

Worldwide increases in petroleum prices in 1973-4 seemed to validate the assumption of progressive scarcity and general rising costs. The political motivations of the OPEC cartel, and a major shift in the cooperative efforts needed to obtain and market petroleum on a worldwide scale brought about the price increase — not actual scarcity of known petroleum deposits.

The timing and nature of the disasters in the computer model depend on hypothetical relationships between various parts of the socioeconomic system, which are nearly impossible to prove or disprove. It is assumed, for instance, that if the average income per person were doubled, then pollution generated per person would be tripled. If the investment per person in agriculture were six times greater than today, the model assumes that the worldwide average production of food per person would be only 2.2 times greater. While such dubious assumptions contribute to the disaster, the fundamental cause of the collapse of civilization, forecast by the model, is the assumed rise in costs of raw materials due to impending scarcity. Although the authors of the study were aware of the findings of Barnett and Morse, they chose to incorporate the scarcity hypothesis in the computer model.[3]

In October 1975 I attended a conference near Houston, Texas, planned as the first of five biennial meetings on the problems of transitioning from exponential growth of population and production to some sort of steady, state equilibrium. That first meeting, Limits to Growth '75, was organized by Dennis L. Meadows, principal investigator of the 1972 study and one of the co-authors of the popular report. The overwhelming majority of the invited speakers were neo-Malthusians; one of the few exceptions was Herman Kahn, a noted champion of technological optimism and continued growth.

One afternoon the program featured a debate between Meadows and Kahn. Aside from profound questions about the validity of any computer model of the socioeconomic system, Kahn attacked the computer model for its failure to allow for the substitutability of materials. He posited that

---

[3]D.H. Meadows et al., *Dynamics of Growth in a Finite World*, (Cambridge, Mass.: Wright-Allen Press, 1973). *The Limits to Growth* does not mention this point. The authors, however, acknowledge the Barnett and Morse findings in a detailed, technical report on the computer model.

through new technologies, scarce resources can be replaced by abundant materials which have been adapted to serve the same functions as depleted materials. Meadows asserted that we are running out of too many minerals, too fast for social institutions to react in time and for the necessary research to be done. Kahn insisted that we have always responded in time; that no forseeable shortages were so serious or so imminent that we could not avert difficulties. Meadows in turn asked how we could trust that new discoveries and innovations would continue to be made rapidly enough to avert disaster. Besides, he argued, every "technological fix" created five new problems in its wake . . . .

By this point, the "debate" had become rather boring, having degenerated to the level of exchanges like this: "Yes, it is." "No, it isn't." "It is so!" "No, it's not!" "You're wrong!" "You don't know what you're talking about!"

The confrontation between the opposing schools of thought was disappointing. The underlying disagreement was not about verifiable facts, but discrepancies about fundamental philosophical views of reality. These differences were never addressed or even acknowledged.

The entire debate about the long term prospects for economic wealth needs to be reformulated. It is not a question of how long resources X, Y, or Z will last under present consumption patterns. The real questions are: *What are the ultimate limits to knowledge? How can we maximize cooperative efforts to put our knowledge to constructive uses?* When the debate is formulated in this way, our perspective about the future is immediately altered. It is entirely possible that economic wealth has no intrinsic limit, since we can certainly see no intrinsic limits to knowledge.

Instead of fearing the future, we are challenged to work together to create and use new knowledge. We can doom ourselves to a future even more bleak than that computed by Meadows and his colleagues, if we draw imaginary boundaries which obstruct the flow of knowledge, or impede cooperative efforts to use that knowledge constructively. The greater wisdom is to remove barriers in our basic world views. Then we can create the humane and positive future we desire. The world in which we live is no more closed than the Earth is flat.

9. The Arms Race and Other Follies of the Zero-Sum Game

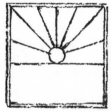The card game, poker, is an archetype of "zero-sum games," games for which the sum of the winnings and the losses (counted as negative winnings) of all the players is exactly zero. In poker, two or more players are necessary, with seven or eight being a practical maximum. Before each hand is dealt, each player who wishes to participate in the hand antes up, or contributes an agreed entrance fee to the "pot." With countless variations and options, several rounds of betting on the strengths of the players' hands may take place as the cards are dealt out or exchanged.

One player, with a reasonably strong hand, will likely bet some additional money, increasing the size of the pot. All other players must see the bet (match it) or fold (drop out of the game, forfeiting the money contributed to the pot during the hand). Any player still in the game can raise the bet (bet a larger amount) and all other players, including the original bettor, must see the raise or fold.

Strengths of poker hands are based on the relative probabilities of occurrence of the combinations of face values and suits of the cards in a player's hand. At the end of the last round of betting, surviving players compare hands with variations in who shows his or her hand first. Weaker hands need not be revealed, and the strongest hand shown wins the pot. Occasionally, a player with a weak hand succeeds in bluffing, so that other players who in fact have hands of average strength fold early; and, on rare occasions, the weakest hand wins the entire pot. If a player has a poor poker face, revealing inadvertently that he or she has a strong hand, other players will drop out of the betting early, the pot remains small, and the strongest hand wins a disproportionately small reward.

Assuming all the players have comparable skills in bluffing and that none of them cheat, no individual player can gain a lasting advantage, although long winning and losing streaks may occur. As long as all of the players recognize that it is only a game, and as long as no player gets "deeper in the hole" than he or she can afford, such zero-sum games can be highly entertaining and enjoyable. But in real life, zero-sum games can be dangerous and deadly.

Hunting and gathering societies do not live by the rules of a zero-sum game. If one person picks a handful of berries or nuts, it does not deprive another of berries or nuts, because everyone will share what each member of the group has gathered. The system is open: if one person desires more berries or nuts, he or she can pick from another bush or tree.

But if necessary resources are believed to be scarce, then whatever one nation takes or uses is denied other nations. Various features of zero-sum games appear, but it is transformed into a sinister and dangerous game — no longer for entertainment — but for survival. The stronger players constantly redefine the rules of the game, in their favor, while all the players attempt to evade the rules without being caught in the act. Bluffing becomes very important, at stakes which sometimes threaten to change the game into a negative-sum game. Until recently, if a card player in Texas shot another card player for cheating during a round of gambling for money, justifiable homocide was an acceptable legal defense against an indictment for murder.

The arms race between the United States and the Soviet Union persists because, within the context of the zero-sum game, both counties assume tacitly that any increase in the other country's political — and thus economic — influence is a decrease in its own power. For centuries, Russia has been the victim of invasions from east and west; by the Tarters and the Poles, by the French under Napoleon, by the Germans under Hitler, and she has become distinctly paranoid about her territorial integrity. Given what seems to be a closed world, of dwindling resources, that paranoia inevitably will be carried over into the struggle for limited resources. Clear and convincing evidence that the world system is open-ended, that more for other nations does not mean less for the Soviet Union (or for the United States), would provide an antidote for this situation. But the nature of the zero-sum game is such that neither side can realistically withdraw unilaterally.

In family life people normally do not apply zero-sum game rules. If a husband and wife begin to draw boundary lines in the bedroom or in household tasks, family life would be in dire straits. In many other areas of human endeavor, we fail frequently to apply principles of cooperation, which come naturally in the family setting. Labor unions, acting in the belief that jobs are inherently scarce, erect arbitrary and rigid boundaries between various trades. In the United States, if a carpenter is erecting rafters atop a new house, the unskilled laborer, who unloads the lumber from the truck, may not lean the rafters against the wall of the house. He must place them flat on the ground, because it is the job of the carpenter's helper to lift them into the upright position, so the carpenter can pull them up to the top of the framing for installation. Without such rigid boundaries between trades, the carpenter's helper would have nothing to do; and the unions assume that fewer jobs would be available in the building trades. In the face of the conviction that it is a zero-sum game in which jobs are scarce, it is useless to point out that lower housing costs could make it possible for more families to buy homes, thus increasing the number of jobs available in construction.

Many environmentalists argue that it is healthy for Western civilization to recognize the limits of a closed system and how to live harmoniously within it. The perception of unlimited abundance, they suggest, corrupted our ancestors who immigrated to the New World and proceeded to rape this magnificent land, which the American Indians had tended to so gracefully. This perspective, I would suggest, reverses cause and effect. The Europeans who emigrated to the New World in the sixteenth and seventeenth centuries were, for the most part, the poor and the criminal who had lived most of their lives as victims of the zero-sum game. Most of the pioneers, in the westward expansion of the United States during the eighteenth and nineteenth centuries, came from similarly downtrodden strata of eastern seaboard society.

Given the mindset of the zero-sum game, it is inevitable that people, moving into a frontier where resources are readily available, will grab as much as they can for fear of losing the resources to someone else. The ultimate caricature of this mentality occurred on the day the Oklahoma Territory was opened legally for settlement by non-Indians. Some ten thousand would-be settlers lined up, for the firing of a gun, before rushing out in a mad race to stake their claims to a limited supply of land.

If we know that the world is open-ended, with more than enough for everyone, then we can afford a leisurely pace, taking only what is needed, when it is needed. If we can exorcise the mentality of the zero-sum game, we can be as kind to the environment as the Indians were, and recognize the boundlessness surrounding us.

African continent from the
Mediterranean Sea to the Antarctica ice cap,
Apollo 17, 1972.

III.

The Living Earth

*View of the Earth
from Apollo 11, 1969.*

10. The Raiment of Gaia

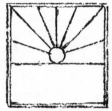 So far I have examined some of the more philosophical aspects of our role in creating the future. If we are to continue to inhabit this planet far into the future, our use of the planet must ensure the continued health of the entire biosphere—not only our own comfort on this planet. I want, now, to consider our relation to the rest of the biosphere.

Ecology can be defined as the study of the balances in the biosphere. The central reality of the biosphere, however, is that it is constantly evolving and changing. In a sense, the subject matter of ecology is a single frame from the movie of evolution. We can no more comprehend Gaia than we can grasp the full impact of the movie, *Gone With the Wind*, by studying a few still shots.

Yosemite Valley in the Sierra Nevada mountains of California is one of my favorite places on Earth. When the glaciers, which formed its sheer vertical walls, receded some ten thousand years ago, they left a large lake in the upper half of the valley, dammed up behind the detritus of gravel and boulders deposited by the melting ice at the lower margin of the active glacier. Over a few thousand years, the lake silted up, creating the flat floor of the valley. When tourists first began visiting the valley in large numbers, less than a century ago, the valley floor was a mix of forest and meadow, with a large, clear lake at the upper end of the valley, reflecting the spectacular granite faces which surround it—Cloud's Rest, Half Dome, North Dome, and Washington Column. Today the forests have taken over more of the valley floor, and the siltation of Mirror Lake continues, so than even in years of normal precipitation the lake is reduced to an expanse of mud with a small stream meandering through one side during half the summer and fall.

A conservation ethic, dedicated to the preservation of the biosphere in its status quo, would be just as lethal — both to ourselves and to the rest of the system—as it would be to pave the entire planet with concrete and asphalt. If we were to attempt to preserve Yosemite Valley, unchanged forever, which Yosemite should be preserved: the glacial lake, the silted marshland of a few thousand years ago, the Yosemite our grandparents knew, or the Yosemite yet to come, with very little meadow space and no Mirror Lake?

How shall we use and shape the planet? Many environmentalists, especially in the United States, point to the English landscape as an example of harmony between the human and the natural environments. But as

Doomsday Has Been Cancelled

biologist René Dubos has pointed out,

> . . . the English landscape, admirable as it is, is far different from what it was in the state of wilderness. . . the prodigious and continuous efforts of settlers and farmers have created an astonishing diversity of ecosystems that appear natural only because they are familiar, but that are really of human origin. For example, the enclosures so characteristic of East Anglia were created in the 18th century to facilitate certain types of agricultural improvements. At that time, the farming country was divided by law into a patchwork of semirectangular fields, each 5 to 10 acres in area, often without much regard to the natural contour of the land. The fields were divided by drainage ditches and straight lines of hawthorn hedges, and trees were planted in regular rows. This famous landscape is thus a very artificial human creation. When it first came into being, in fact, it greatly shocked farmers, nature lovers, and landscape architects . . . .
>
> The English landscape architects transformed the humanized land of East Anglia by taking their inspiration from bucolic but imaginary landscapes painted by Claude Lorrain, Nicholas Poussin, and Salvatore Rosa. They obviously did not believe that "nature knows best," but instead tried to improve on it by rearranging the elements.[1]

We clothe our bodies to keep ourselves warm in the winter, cool in the summer, and dry when it rains or snows. In making or selecting clothes to wear, we consider also whether our clothing will protect us from dangers such as sunburn, mosquitos, chapparal, or mud. Once we have satisfied these utilitarian functions, however, we usually make some effort to dress ourselves attractively, highlighting our personal appearance, by careful selection of the textures, colors, and shapes of fabrics, metals, and gemstones.

In the emerging relationship between *Homo sapiens* and the rest of the biosphere, we are coming to accept our role as the consciousness of Gaia; we must likewise consider both the functional effects and the aesthetic qualities of the ever-changing raiment in which we choose to clothe her planetary flesh.

One of the most important functional effects of human civilization and its alteration of the landscapes of the Earth is the effect on the thermal balance of the biosphere. The direct release of energy into the lower layers of the atmosphere, or into the oceans, is projected for the next century or more to total far less than the solar energy deposited in these layers of the atmosphere, in the waters of the oceans, and in the top layers of soil and rock. But the indirect effects of human activities could be large; so it is of considerable importance to understand how Gaia has controlled her tem-

[1]René Dubos, "Symbiosis Between the Earth and Humankind," *Science*, 6 August 1976, pp. 459-462.

perature within a few degrees if 15⁰ C (59⁰ F) for several hundred million years. As yet, the picture is only fragmentary; the effects of slow changes in the shape of the Earth's orbit, and of variations in the tilt of the Earth's axis of rotation, apparently can account for the major cycles of glacial advance and retreat during the last two million years or so,[2] but the possible role of changes in the brightness of the Sun itself remain unknown. The composition of the atmosphere affects the absorption of sunlight and the emission of thermal (infrared) radiation; the composition is determined by all the lifeforms on Earth as well as by the emissions of airplanes and rockets passing through the stratosphere.

Once we come to understand the heat balancing mechanisms more thoroughly, we can begin to supplement existing regulatory interactions with consciously implemented mechanisms. Should we find it desirable, we will be able to turn the Sahara Desert into farms and forests, or remake the landscape of New England, while we create the kind of future we dream.

> Nature is like a great river of materials and forces that can be directed in this or that channel by human intervention. Such intervention is justified because the natural channels are not necessarily the most desirable, either for the human species or for other species. It is not true that "nature knows best." It often creates ecosystems that are inefficient, wasteful, and destructive. By using reason and knowledge, we can manipulate the raw stuff of nature and shape it into ecosystems that have qualities not found in wilderness. Many potentialities of the earth become manifest only when they have been brought out by human imagination and toil . . . .
>
> Symbiotic relationships mean creative partnerships . . . Millenia of experience show that by entering into a symbiotic relationship with nature, humankind can invent and generate futures not predictable from the deterministic order of things, and thus can engage in a continuous process of creation.[3]

We are the legitimate children of Gaia; we need not be ashamed that we are altering the landscapes and the ecosystems of Earth. But we do owe our mother careful attention to our handiwork and to our treatment of Gaia's other species of life.

---

[2]Nigel Calder, "Head South With All Deliberate Speed: Ice May Return in a Few Thousand Years," *Smithsonian*, January 1978, pp. 32-41. Presents a very readable account of the Milankovitch theory of the ice ages of the last two million years.
[3]Dubos, "Symbiosis."

Weather satellite catches the eye of hurricane Katrina
off the coast of Baja California, September 3, 1975.

11. Feasts and Famines

 Environmentalists frequently warn us that a population of any particular species cannot be maintained indefinitely at levels above the "carrying capacity" of the environment. The number of wolves and cougars that can be supported in a given area, for example, depends on the numbers of deer, rabbits, squirrels, and other animals on which the carnivores prey. The number of deer that same area can sustain depends on the population and luxuriance of the plants which are edible by the deer. Should the wolf population increase dramatically, the deer population would dwindle correspondingly. After some time, the favorite foliage of the deer would grow more lushly, while the wolves and the cougars begin to starve, permitting an increase in the number of deer. Under a given set of circumstances, the wolf population regularly oscillates around some optimum level, the carrying capacity of that particular environment for wolves.

Carrying capacity is a relative term: it depends on the particular set of circumstances. If all the cougars were removed from the area I just described, the carrying capacity of that area for wolves would increase, and the relative populations of deer, rabbits, and squirrels would all shift slightly, because of differences in the preying tactics and taste preferences of wolves and cougars. These shifts would slightly alter the mix of forage plants, which would change the relative populations of herbivorous and carnivorous invertebrates and, ultimately, the ratios among the populations of various scavengers in the system, such as carrion beetles, vultures, earthworms, and mushrooms.

If rainfall and average temperature in the area were to increase slightly, the vegetation on which the deer, rabbits, and squirrels feed would grow more luxuriantly, and the carrying capacity of the area for all the herbivores, carnivores, and scavengers would increase slightly, again with some shifts in the relative numbers of virtually every species of plant and animal.

The greatest difficulty with the concept of carrying capacity comes in applying it to the human population or to the biosphere as a whole. *What is the carrying capacity of the planet Earth for human beings?* This question is objectionable for three reasons: it is incomplete, since the particular circumstances are not specified; it tacitly assumes that the carrying capacity is immutably fixed at a level determined entirely by unconscious natural processes; and it assumes that the biosphere itself has reached its maximum growth.

Clearly, the carrying capacity of the planet Earth for human beings would be enormously larger than the present population of some four billion people, if we were all to live in high-rise apartments or subterranean cities, with every acre of land and every rooftop covered with greenhouses, enclosing intensive farms. With careful integration of the entire agricultural system, we could raise an optimum mixture of plants and animals to provide a balanced diet as well as sufficient fuels for energy derived from plant and animal wastes. No one would be hungry or cold, and not a gram of plant or animal refuse would escape, unused. Short of such an absurd extreme, however, immense freedom of choice is available in the mix of agricultural practices, diets, social priorities, and land use policies — with due consideration for preservation of wilderness — which could sustain many times the present population of the world.

The cultural history of the human species has been dominated by our efforts and successes in applying knowledge to overcome the apparent restrictions and limitations of unconscious natural processes. It now appears that a twelve-year, worldwide campaign has succeeded in eradicating the smallpox virus, which has scourged the human species since ancient times, overcoming one particularly miserable limitation on human population. Few would mourn the extinction of the wild smallpox virus. A serious debate is developing concerning whether small populations of smallpox viruses in captivity, in pharmaceutical laboratories, should also be extinguished or preserved in perpetuity. Meanwhile, the carrying capacity of the Earth for human beings has been altered by this single program, whose total cost was only about $120 million.

How big is the biosphere itself? The total mass of living things and organic debris, such as fallen leaves and branches, dead animals, manure, and partially decomposed materials, mixed into the mud at the bottoms of lakes and streams, amounts to 1.02 million million kilograms (2.42 million million pounds). While this seems like an enormous quantity, it is less than one-sixth of one-millionth, of one-millionth, of the total mass of the planet Earth. Averaged over the entire surface of the Earth, the total biomass amounts to a thin layer of a bit less than 200 metric tons per hectare (or 89 short tons per acre). The four light elements (oxygen, carbon, hydrogen, and nitrogen) account for 99% of the total mass, and the greatest fraction of the total is in the form of cellulose, which contains only oxygen, carbon, and hydrogen.[1] The amount of each of the four principal elements of the biomass of the planet, which are available in the atmosphere, the oceans, and in oil shale or limestone deposits, is, in each case, at least one million times greater

[1]Edward S. Deevey, Jr., *The Biosphere*, (San Francisco: Scientific American and W.H. Freeman, 1970), pp. 83-84.

than the total mass of that element in the biomass of the planet. Thus the carrying capacity of the Earth for all life is not limited by the stocks of raw materials, but rather by the organization and the structure of the flows of materials, energy, and information.

In studying the progression of growth of an ecosystem, such as a forest taking over a meadow or growing back after a forest fire, ecologists have developed the concept of "climax forest," in which the distribution of plants and animals by species, age, size, and location has reached a kind of equilibrium, and the total loss of leaves, branches, and dead animals each year is exactly balanced by new growth and new births. Yet in every case examined, in recent years, of an ecosystem which was believed to be a climax forest, careful measurements of the flows of minerals into and out of the ecosystem indicate a rate of increase in the biomass of the area of about 1% a year.[2] It is interesting to speculate whether this finding is due to an incorrect conception of climax growth, or whether it may be part of the long term recovery of the biosphere from the last glaciation. It may also be the result of human activities, such as release of carbon dioxide into the atmosphere, by the burning of fossil fuels, and progressive deforestation of most inhabited regions of the Earth.

Although a growth rate of 1% a year (if applied to all of the biosphere) may seem alarming, the prospect of civilization becoming engulfed in greenery in the forseeable future is most unlikely. Certainly much more research is needed to understand the magnitudes and structures of material cycles in the biosphere, including nitrates, phosphates, sulfur, carbon, and nitrogen, and to define the extent to which human activities affect these flows. In the past the biosphere has experienced periods of rapid expansion, most notably after the beginning of photosynthesis. It seems clear that the biosphere can grow larger; if it actually is growing larger at the present time, expansion may mark another transition for Gaia, as significant as the invention of photosynthesis. We shall determine the carrying capacity of the Earth for human beings and all life, as we better understand the flows in the system.

[2]Deevey, *The Biosphere*, p. 92.

Infrared photograph of
the Amazon and Purus Rivers, 1972.

12. Enough to Eat

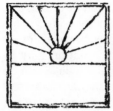A healthy, adult, human being can maintain consciousness for perhaps two minutes without breathing oxygen, but will suffer irreversible brain damage in less than six minutes. Given air to breathe, an adult can survive for several days, perhaps two weeks depending on air temperature and humidity, without water to drink. With sufficient air and water, clothing, and shelter, or fire to maintain body heat in cooler climates, an adult can survive for several weeks, even a few months, without food; but even the first few days of fasting will result in significant decreases in the ability to perform physical or mental work.

If we are to have a humane and positive future, the production of food for human consumption must expand as the human population increases. Since the end of World War II, the Food and Agriculture Organization (FAO) of the United Nations has issued a series of World Food Surveys which have attempted to monitor the balance between global population and food supply. Generally speaking, these reports have not been very hopeful, and have contributed heavily to the climate of despair in the West during the past two or three decades. In the wake of these reports, the spectre of global famine lurks behind every major political or economic event.

Considered individually, any one of these FAO surveys appears incontrovertible in its documentation of rampant starvation and malnutrition; taken *in toto*, however, the differences in methodologies, assumptions, and conclusions among the successive reports, stimulate skepticism in all the reports.[1] The FAO has insufficient resources — of money or staff — to collect and interpret detailed data from all over the world; it relies, instead, on data provided by the member governments of FAO and on some very limited field studies. The economic system in Third World countries is underdeveloped, and so is the mechanism for collecting data on income distribution, personal expenditures for food, market prices of agricultural commodities, and actual food production, let alone reliable census information. In the face of inadequate information, the FAO's approach has been to assume homogeneous dietary patterns throughout each country. On this basis, the FAO computes a hypothetical, average daily intake of calories and proteins

[1]Thomas T. Poleman, "World Food: A Perspective," *Science*, Vol. 188, 1975, p. 510. Poleman presents what seems to be a balanced critique of food surveys published by the FAO and the U.S. Department of Agriculture.

and compares it to the recommended daily nutritional allowances, formulated by such groups as the World Health Organization (WHO) of the United Nations, the Food and Nutrition Board of the National Research Council in the United States, and the FAO itself.

This approach is dangerous, at best. Even in industrialized nations like the United States, where the same kinds of foods are available in every city, enormous differences in dietary patterns exist among different ethnic and economic subgroups. In countries where dietary staples vary widely from place to place, variations in dietary patterns are likely to be even greater; so that the assumption of dietary homogeneity throughout a nation may be very misleading. The entire question of human nutritional needs is still far from being understood. As the science of nutrition matures, estimates of minimum daily needs are continually revised downward, so that the criteria for determining malnutrition or starvation have changed, from one FAO survey to the next. The FAO has failed to consider the decreased caloric intake in the warmer climates of most of the Third World, further aggravating the apparent imbalance between food production and population.

The results of juxtaposing such uncritical averages, to draw conclusions about the real world, can be illustrated by considering what sort of conclusions might be drawn casually from several independently appropriate averages. Suppose careful surveys of some hypothetical country showed the following facts:

- The average age of the population is 28 years.
- The average minimum daily requirement for a 28-year old adult in that climate is 2,350 calories.
- The average daily diet provides 1,900 calories per person, per day.

To draw the conclusion that starvation is rampant in such a country would be unjustifiable, since the daily needs of the significant fraction of the population in the prepubertal and elderly age brackets are much lower than those of twenty-eight-year old adults. The *average needs per person* would be substantially lower than the *needs of the average-aged person*. In the face of inadequate data, the FAO surveys have drawn equally inappropriate conclusions.

Despite the failings of the FAO's reports, it would be irresponsible to deny that food production and distribution pose important problems; the famine in the sub-Saharan countries of Africa in the early 1970s was certainly real. I cannot provide a comprehensive and definitive review of global agriculture here; instead, I want to point out some ideas and perspectives which offer realistic hopes that everyone on Earth can have enough to eat throughout the forseeable future.

For most of the history of the human species we have been hunters and gatherers. Deliberately planting seeds, cultivating the soil, irrigating the fields, and harvesting the yields became widely adopted independently, and more or less simultaneously in at least five different parts of the globe, about ten thousand years ago. Domestication of a number of species of birds and mammals began at about the same time. Deliberate and continual breeding of plants and animals, to enhance desirable traits, has existed since the very beginnings of agriculture.

In the wake of this transition, the human population began a rapid increase, and human social structures were transformed so dramatically that the transition is described as the Neolithic (New Stone Age) Revolution. The usual view of this transformation of human society is that our ancestors adopted the sedentary farming life out of a desire for the security of the food surpluses which could be produced by tilling the soil; surely that must have been preferable to the unreliability of hunting and gathering, and to the sporadic famines to which hunters and gatherers presumably were vulnerable. Once villages formed, social arrangements altered radically, and people began to acquire and hoard personal belongings.

The actual reasons for the transition, from nomadic hunting and gathering to sedentary farming villages, is still open to speculation. Anthropologists are studying the few remaining hunting and gathering societies scattered around the Earth, before they, too, are caught up in the Neolithic Revolution. Some of their findings are rather surprising. Our remote ancestors may have made the transition because they desired the changes in social arrangements and the possibility of acquiring personal belongings.

Even the inhospitable Kalahari Desert of Africa affords hunting and gathering, Bush peoples a steady supply of abundant food year round. The typical adult of the !Kung tribes spends only two or three days, on the average, out of seven actively procuring food for the group. Much of the remaining time he or she spends socializing — hardly a picture of marginal subsistence.[2]

The !Kung have very few personal or tribal possessions, since all such possessions must be either carried along when the group changes base camp or be abandoned. Thus even bodily adornments are very limited. Since they store no foods, in the dry season, before the summer rains come to the Kalahari, the dietary staples are insipid, tasteless, root vegetables, eaten without pleasure or appetite. During routine foraging for fruits, nuts, and vegetables, or whenever the group moves camp, the mothers must carry their infants and toddlers up to three to five years of age. Thus the usual spacing between siblings is three to five years.

It is entirely possible, then, that the transition to fixed agriculture was

[2]Richard Lee Borshay, "The !Kung Bushman of Botswana," in M.G. Bicchieri, ed., *Hunters and Gatherers Today*, (New York: Holt, Rinehart & Winston, 1972).

motivated — not by survival needs — by the desire for a place to store more personal belongings;[3] the desire to store out-of-season foods; and the desire — expressed by many !Kung women — for more children.

Whatever the prehistoric motivations may have been, the human population today can no longer be supported solely by hunting and gathering. Agriculture is no longer optional if more than a few percent of humanity is to survive. Although food production, averaged around the whole world, has kept pace with population growth, a number of myths about the food situation are impeding real progress in improving the food supply for the world's poorest people.[4]

Lappé and Collins argue that scarcities of food and agricultural land are not the reason for hunger on Earth. Even during the worst famines of the early 1970s, the world's production of staple grains alone was sufficient to provide more than 3,000 calories a day for every human being. Population density does not correlate with hunger:

> Bangladesh, for example, has just half the people per cultivated acre that Taiwan has. Yet Taiwan has no starvation while Bangladesh is thought of as the world's worst basket case. China has twice as many people for each cultivated acre as India. Yet in China people are not hungry.[5]

One cannot argue that we have run out of arable lands when large fractions of the cultivated land in Third World countries are dedicated for crops for export, including coffee, tea, and cotton.

Defining the problem as one of scarcity results in excessive attention to reducing population growth and to technological methods of increasing productivity per acre (as admirable as the latter goal may be), with insufficient attention to social and political reforms. Following agribusiness in the United States, in different social, economic, and political surroundings, has tended to cut small farmers and marginal producers out of the economy altogether, despite the fact that these small farms are often much more productive per acre.

> A study of Argentina, Brazil, Chile, Columbia, Equador, and Guatemala found the small farmer to be three to fourteen times more productive per acre than the larger farmer. In Thailand plots of two to four acres yield

---

[3]C.S. Lewis, *Perelandra*, Vol. 2, of trilogy *Silent Planet*, (New York: Macmillan, 1958). In this allegorical science fiction trilogy, C.S. Lewis describes the temptation of the planet Venus's equivalent of Eve. The first woman on Venus and her mate are preternaturally guileless, free-wandering food gatherers. A handsome demon attempts, unsuccessfully, to seduce her into evil, using as his most powerful temptation, the suggestion that by living in a fixed place, she could accumulate beautiful adornments for her body.

[4]F.M. Lappé and J. Collins, *Food First!*, (New York: Houghton Mifflin, 1977).

[5]F.M. Lappé and J. Collins, *Food First!*, *Renaissance Universal Journal*, Fall 1976, pp. 38-43.

almost sixty percent more rice per acre than farms of 140 acres or more. Other evidence that justice for the small farmer increases production comes from the experience of countries in which the redistribution of land and other basic agricultural resources like water has resulted in rapid growth in agricultural production: Japan, Taiwan, and China stand out . . . Worldwide studies of the 'Green Revolution' have shown that even when the larger farmers are favored with heavy investment in the new seed-fertilizer technology, the net return per acre continues to be less on large farms than on the small where large amounts of work . . . more than compensate for the big doses of capital investment on the large.[6]

It is a myth that the world cannot afford the "luxury" of land reform in the face of population growth.

If we place the entire focus of increasing productivity on technological means, then it is natural that we will also accept the myth that we can meet the world's needs for increased food production only at the expense of the environment, with ever greater use of pesticides and with extensive erosion resulting from the exploitation of marginal lands. (This myth was explicitly incorporated in the mathematical assumptions of the computer model used in *The Limits to Growth*.) If agribusiness preempts the best lands to raise non-food crops for export, small farmers, trying to earn a living by providing food crops for local markets, will begin to till unsuitable land. The resulting environmental damage will not be the result of excess population, beyond ecological limits, but of inappropriate land use.

Even in the United States pesticide pollution is not forced upon us by the necessity of raising food for ourselves and many other countries around the globe. Nearly half the pesticides consumed are used on parks, golf courses, and lawns — not on farms. Of all insecticides used on farms, nearly half are used for cotton rather than for food. Were all pesticides eliminated from commercial agriculture, the U.S. Department of Agriculture estimates that total farm yields of food crops would decrease by only 11%.

Lappé and Collins conclude that "There is no country without sufficient agricultural resources for the people to feed themselves and then some." We should emphasize food for domestic consumption first in agricultural policy, followed by the development of cash crops for export. Land reform is the top priority; successful long-term solutions to this internal social and political problem must come from within each country, not by mandate or fiat from outside.

What is the proper role for developed countries in improving the global outlook for food production and distribution? We must recognize that the "food problem" is not that we have too many people and too little planet, but rather that we have social inequities. We can afford the necessary studies for each country (with their consent and participation) to document the

[6]Ibid.

extent to which inequities create the food shortages, political instabilities, and economic losses. We can also clarify the extent to which technological advances in agriculture are successful only when the small farmers have equity. The "green revolution" has been highly successful in India's Punjab State, where most of the farms are family owned and operated, but it has had very limited success — and has occasionally been counterproductive — in other parts of India, where land ownership is highly concentrated. The governments of less developed countries cannot be expected to take effective action to remedy these problems until the true nature of the problem is recognized.

We, in the developed countries, are uniquely qualified to do the research to develop further technical improvements in agriculture, especially focussing on methods which require minimal capital investment and can be adapted to an intensive labor pool. Coupling new methods with social and political reforms, as they occur, and helping to disseminate their use where reforms have already been made, will likely prove to be the greatest contribution we can make to providing enough to eat for everyone on Earth.

13. The Enduring Neolithic Revolution

 While land reform can bring about major increases in food production in most Third World countries within a fairly short time—the improvements seen in Japan, Taiwan, and China have all occurred in less than three decades—what prospects do we have for further improvements by technological means? Have we reached the ultimate limits in agricultural technology?

One of the earliest agricultural systems invented by our prehistoric ancestors is still in use in many parts of the Third World. In this system, the natural growth of trees, shrubs, and grasses is cleared by cutting down the larger plants and setting fire to the entire field. Crops are planted, and the seeds sprout and become established before the wind or animal carriers reintroduce weed seeds. Burning the original biomass releases minerals such as phosphorus and potassium in soluble forms, but much of the soluble nitrogen compounds are lost in volatile forms by the flames. After one or two growing seasons, the nutrients, liberated by the fire, are depleted, and weeds recolonize the area. The farmer has to move on to repeat the process on a different plot of land, allowing the first plot to lie fallow for several years, during which wild vegetation restores the potential fertility of the area, building up soluble nitrogen compounds again, with the assistance of soil microbes.

As the need for food rose gradually, prehistoric farmers increased the total flow of food production by reducing, or even eliminating, the fallow years of a particular plot. In some instances, this had disastrous long term effects, as the soil became progressively depleted of nutrients and more vulnerable to erosion. In many instances, techniques for long term, sustained yields were developed, many of which are still relevant today.

One technique invented in prehistoric times, to permit continual farming of the same land for centuries, is irrigation. In the Nile Valley and in parts of Japan, irrigation systems took advantage of annual flooding by the major river which deposited a layer of silt each year, restoring the fertility of the soil with the nutrients transported from far upstream. In other parts of the world, especially where the river originates in barren or highly eroded regions, the water is apt to contain a great deal of dissolved salt. Unless drainage is excellent and the water table beneath the irrigated areas remains sufficiently deep, irrigation, under such circumstances, can deposit as much as ten tons of salt per acre in the topsoil. If sufficient water flows through each year, the flow takes away as much salt as it deposits, permitting a long term equilibrium. But if the flow of water, necessary to sustain the crops, is very large, the water table may rise, preventing salts from being flushed out as rapidly as they are deposited. The accumulation of salt in the irrigated fields of Sumer, over a millenium or more, appears to have contributed to the decline of that early civilization.

In many parts of the world where abundant sunshine is available for photosynthesis, rainfall is distributed poorly during the year. One of the most important agricultural areas in the world today is the Central Valley of California. During eight or nine, out of every ten years, no rainfall occurs from May to October. The enormous agricultural productivity of the area is possible because of extensive dam and canal systems, which divert the runoff of melted snow accumulated in the Sierra Nevada Mountains during the previous winter. Instead of running directly into the Pacific Ocean, these waters first pass through the fields of the Central Valley and continue out to sea.

Similarly, the Ganges Plain of India has abundant water resources available from the monsoon snows in the Himalayan headwaters of the Ganges River. During the growing season, the water level in the river is low and little rain falls. Presently the population of this area is about 250 million. If the water resources of the area could be harnessed effectively, by building dams, storing water in underground aquifers, drilling tube wells to tap ground water and underground aquifers, and building irrigation canals, the area could provide a satisfactory diet for more than 600 million people. The total cost of such a development project would be large, but the cost per hectare irrigated would be less than $50 per year, far less than the $500 value of cereal crops which each hectare could then produce annually.[1] Making the river navigable all year round, additionally would benefit the economic development of India and Bangladesh. Whether or not such a large scale project can be organized and undertaken in the near future depends on the appropriate governmental jurisdictions recognizing that food production is the first priority in development.

Agriculture in China, sustained over several millenia, has relied on irrigation and the deliberate return of nutrients to the soil, in the forms of table scraps, nightsoil (human wastes), and animal manures. While this practice has maintained the fertility of the soil in major agricultural areas, until recently it had serious, lethal side effects. In its potential for killing people, human fecal contamination of food and drinking water is unrivalled by any large scale industrial pollutant presently found in the United States. Fecal contamination provides a channel for the transmission of a host of infectious diseases, including hepatitis, polio, dysentery, cholera, and

[1]R. Revelle and V. Lakshminarayana, "The Ganges Water Machine," *Science*, Vol. 188, 1975, p. 611.

typhoid. The use of raw human sewage in agriculture persisted in China and Korea until as recently as the 1950s. The People's Republic of China now meets the requirements of public health by carefully composting wet garbage and nightsoil before they are returned to the fields. Proper composting destroys pathegenic microbes without loss of the valuable organic nutrients and humus.

The original prehistoric system alternates a few productive seasons with a number of fallow years; it balances the flow of nutrients from the land to the table, by a slower flow of oxygen, carbon, nitrogen, hydrogen, phosphorus, sulfur, and another dozen or more trace minerals back into the land by rain, windborne dust and detritus, animals, and new plant growth, absorbing these substances from the air. The Chinese system balances the flow from the land to the table by a deliberate but much more rapid flow, back from the table and the chamber pot to the land, thereby enlarging the total flow of food production per acre over the flow achievable in the fallow system.

Another system which enlarges the flow by accelerating the return flow of nutrients, has been the subject of an experimental program since 1972 under the sponsorship of Ecology Action of the Midpeninsula in northern California. This method, the biodynamic/French intensive method or organic horticulture, is based on raised beds; careful cultivation of the soil to a depth of 18 inches (45 cm) or more; extensive use of composts (excluding human wastes); close planting, so that the crops provide their own mulch, both inhibiting the growth of weeds and minimizing evaporation of water from the soil; and interplanting different kinds of plants for synergistic effects. Preliminary results of this program suggest yields per acre approximately double those of commercial farms in the United States, even in mediocre soils, with far less water and far less fertilizer (frequently none).[2] These method are particularly well adapted to small farms and can be highly labor intensive, making them especially suitable for developing countries where rural unemployment is a major social and economic problem.

While the Chinese agricultural system and the biodynamic/French intensive organic system both rely on closing the cycle of nutrient flows from the land, to the table, and back to the land (largely imitating the predominantly closed cycles of natural forest ecosystems in temperate climates), one should not conclude that only closed-cycle systems are compatible with the natural environment. The Nile system, for example, was not a closed cycle: the river's annual flood stage brought in new topsoil from distant lands, carrying away garbage from the cities and towns of Egypt all year round. Many cycles of the major elements involved in the biosphere are open-

[2]John Jeavons, *How to Grow More Vegetables Than You Ever Thought Possible on Less Land Than You Can Imagine*, (Palo Alto: Ecology Action of the Midpeninsula, 1974). 2225 El Camino Real, Palo Alto, California, 94306.

ended, or closed only geologically long timescales.

Ever since the Neolithic Period we have been engaged in another approach to accelerating the flow of food production: by increasing the usable fraction of the biomass produced per acre of cultivated land. The principal tool in this approach has been plant and animal breeding. Since the earliest farmers in Central and South America began to cultivate the primitive ancestors of maize, the yield per plant has increased about a hundredfold. Similar increases have been obtained in most of the staple grains around the world, including wheat, rice, millet, rye, oats, and sorghum, each of which has been cultivated and selected for better yields of up to ten thousand generations of each species.

Smaller gains have been obtained among the domesticated fruits which have been cultivated only in historical times, including dates, figs, pomegranates, grapes, and olives. The sizes of individual fruits have increased two to ten times over wild strains of these fruits, with increased numbers of fruits produced in each crop contributing modestly to increased yields as well. Dwarfing techniques have provided a major advance in fruit production within the last century or so, by reducing the time for an orchard to come into production, from as long as ten or fifteen years to as little as three to five years, with equal or greater yields per acre.

The sophisticated plant breeding techniques of the "green revolution" have accelerated these developments further, dedicating efforts primarily to the staple grain crops, because they form such an important part of the diet in most of the world. Attempts are underway to improve the yields of major root crops, such as cassava, with the potential of major improvements in productivity per acre.

Techniques of genetic manipulation are just beginning to be used to accelerate the development of improved crops. The first new cereal crop developed since the Neolithic is triticale: produced by crossing wheat with rye and manipulating the nuclei of the germ cells to maintain the full complement of chromosomes from both ancestors. The resulting hybrid grain is fertile and breeds true, having some of the rust resistance of rye and a protein content somewhat higher than wheat, with a better balance of essential amino acids. Triticale bread is now regularly available in U.S. supermarkets, with a flavor I would describe as a slightly more robust whole wheat bread.

A long term challenge for genetic manipulation and molecular biology is the improvement of the photosynthetic process itself. Theoretically, the photosynthesis reactions should allow up to 6% (or 8% in some types of plants, using a slightly different chemical reaction) of the solar energy falling on plant leaves to be converted into chemical energy. Actual efficiencies are typically only 1%, partly due to photorespiration during the hours of darkness, in which some of the chemical synthesis accomplished during the day is undone. Photorespiration is mediated by an enzyme which apparently serves no other purpose in the metabolism of plant cells. By modifying or controlling the expression of the gene, which controls production of this enzyme, the net efficiency of photosynthesis would be improved, further increasing yields per acre.

Within the last century and a half another approach to increasing the useful fraction of biomass produced per acre has been the control of animal diseases. In 1971 a new vaccine was introduced in the poultry industry to control Marek's disease, which had taken a large toll among laying hens. Within months egg prices in the United States fell to an all-time low. In Africa the use of cattle and other domesticated ungulates has been severely limited by trypanosomiasis (sleeping sickness) and theileriasis (east coast fever and related less common diseases). These diseases are the targets of a major effort by the International Laboratory for Research on Animal Diseases (ILRAD) in Nairobi, Kenya; the potential impact of success in these efforts in enormous, but care should be taken to ensure that widespread use of cattle does not eradicate native herds of ungulates.

Over the past three years, I have been using the biodynamic/French intensive method in my own side yard. A large pile of shrub trimmings which had been piled up for several years without perceptible decomposition, run through a shredding machine, was combined with composted grass and kitchen wastes to transform a piece of California adobe soil into a lush patch of ground supporting a wide variety of hybrid squash, tomato, bean, radish, corn, lettuce, cabbage, melon, and cucumber plants. While I water the raised bed or pick their produce several times a week, I sense a continuity and kinship with our Neolithic ancestors who began the process, still continuing, of directing the flows of matter and energy through the parts of the biosphere we call farms and gardens. The end is nowhere in sight; the Neolithic Revolution endures.[3]

[3]Philip H. Abelson, ed., *Food: Politics, Economics, Nutrition, and Research*, (Washington, D.C.: American Association for the Advancement of Science, 1975). Provides a representative sampling of the countless directions of research which promise to increase agricultural yields and improve food storage and distribution. Many of the specific examples given in this chapter are discussed in the articles in this compendium.

A conceptual mass driver, several kilometers long, transporting a one-million ton asteroid to a space manufacturing facility for use in satellite power stations and habitats. Asteroids may also be a 21st century source of metals (cobalt and nickel) for the Earth.

14. Endless Mineral Resources

 A recurrent theme in doomsday literature has been the idea that depletion of nonrenewable resources will lead to a catastrophic collapse of industrial societies, as the costs for mining and refining progressively lower grade ores climb higher. Technological optimists have countered this argument by pointing to the historical record of technological progress which has more than compensated for the exhaustion of high grade ores and will continue to do so. Neo-Malthusians have insisted, on the other hand, that it would be foolish to put all our eggs in the basket of wishful thinking, since no one can guarantee that technological progress will continue to be made rapidly enough to forestall disaster. Here I would like to present some alternate ways of thinking about these issues, which can provide a more credible assessment of our prospects with respect to mineral resources.

It makes good headlines to announce that the world reserves of copper ore will be exhausted in less than twenty years, and that shortly thereafter we will have to abandon electrical power networks and electrical appliances. Most of the copper mined in all of human history, however, has not been "consumed" but is still to be found, above ground, in highly refined forms, either as elemental copper metal or in such alloys as brass and bronze. Herman Kahn describes in detail what would be likely to happen if the price of copper suddenly rose from about $1 a pound to $10 a pound in the next ten years. The eighty million tons of copper above ground in the United States, in a wide range of artifacts, would have a value of some $6000 per person. Within a few months, electric utility companies would begin to replace the copper wire in their generators and transformers with aluminum wire, because it would be immensely profitable to do so even with new equipment needing to be installed. New construction and renovation of older homes and buildings would switch to aluminum wiring. Plumbers would be in demand to replace copper pipes in homes and offices with plastic or galvanized pipes. Several million tons of brass lamps, doorknobs, and bedframes would be exhumed from basements and attics and sold to scrap metal dealers at handsome prices.

Meanwhile, techniques to extract copper from volcanic rocks at $4 or $5 a pound would become highly attractive to copper producers, providing a virtually endless supply of copper. The net result of the originally shocking price rise in copper would be the rapid and extensive substitution of different materials for most of the present copper usage, with the collapse of the price of copper to levels about equal to, or slightly lower than, present prices (since the market for copper would have permanently collapsed to those few applications where no substitute would perform as well, such as electrical wiring in airplanes).[1] Copper jewelry would probably become very popular for at least a few years after the transition.

At present, known reserves of copper ore are sufficient for the projected demand for the next two or three decades. Is this cause for panic? Suppose you were on the Board of Directors of a mining company which presently holds leases for mining rights on enough ore for the next thirty years of production by that company. Would you authorize the expenditure of several million dollars by the company's geologists to prospect for more copper ore? If you did authorize this expenditure, and the geologists did find a lode which would extend the company's production for ten more years, would you authorize the expenditure of millions of dollars to obtain and hold leases on that lode for the next thirty years, during which time the company will not earn a single dime from that lode? If you did authorize either of these expenditures, or both of them, the stockholders would be justified in tarring and feathering you at the next annual meeting of the company.

For this reason, it is usually accidental that known reserves of minerals exceed a few decades: reserves in excess of a few decades were found, not because someone was looking for them, but because they accidentally stumbled over them while prospecting for something else.

I would like to consider the question of resources from a different economic approach. Suppose, for the sake of argument, that we do not manage in the future to make the kinds of advances assumed by the technological optimists, and are thus forced to make do with lower and lower grade ores for the same uses. Just how disruptive would this be to our economy? To answer this we must consider in some detail just what kinds of minerals we presently use, how much of these we use, how much is available at various concentrations of ores in the ground, and how much energy is required to extract and process minerals from different grades of ores.

During 1968 the total quantity of nonrenewable mineral resources extracted from the crust of the Earth, from the oceans and rivers, and from the atmosphere, was some 3.36 billion tons for use worldwide. (These numbers are for the refined minerals, not for raw ores, and do not include recycled materials.) The market values for these materials totalled $42.2 billion for the U.S. and $158.5 billion worldwide.[2] Although the totals look

[1] H. Kahn, W. Brown, and L. Martel, *The Next 200 Years: A Scenario for America and the World*, (New York: William Morrow & Company, 1976).

[2] H.E. Goeller and Alvin M. Weinberg, "The Age of Substitutability," *Science*, Vol. 191, 1976, p. 683.

Endless Mineral Resources

Table I

NONRENEWABLE RESOURCES EXTRACTED IN 1975 FOR USE IN THE UNITED STATES*

Mineral	Weight per capita (lbs)	Fraction of all minerals (%)	Fraction of group (%)	World supply (years)**
FOSSIL FUELS	17,050	45.95	100.00	few $\times$ 10^3
Petroleum	7,650		44.87	
Coal, lignite	5,200		30.50	
Natural gas	4,200		24.63	
NON-METALS	18,940	51.04	100.00	
Sand, gravel	8,000		42.24	5×10^6
Stone	8,000		42.24	few $\times$ 10^6
Cement	660		3.48	4×10^6
Clay	450		2.38	few $\times$ 10^6
Salt	430		2.27	300×10^6
Phosphate	315		1.66	1.3×10^3
Other	1,085		5.73	$30\text{-}100 \times 10^6$
METALS	1,118	3.01	100.00	
Iron (steel)	1,000		84.45	4.5×10^6
Aluminum	46		4.11	200×10^6
Copper	16		1.43	few $\times$ 10^0
Zinc	14		1.25	few $\times$ 10^0
Lead	11		0.98	few $\times$ 10^0
Other	31		2.77	few $\times$ $10^{0\text{-}6}$
TOTAL MINERALS	37,108	100.00		

*Table adapted from John D. Morgan, "The World Supply/Demand Outlook for Minerals," in A.G. Chynoweth and W.M. Walsh, eds., *Materials Technology – 1976*, AIP Conference Proceedings No. 32, New York, American Institute of Physics, 1976.

**Data in this column taken from H.E. Goeller and Alvin M. Weinberg, "The Age of Substitutability," *Science*, Vol. 191, 1976, p. 683.

impressive, they represent small fractions of the total economic activity, amounting, respectively, to 4.8% of U.S. gross national product for that year and to about 8% of gross world product.

Because these fractions are so small, it is clear that even if the average cost for these raw materials were to increase two or three fold, civilization would not collapse as projected in *The Limits to Growth*, provided only that the rise in costs were reasonably gradual.

The pattern of minerals used in the United States is indicated by Table I, showing minerals extracted in 1975. First notice the large share of the total represented by fossil fuels, those hydrocarbon minerals which can be extracted from the Earth with an expenditure of energy smaller than the energy which can be obtained from burning them as fuel. On the timescale of the survival of the human species, fossil fuels are indeed in short supply, and no one disputes the conclusion that we will have to shift over to other sources of energy at some point in the not-too-remote future.

Hydrocarbons have another important use as basic raw materials for the synthesis of complex organic compounds, including plastics, lubricants, and pharmaceutical products. For these purposes, the vast quantities of oil shale, in just the uppermost kilometer of the Earth's crust, are sufficient for at least 3.5 million years, at current worldwide consumption rates. For these applications of hydrocarbons it does not matter that more energy might be required to extract the oil from the shale than could be obtained by burning that oil. Yet it would be preferable to save as much as possible of the high grade, easily extractable fossil fuels for chemical synthesis purposes, by switching to newer energy sources at the earliest opportunity.

We have a few centuries to go before depletion of fossil fuels becomes a serious threat to civilization. Environmental issues associated with coal mining and burning, including emission of radioactive materials trapped from volcanic ashes by the coal-producing swamps of eons past, on the other hand, lend urgency to the need for a transition to other sources of energy.

The next major group of minerals to consider is the nonmetals. Sand and gravel are used in making glass and concrete; various kinds of stone are used in the construction of dams, opera houses, highways, homes, and for some furnishings such as fireplaces, tables, and sinks; limestone is used to make Portland cement; clay is used for ceramic products including bricks and for a glossy finish on some varieties of paper; and salt is used in numerous industrial processes as well as in cooking and preserving food. All of these minerals are abundantly available. At present worldwide rates of consumption, the Earth's stocks of these materials would suffice for millions of years!

The only important nonmetal in limited supply is phosphate rock, used primarily as an agricultural fertilizer. World reserves are presently estimated sufficient for 1,300 years, at current worldwide consumption rates. But phosphate is also a renewable resource. Animal bones concentrate phosphorus from the plants consumed; increased recycling of organic wastes (sewage sludge, feedlot wastes, wastes from canneries, etc.) could reduce enormously future demand for phosphate rock. Similar considerations also apply to a number of trace elements necessary for plant and animal growth and vigor. With an abundant and inexpensive energy source for the long term future, the virtually inexhaustible supply of phosphorus salts dissolved in the oceans, would also become available. Since the costs of phosphate are such a tiny part of the total costs of agriculture, the economic system would hardly collapse if we had to obtain phosphorus from sea water, even though it might be much more expensive than mining phosphate rock.

Finally we must consider the metals we use. The stages of humanity's ascent from the caves have often been characterized by the materials which dominated the economic activities of each cultural stage, from the Stone Ages through the Bronze Age and the Iron Age, into the present Steel Age. Iron overwhelmingly dominates the metals extracted from the Earth, primarily because of its use in steel. The principal source of iron at the present time is taconite ore, containing about 15% iron by weight. Presently known taconite ores are sufficient for several centuries at present rates of use.

The next major source of iron is lateritic iron ore, containing about 5% iron by weight. The processing technology for extracting iron from these ores is already available, but as long as taconite is abundant, it is not economically advantageous to use laterite. Although laterite contains less iron, and thus larger tonnages of ore must be processed to extract the same quantity of iron, the difference in energy per ton of finished steel would be only 17% more than at present. Since the known supply of lateritic iron ores is sufficient for about 4.5 million years, it is safe to conclude that civilization will not collapse very soon from the exhaustion of iron ore.

Steel, of course, contains other elements in addition to iron. Among these are manganese, chromium, vanadium, cobalt, and columbium, and the outlook for supplies of these minerals is much more limited. Known supplies, economically extractable by techniques currently in use, may last as little as thirty or forty years. What do we do then? Considering the energy requirements for extracting these metals from less concentrated ores (presently considered uneconomical) would, in most cases, increase the energy per ton of finished metal less than two-fold. If the cost per ton doubled or even quadrupled, the cost of steel would increase only modestly, since these other elements form only a few percent, by weight, of steel. Alternative metals, however, would gain in competitive position in relation to steel. In most applications, stainless steel can be replaced by titanium, which is almost as abundant as aluminum and iron; high-strength, high-temperature-resistant steel alloys can often be replaced by tungsten.

Such consideration, element by element, strongly suggests that we can find substitutions for virtually every material we now use in economically significant quantities, with the exceptions of fossil fuels and phosphate rock. H.E. Goeller and Alvin M. Weinberg have suggested that, in the long run, we can make the transition to an "Age of Substitutability," in which virtually all of the relatively scarce materials we presently use will have been replaced by substitutes, based on materials which are virtually unlimited. These materials would include plastics, wood, glass, cement, stone, iron, aluminum, and magnesium. To maintain a standard of living comparable to that in North America today would require an energy expenditure per person of only about one-third greater than today.

But won't we, in the Age of Substitutability, end up buried in mine tailings? During the 1960s mining activities in the United States alone produced about five billion tons of mine tailings and rock overburden — about sixteen times more mass than all the sewage and rubbish produced by our homes, offices, shops, schools, and factories. Some of these mine wastes produce biocidal substances such as sulfuric acid, when water percolates through them. If these pollutants are allowed to leak into nearby streams, they can wreak havoc with the environment.

But if we consider Table I again, the picture is not as bleak as I have just portrayed it. Sand, gravel, stone, cement, and clay together account for about 46% of the minerals produced for consumption in the United States, and more than 67% of the minerals produced for use worldwide. Very few mine wastes result from the extraction of these minerals, with virtually no biotoxic leachates. The principal environmental impact of mining these materials is the alteration of the landscape by the quarrying operations. In most cases, we already have the knowledge to rehabilitate the landscape without a tremendous increase in production costs for the overall mining operation. Modest institutional changes, in combination with growing public sensitivity to the aesthetics of the landscape, can produce significant improvements in this area. In many cases, depleted quarries can be converted into reservoirs or recreational facilities for public use, at minimal expense, with major social and environmental benefit.

Fossil fuels (especially coal) produce large quantities of mine wastes whose leachates are often severely polluting to nearby waters. In the United States, each ton of coal produced, typically results in eight tons of mine spoils, and the tailings associated with coal production add up to more than twenty times the mine wastes due to all metals combined. Everyone agrees that mining fossil fuels for energy will be replaced by alternative energy sources; the largest share of mine wastes — including many of the most biotoxic — will then vanish. Iron will continue to dominate metals, but the wastes will be limited strictly as we go to lower grade ores, since the lateritic ores are, practically speaking, unlimited, entailing only a three-fold increase in wastes, compared to the taconite ores we presently mine. Thus total mine spoils per capita will still be small compared to those from coal alone, at the present time, and modest improvements in technology, combined with somewhat greater social attention to the location of tailing dumps, can further alleviate the environmental impact of future mining operations.

Although sudden shortages of certain key minerals can create temporary dislocations within our economic systems, they cannot totally destroy civilization. Like all living things, human civilization is dynamic, continually evolving and adapting to its changing environment. As economic patterns and technologies change in time, the material and energy – use patterns will change as well. If stone is not available, a society will make do with whatever alternatives are at hand. As England became progressively deforested, and wood for houses became scarce and expensive, the English built homes of brick and stone instead.

Insofar as material resources alone are concerned, the survival of industrialized civilization on Earth can be assured for a population as large as ten or twenty billion people, at a standard of living comparable to the United States and Canada today for at least several million years, provided alternative, environmentally sound, sources of energy have been implemented. Substitution of relatively scarce materials by abundant materials, suitably adapted and tailored, is unquestionably attainable. Modest levels of research on such substitutions will hasten the arrival of the Age of Substitutability.

Skylab 3 view of solar prominence
which sent an arch of helium 500,000 miles
into the solar corona, 1973.

15. The Fires of Prometheus

 In Greek mythology the earliest humans were believed to have been rude creatures living like beasts, without benefit of language, clothing, or artifacts, who were compelled to eat their food raw like animals. The demigod, Prometheus took pity on them and taught them to speak, dress themselves against the elements, and make tools. The gods on Mount Olympus considered his philanthropy a harmless eccentricity, but when Prometheus asked the gods for their consent to a final gift of civilization, the gods refused to share the fire on Mount Olympus, which they guarded jealously, for their own use. Prometheus defied the gods, stole flames from the Olympian fires, and altered humanity forever.

This familiar myth recognizes the control and application of energies (beyond those of our muscles and metabolism) as central to human culture. Even the earliest remains of hominid tools are often found in close association with traces of fire; so it is no coincidence that *Homo sapiens* alone, among all land vertebrates, have no instinctive fear of flames.

Fire can ward off the chill of the night; it can cook our meals (allowing us to make use of a far wider range of foods than our teeth and digestive systems would otherwise accept); it can alter the physical and chemical states of matter in ways that would seem magical if they were not so commonplace to us. But fire can also kill or maim; in minutes it can destroy an entire season's harvest or level shelters which may have taken weeks to build.

The Olympian gods were enraged that Prometheus had raised humanity to a level near the gods, by stealing flames from their fire. Zeus punished Prometheus by chaining him to a mountain crag where an eagle came each day to feast on his liver which grew back each night. This torment lasted for centuries until Hercules set Prometheus free. It may be closer to the truth that the first fire-giver was chained to a rock by those who saw only the dangers of fire, lacking the vision of its potential for good, who punished him rather than admit their fears.

Depending on size, stature, gender, daily occupations, and climate, the average adult human being consumes between 1,500 and 4,000 calories of energy daily in the form of chemical energy locked up in food. A small fraction of that energy can be converted into mechanical work on material objects—cultivating the land, preparing the food, chipping rocks into arrowheadsd and axes, or carving bone and wood into ornaments and tools. When fire was harnessed and became inextricably integrated with our diet, the average consumption of energy per person increased to about 12,000 calories a day, (the increased consumption being equivalent to the energy released in gathering and burning about one ton of dried firewood anually per person, as is still the case in much of the Third World). The domestication of draft animals such as oxen, donkeys, reindeer, yaks, or llamas again doubled or tripled the energy commanded per person. While the metallurgical advances of the Bronze Age and the early Iron Age required far more concentrated energies, the average consumption of energy per capita remained very limited until the Industrial Revolution made metal products available to a large segment of the population.

With the Industrial Revolution the energy of fire could be directed in many more ways than ever before. The steam engine of Simon Newcombe, improved by James Watt, provided the means to convert chemical energy into thermal energy and thence into mechanical energy, more practically, and on a larger scale, than had ever before been attempted. The concurrent transition from charcoal to coal brought about rapid advances in the metallurgy of iron and steel, and metal products became sufficiently inexpensive and abundant that everyone could afford them. Thomas Edison's refinement of the electrical dynamo and his invention of the electric light bulb took the entire process two steps further: permitting chemical energy, originally converted from sunlight, to be transformed first into thermal energy; then to mechanical energy; then into electrical energy; and finally back into light.

Today in the United States energy consumption per capita is about 235,000 calories per day, including all mining, manufacturing, agricultural, commercial, transportation, and household applications. Our material affluence is directly attributable to the diversified control we have over the manifold forms of the fires of Prometheus. We find ourselves in a bind as our energy consumption continues to rise while our principle sources— petroleum and natural gas—seem to dwindle in supply and increase in price (for reasons which are more political than material). When the wells are turned off at last, will we fall back to the sub-barbarian level from which we were lifted so long ago, by the discovery of fire?

It is precisely because energy use is so intricately entangled with every aspect of civilization and culture that energy policy has become so controversial and so politicized since the "energy crisis" of the early 1970s. Simple answers elude us; perhaps because it is so difficult to formulate the proper questions. I propose to discuss a few perspectives on the energy question which may help to cut through parts of the Gordian knot and to show that we have far more options and opportunities than the phrase "energy crisis" suggests.

In the discussion of living systems I showed how industrial society is based on a continuing flow of entropy through the system. While the biosphere uses the entropy flow originating from the conversion of highly organized sunlight into disorganized thermal (infrared) radiation, industrial society today uses the entropy flow produced by converting the highly organized molecules of complex hydrocarbon chains and rings, making up petroleum and coal, into disorganized molecules of water vapor and carbon dioxide. Our useful energy comes from the entropy changes in the flow of materials — the fossil fuels we burn.

The cleanest of our fossil fuels is natural gas, which consists mostly of methane (CH_4) with small admixtures of more complex hydrocarbons such as ethylene (C_2H_4) and ethane (C_2H_6). Natural gas can be transmitted by pipeline very economically and safely, with minimal environmental damage, even in the short term associated with construction of the pipeline. In its conventional forms, natural gas occurs in porous rock formations, trapped by suitably convoluted impervious layers of rock, usually in conjunction with petroleum deposits. But the world supplies of natural gas — and certainly the supply in the United States — appears to be very limited, with perhaps as little as fifteen or twenty years of production remaining before extraction costs exceed the federal price ceiling.

But natural gas also occurs in geopresurized deposits in the coastal regions of Louisiana, Texas, and northern Mexico and in the continental shelf of the Gulf of Mexico. The natural gas is dissolved in salt water trapped in porous rock layers at depths of 8,000 to 26,000 feet. The weight of the rock layers above keeps the pressure in the fluid far higher than that of open water at equal depth, accounting for the term *geopressurized natural gas*. The technology for bringing the mixture of brine and gas to the surface, extracting the natural gas, and returning the brine into the ground is reasonably well developed. Some estimates suggest that natural gas could be produced from such wells at a cost less than twice the current regulated price of natural gas. Since natural gas is presently underpriced by 50 to 70% in comparison with imported petroleum, for equal energy content, this new source of natural gas would be highly competitive with petroleum or imported, liquified natural gas (LNG). Deregulation of natural gas prices domestically is clearly indicated.

How far could these deposits stretch our supply of natural gas? Should current exploration and experiments in extracting this gas from the brine solution verify current estimates, these Gulf reserves alone may contain enough energy to meet the total energy needs of the United States for 300 to 1,500 years at present rates of consumption. Moreover, geologists believe that this type of formation probably occurs in several other places in North America, and certainly a handful of comparable deposits should be found elsewhere on Earth.[1]

[1]William M. Brown, "A Huge New Reserve of Natural Gas Comes Within Reach," *Fortune*, October 1976, p. 219.

Doomsday Has Been Cancelled

The flows of entropy we need to sustain industrial civilization can be provided by many different flows of materials other than the combustion of fossil fuels. Nuclear reactions (either fission or fusion) are one widely discussed possibility, with well known advantages and disadvantages. Other possibilities have received less attention, including tapping the flow of entropy associated with the mixing of fresh water with salt water, near the mouths of large rivers such as the Mississippi, the Columbia, or the St. Lawrence. The scale of such projects pushes these schemes farther into the future than most people are willing to consider today.

A strong argument can be made in favor of tapping into the entropy flows associated with changes in the entropy of natural energy flows such as solar energy. These arguments have degenerated often into ideological disputes concerning centralization versus decentralization, in which many of the solar advocates seem to be saying that it is morally wrong for city dwellers to rely on a centralized utility company for their energy supply. Yet it seems to me that the overwhelming majority of urbanites would be perfectly content to rely on the utility company for power, rather than have to maintain their own independent solar collectors on the roof (which, at the present time, cannot yet compete economically with the utility companies unless such devices are subsidized by other citizens through various tax incentives).

Much of the rancor in the debate between the centralized and decentralized energy advocates might be reduced if both sides were to remember that the underlying difference concerns the respective visions of quality of life, and neither side is right or wrong. The advocates of decentralization yearn for self-reliance and a sense of mastery over the hardware and technology directly involved in their daily lives; while other urbanites would prefer to pay the monthly utility bill and spend their time and effort in directions other than energy.

In the long run it seems that solar energy, in some form, will have to be our ultimate energy source. My own view is that the transformation to solar energy will come primarily through Solar Power Satellites, large arrays in space which gather solar power in orbit, high above the Earth's atmosphere, convert it into suitable form for beaming to the Earth, where it can be converted into electricity or chemical form for use by conventional means.

In the meantime how can we tide over most effectively in the next few decades? Debates in the 1970s about energy supplies, energy demand, and energy needs are common. Those who believe the scarcity hypothesis regarding natural resources have often drawn distinctions between the energy we *need* and the energy we *demand*. This distinction generally alienates the public at large, because it is most unpleasant to be lectured, "You don't need to drive your car 1,300 miles every month. Don't be so greedy in your demands." Each of us has our own valid notions of what constitutes quality

90

of life for us, and we feel irritated and annoyed if someone else tells us we ought to have different values; that we ought to find different things desirable and pleasing. From a strictly rational point of view, our energy needs, for physical survival, could be as little as 12,000 calories a day (that sufficed for our cave-dwelling anscestors who used fire for cooking), or even the 1,500 to 4,000 calories (of our more primitive ancestors who ate only raw food). Few of us would find that kind of lifestyle within the acceptable range.

Perhaps a more useful distinction than between needs and demands is between energy *actually applied* to a given task and energy *expended* for accomplishing that task. For many people, a high quality of life includes a great deal of travel by private automobile. What is essential for fulfillment of this goal, however, is not the expenditure of so many gallons of gasoline, but the application of enough energy to move the automobile, with its passengers and cargo, along the desired journey. Typical automobiles in the United States today expend about twelve gallons of gasoline to obtain energy of motion equivalent to the chemical energy content of just one gallon of gasoline (so that the overall "efficiency" in converting chemical energy into energy of motion is about 8%). The energy of motion involved for a given trip, in a smaller car, is less than for a heavier car, but the ratio of energy applied to the energy expended varies only slightly with the weight of the car.

The internal combustion, gasoline engine converts about 30% of the chemical energy of the gasoline burned into energy of motion, but some three-quarters of that energy of motion is subsequently lost to friction and thus to low grade thermal energy in the transmission, drive shaft, differential gears, bearings, and tires, leaving considerable room for improvement in efficiency.

How can we gauge progress by improving efficiency? We have to know something about the maximum possible efficiency under ideal conditions, before we can say how much remains to be done in improving any particular system. The laws of thermodynamics provide the key. The first law of thermodynamics states that energy can be neither created nor destroyed; energy can only be altered in form. The second law tells us the limits of extracting useful work or energy from any given process of conversion from one form of energy to another. If we try to obtain useful mechanical work from thermal energy, only a limited fraction of the heat can be turned into useful work, regardless of the materials or design I use to build a heat engine. The efficiency of converting heat energy into useful work is limited by the temperatures between which the heat engine operates.

For the temperatures practically achievable in internal combustion engines, using present day materials, the maximum possible efficiency of the mass-produced automobile engine is about 35%, so that further improvements beyond the current 30% or so will not be significant unless operating temperatures were raised by hundreds of degrees, with major increases in engine weight, maintenance costs, engine complexity, and public hazard.

The usual definition of *efficiency* compares to the energy actually *applied* to a given task by the equipment in hand to the energy *expended* by that equipment. By this definition, gas furnaces used to heat homes in the United States typically deliver about 60% of the energy released by burning natural gas, in the form of useful heat inside the house. It would seem we can only hope for modest improvements in the efficiency of heating our homes, offices, and factories.

A hidden assumption has slipped past us. Suppose that, instead of asking how efficient a furnace can be, we ask an altogether different question: How little energy could be expended if we used some other kind of equipment, if in fact we use the best possible means of doing the desired task?

Buildings can be heated in the middle of winter by pumping low grade heat from the air, soil, stream or pond, into the building with a heat pump. A refrigerator is, in effect, a kind of heat pump: it extracts low grade heat from the cold air inside the refrigerator and dumps it, along with heat from the electrical motor, which runs the refrigerator, into the warm kitchen air around the refrigerator. Heat pumps, used for heating buildings, are often made so that they can operate backwards as well, cooling the interior of the house in the summer. Such a heat pump replaces the functions of both furnace and air conditioner.

If the temperature of the soil two feet below my lawn is 10° C (50° F) during the winter and I want to keep the inside of my house at 20° C (68° F), an ideal heat pump could bring 96.6 British Thermal Units (BTU) of heat into my house every hour while expending only 3.4 BTU an hour of heating. A conventional furnace, on the other hand, operating at 60% efficiency, would have to expend 167 BTU an hour, nearly fifty times as much, to achieve the same effect.

Heat pumps commercially available today do not operate quite as well as the ideal device I have just described, but they are more efficient than furnaces. As yet they are more expensive to install than furnaces and air conditioners, although the total cost over the lifetimes of the two alternative appliance installations are competitive. The volume of manufacturing is small, keeping the initial price higher. Because of the smaller volume, practical engineering has not yet advanced as far, so maintenance and repair costs have tended to be higher than for more conventional appliances. Significant advances probably could be made, if one or more large construction projects (whether by the U.S. government, for a major office building and commercial center, or for a very large housing tract), ordered a large number of heat pumps from a single manufacturer, with extended maintenance or warranty contracts included in the purchase.

The Fires of Prometheus

On the basis of case-by-case examinations of the energy actually expended in relation to the minimum possible expenditure of energy for a variety of common tasks, it is possible to show that total expenditure of energy in the United States during the next decade or so need not increase significantly; provided we take advantage of opportunities to retrofit our homes, businesses, and industries with devices of higher efficiency whenever current devices need to be replaced. Such an approach need have no adverse economic effects and does not require the kinds of changes in lifestyle implied by shifting from private automobiles for commuting to work, for example, to car pools and mass transit systems.[2]

This strategy, however, is not likely to succeed as long as the rhetoric from Washington continues to emphasize conservation. Conservation seems to demand giving up much of what is considered essential to personal lifestyles; it connotes a Puritanical judgment of personal values. To emphasize efficiency, on the other hand, would be more than a semantic shift. Greater efficiency in achieving our desired ends is a positive goal: much more palatable to most of us, much more challenging to Yankee ingenuity than the negative goal of restraint and reduction in our personal desires and our visions of quality of life. Either conservation or greater efficiency will achieve the same end — stretching out the supply of fossil fuels and reducing our dependence on imported petroleum. Greater efficiency, however, will not demoralize us, and in its encouragement of technical innovation, it is more likely to produce inventions and discoveries which lead us to new sources of energy supply.

The emphasis on greater efficiency is appropriate for the underdeveloped nations of the world, as well as for the United States. Third World countries are literally starving for energy; to admonish them to restrain their demands and to conserve fossil fuels is in grievously poor taste. To promote greater efficiency in energy use, however, is as appropriate there as it is here.

The average consumption of firewood or dried animal manures for cooking fuel alone averages one ton per person per year in much of the Third World. Yet the stoves used in such countries, typically deliver only 9% of the chemical energy released in combustion, into the food being cooked. Electric and gas ranges in the United States, on the other hand, deliver an average of about 36% of the thermal energy released at each burner into the food being cooked. The design and construction of large numbers of inexpensive and simple cooking stoves, of greater efficiency, for use in the Third World, would be a major boon for economic development.

While the cheapest and fastest method of relieving our present "energy

[2]Marc H. Ross and Robert H. Williams, "Energy Efficiency: Our Most Underrated Resource," *Bulletin of the Atomic Scientists*, November 1976. Presents a lucid discussion of the prospects for improved energy efficiency.

crisis" is improved efficiency in the application of energy to our desired ends, we can only meet the long term energy challenge by focussing research efforts on long term energy sources where basic scientific understanding is most needed.[3] The transition to a solar economy with abundant, inexpensive, and environmentally sound supplies of energy, is just around the corner, if we just get on with the work.

[3]Philip H. Abelson, ed., *Energy: Use Conservation and Supply*, (Washington, D.C.: American Association for the Advancement of Science, 1975). A representative cross-section of expert opinion on energy policy and energy technologies.

16. Doing More With Less

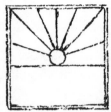

When life first appeared on the Earth, it depended for its nutrients on complex organic molecules synthesized by abiotic processes such as lightning, ultraviolet light, hot springs, and surf. Thus an enormous area of the planetary surface was required in order to support each kilogram of living organisms. The invention of photosynthesis two billion years ago radically altered the picture, so that at the present time, averaging over the entire surface of the Earth, less than half a square meter now supports one kilogram of life.

Human civilization has come to use large quantities of materials and energy to support each person, in sharp contrast to the few pounds of personal and tribal belongings of hunters and gatherers in tropical climates. With increasing affluence, we seem to accumulate more and more personal possessions of ever-widening diversity. Yet this trend, which seems so obvious and alarming to environmental activists, is countered increasingly by a more subtle trend toward *ephemeralization* — toward ever increasing efficiency in the utilization of matter — paralleling the course of biological evolution. A few examples will suggest how universal this trend is in modern civilization.

When Charles Lindbergh crossed the Atlantic Ocean in 1927, his airplane had an empty weight of about 2,150 pounds and achieved an average speed of one hundred miles an hour. In 1978, an airplane of comparable dimensions weighs only 1900 pounds and cruises at about 160 miles an hour. These differences in weight and speed may seem to be rather minor, until we examine the increased capabilities as well as the decreased weight of the present day airplane. Although today's airplane flies faster, it uses less fuel per mile. Its cabin accomodates four adults in greater comfort than Lindbergh had as sole occupant of the Spirit of St. Louis. All of the occupants of the modern airplane have an excellent view of the countryside through large windows on all sides, while Lindbergh had only a small window on one side of the cockpit and had to look through a periscope to see forward. Today's airplane has a reduced weight even with a variety of navigation and communications equipment. Transatlantic crossings, even by light airplanes, no longer need to rely solely on dead-reckoning, in radio silence, with no advance information on weather conditions.

The differences between the two aircraft are attributable to improvements and advances in materials, science, and engineering techniques. The structural members and the engine block are made of aluminum instead of steel; metal alloys, more resistant to higher temperatures, have allowed the engine to be air-cooled instead of water-cooled; although engine temperatures are higher, permitting higher fuel efficiencies; sheet-metal forming techniques allow the airplane's shape to be aerodynamically more efficient; the use of molybdenum instead of high-temperature steel alloys for piston rings, has increased the time between major overhauls of the engine from two or three hundred hours of operation at cruise power to two thousand hours or more, while significantly reducing oil consumption. The modern airplane, in brief, has far greater capabilities and far more safety features than its predecessor, using far less material of greater sophistication and diversity.

The first electronic computer was built at Los Alamos during the Manhattan Project in World War II. Using vacuum-tube technology, the computer filled two rooms with racks of electronic chassis and required about one hour of repair work for every hour of computing time. The total electronic memory was a few hundred binary digits (bits), and programming the computer was extremely cumbersome. Yet this machine could perform more calculations in one day than a good numerical analyst could do in several years, with a mechanical desk calculator of the types then available.

Today the programmable pocket calculators, available for a few hundred dollars or less, can store ten or twenty numbers with ten-digit accuracy; remember a sequence of two hundred instructions for manipulation of data; and calculate at speeds somewhat greater than the Los Alamos machine all in a volume of about ten cubic inches (less than two hundred cubic centimeters) instead of two whole rooms, with thousands of hours of operation, before having a single failure. Today's large computers, used for scientific and engineering calculations, can remember sequences of a hundred thousand instructions, store a half million numbers with fifteen-digit accuracy, and perform arithmetic and logical operations one to ten million times faster—all in a volume of a few cubic meters, with a time between failure of electronic components of a few hundred hours.

The progressive ephemeralization of computer hardware has resulted from advances in semiconductor materials and fabrication techniques. Vacuum tubes were first replaced by early transistors perhaps one-tenth the size of tubes. As fabrication techniques improved, transistors became smaller and smaller, finally permitting the replacement of conventional sheet-metal chassis by printed circuitboards. Integrated circuits followed, with transistors, resistors, and capacitors, fabricated in a single unit, by a combination of etching, vapor deposition, and vapor diffusion processes. (Because transistors use a tiny fraction of the current used by vacuum tubes performing the equivalent function, the resistors and capacitors used in equivalent circuits could also be tremendously reduced in size, even though advances in materials have not allowed similar reductions in the intrinsic sizes of resistors or capacitors.) The use of metal oxide substrates has allowed the extension of these techniques to large scale, integrated circuits, in which the equivalent of 15,000 vacuum tubes, resistors, and capacitors are compressed into the area of a postage stamp.

But the end is not yet in sight. As wondrous as these advances may seem, the sophistication and miniaturization of the human nervous system far exceeds computers in all respects except speed and accuracy in the manipulation of data which are intrinsically digital. In a mere 1.5 kilograms the human brain has an estimated storage capacity of more than 10^{11} bits; it can simultaneously perform elaborate processing of data from our eyes, ears, skin, tongue, and inner ear, while we climb stairs, carrying a load of books or parcels, also controlling our diaphragm, vocal cords, face, mouth, and throat muscles to produce speech, song, or whistling. We do not understand how the storage and retrieval of data is accomplished, but perhaps individual molecules of neurotransmitter chemicals are transferred across cell boundaries at neural synapses. The energy expenditure in handling each bit of information appears to be very near the ultimate lower limit allowed by thermodynamics, an efficiency millions or billions of times greater than has yet been achieved by the most advanced electronic computers.

Perhaps the ultimate in information storage is the genetic code. The nucleus of each cell of our bodies contains all the information needed to describe completely every detail of human anatomy and also the operating instructions for the incredible diversity of subtle biochemical factories contained in each cell and organ system. The density of information probably approaches 10^{15} bits per cubic centimeter in the cell nucleus, about a billion times more compact than we have managed so far.

Communications technology offers further examples of the trend to ephemeralization. Twenty years ago a transatlantic cable, with a total mass of several million kilograms, was required in order to provide an additional 4,000 telephone circuits between North America and Europe. Today this capacity can be provided by launching one more communication satellite with a mass of less than a thousand kilograms, and the service provided is far more versatile and flexible, providing the potential for communications between any two points in an entire hemisphere.

The study of wear (which has become a science in its own right since 1950), also is accelerating the trend toward reduced consumption. At the present time many of our artifacts are discarded because they have been rendered useless for their original purpose by the wearing away of less than one-tenth of one percent of the total mass of the artifact.

Four basic and distinct mechanisms for wear have been identified: *adhesion*, in which small particles of material are transferred from one surface

97

to another; *abrasion*, in which bits of matter are gouged from one surface by another surface which is hard and sharp; *corrosion*, in which material is removed from the surface, or atomic arrangements in and near the surface are altered, by substances in the environment; and *fatigue*, in which tiny cracks and defects within the material propagate and grow into macroscopic fractures. A better understanding of all of these phenomena can lead to significantly longer lifetimes for the artifacts of civilization, with greater utility from less material substance. Some indication of the potential here is suggested by the fact that

> ...a substantial portion of the steel capacity in the United States is being used to replace corroded and rusted steels already in use....The corrosion problem alone is responsible for annual replacement of materials worth more than $20 billion, most of it attributed to iron-base alloys.[1]

Although Leonardo da Vinci attempted as early as 1500 to study friction systematically, major strides in controlling undesired friction have just begun to accelerate in recent decades. Presently we use lubricants of increasing variety and sophistication, mechanical devices such as roller bearings, and new materials at interfaces between moving parts, with considerable room for improvement. During the last three decades the 1000 mile lubrication and the 2000 mile oil change for automobiles have largely disappeared. Maintenance procedures for new cars typically call for lubrication and oil change at 5000 or 6000 mile intervals, reducing our use of lubricants in transportation three-fold. In applications where friction is desirable, such as in brake linings, newer materials provide better gripping with reduced wear, and lengthen the lifetime for these artifacts.

Yet another direction of ephemeralization is provided by the gradual, but steady, increase in the strengths of materials. We are, as yet, far from the ultimate limits of the laws of nature; the strongest steel alloy available today is still more than one hundred times weaker than the strength it theoretically should have, on the basis of forces acting between atoms and molecules within a solid. Microscopic defects, trace chemical impurities, and small scale crystallization are principal reasons for such gaps between presently attainable strengths and ultimate theoretical limits to the strengths of materials. The effect progress has had, on the quantities of materials we must use for given purposes, can be illustrated by comparing the Great Pyramid to the World Trade Center towers in New York. The Great Pyramid is about 480

[1]R.C. Kirby and A.S. Prokopovitsh, "Technological Insurance Against Shortages in Minerals and Metals," *Science*, Vol. 191, 1976, p. 713. See also: D.A. Vermilyea, The Physics of Corrosion," in A.G. Chynoweth and W.M. Walsh Jr., eds., *Materials Technology – 1976*, (AIP Conference Proceedings, No. 32), (New York: American Institute of Physics, 1976). p. 141. E. Rabinowicz, "Gaps in Our Knowledge of Friction and Wear," in A.G. Chynoweth and W.M. Walsh, Jr., eds., *Materials Technology – 1976*. p. 165.

feet tall and each edge of its base is somewhat more than 500 feet in length. It was constructed with this ratio of height to base, not for aesthetic reasons, but because the stones from which the Pyramid was built have such low strength that the base must widen as the total weight above it increases, lest the entire structure collapse. The high grade steels which support a modern skyscraper like the World Trade Center, which stands more than 1100 feet tall, likewise need to broaden the base of support toward the bottom of the structure, but to such a limited extent as to fit within the envelope of a rectangular shape, less than 200 feet wide at the base.

Continuing development of science and technology does not inevitably spell more and more material consumption per person. Ephemeralization is accelerating, rather than slowing down, and can be expected to continue making important contributions to higher quality of life for all of us.

*Perspective of Earth
from 10,000 miles, Apollo 4, 1967.*

17. The Pig's Squeal

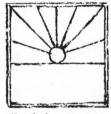Loosely stated, the second law of thermodynamics tells us that in any process the entropy of any finite system and its environment can never decrease. At best, the entropy remains constant; more commonly, the entropy increases. It follows from this principle that no physically achievable heat engine (such as an internal combustion engine, a refrigerator, or a turbogenerator) can convert all of the energy content of the fuel consumed into useful work. Some energy will always be dissipated as waste heat.

The same principle applies to processes whose purpose is the reorganization of raw materials into finished products, whether the process is based on chemical reactions or on mechanical shaping and manipulation: some losses must be expected, some material will be wasted.

It does not follow from this inexorable law of physics that we are doomed to be buried in exponentially mounting accumulations of industrial wastes and pollutants. Just as the total release of energy needed to provide the useful work we actually desire can be reduced by greater attention to the ultimate efficiencies possible, so too can we reduce the ratio of wastes to useful products by greater awareness of the elegance of industrial processing.

Yet we can in a way escape the apparent implications of the second law; in principle, we can reduce the material wastes in any process to as small a quantity as we like, but at the expense of greater energy utilization, shifting the burden of the entropy increase to the energy flow, rather than the material flow. In practice, the most economical process will almost invariably involve some mixture of thermal and material wastes; to shift the full burden of entropy to the energy stream would be prohibitively expensive in virtually every real situation.

In this chapter I will discuss yet another approach to the problem of industrial waste, which is based on changing some of our mental constructs and boundaries. Hog butchering is an ancient art in which it was said that every part of the pig could be used except the squeal. The success in reducing wastes to a minimum was due entirely to an underlying conceptual shift. If we eliminate completely the word *waste* from our vocabulary, and speak instead of *by-products*, then our eyes are opened to a new conception of reality, and we begin to search for economical uses and markets for those substances and materials which are secondary to the initial purpose of the process. Hog butchering was designed initially to remove the meat from the carcass. Varied uses were soon found for the lard; the art of tanning leather created uses for the relatively furless skin of the pig; the intestines themselves came to be used for sausage casings; and even the pig's knuckles, properly pickled, are considered a delicacy by many. Only the squeal is lost, a vestige of the second law of thermodynamics.

Perhaps the best example of a modern industry using the by-product approach is petroleum refining. The crude oil from each oil field is slightly different in composition from oil coming from anywhere else on Earth. At a refinery the crude oil is fed in a continuous stream through a complex system of fractional distillation columns, catalytic "cracking" units, retorts, and reactor vessels, to produce gasolines of various octane ratings, lubricating oils of various viscosities, benzene, kerosene, paraffin, heavy tars, asphalt, and many other products. In the late nineteenth century, the principal product was kerosene for lanterns. Other substances produced by refineries today gradually emerged from "by-products" into commercially important products. These are dominated today by gasoline and heating oil, with kerosene considered a minor by-product.

Just how much of each of these products emerges from a refinery depends on the initial composition of the crude oil; on the kinds and quantities of other chemicals added to the stream; on the temperatures of the various stages of each fractional distillation column; and on the temperature and pressure of the catalytic cracking units. The wastes, amounting to a tiny fraction of the weight and volume of the crude oil, are a few sticky tar-like residues, some volatile gases, and varying amounts of sulfur, depending on the composition of the crude oil. Some attempts are being made to find new uses for the sticky residues as well.

From the point of view of the shareholders of the oil company, the goal of the refinery is to maximize the revenues, while minimizing the costs for the refinery as a whole. The price and demand for each of the dozens of products produced by the refinery are constantly changing, as are the costs of the crude oil and the chemicals added in the refining process. The problem of maximizing the monetary returns for oil refineries has stimulated the development of an entire branch of applied mathematics called "linear programming." Refinery operations are typically managed by computers which continually analyze the refinery's mix of outputs, to achieve the maximum possible monetary return, subject to certain constraints. These constraints include the composition of available crude oils, current inventories of petroleum products, storage costs associated with each, projected demands and prices for each product, and so forth. The operating conditions (temperatures, pressures, additives) are then constantly adjusted to provide the best economic use of the available resources.

Instead of considering specifically a petroleum refinery, we can broaden our perspective, to include a general chemical or manufacturing plant, industry, or even a farm. A stream of materials A, B, C...flows into the system. These materials are combined or altered in a variety of ways inside the system, and a stream of materials or products P, Q, R...pours out of the factory or farm, along with streams of by-products, U, V, W.... The purpose of the system is to maximize profits subject to certain constraints.

But as long as we define the side streams U, V, W,...to be wastes, we will have a "waste disposal problem"; for the mental barrier we have erected in our minds, by labeling these side streams as wastes, will prevent us from including U, V, W,...in the calculation of profits. In actual industrial practice, the disposal of wastes is often relegated to the purchasing office, which naturally seeks to eliminate them by the cheapest and bureaucratically easiest method available.

Under present conditions in the United States, the cheapest method of disposal is dumping, largely because of the hidden public subsidies dumping enjoys. At the state and county level, the government accepts the costs of operating dumps; costs of hiring geologists to find sites suitable for the dumping of potentially hazardous materials; costs of cleaning up the vicinity in the event hazardous materials do escape from the dumpsite. None of these costs is charged back to the dumpsite user.

Large plants such as steel mills and lumber mills can recycle by-products relatively easily, merging the by-product streams back in with the streams of input materials, but this is not feasible for the small or medium-sized factory or shop. A small shop which fabricates custom-made aluminum windows, screens, and doors has no way of merging the stream of metal snippets back into the input stream of fabricated metal stock and screening. A marketplace through which small and medium-sized factories, shops, and laboratories can recycle their by-products at economic gain is thus needed in industrialized countries.

Such marketplaces have already begun to emerge. Recycling glass, aluminum, steel, and newsprint has become an important means of fund-raising for civic organizations, ranging from churches to community ecology centers, because the labor-intensive nature of these operations is well-matched by the volunteer labor forces such groups can muster. At least one company dedicated to providing a marketplace for surplus and waste industrial chemicals, has found the recycling of these substances profitable.[1] Many by-product or surplus chemicals can be sold to other users at prices below those of virgin materials; they can be given away or sold at low prices to such a marketplace much more advantageously than by paying to have them hauled away to a dumpsite (where an additional fee is charged for the privilege of disposal).

Individual companies can make significant contributions to everyone's

[1]Zero Waste Systems, Inc., 2928 Poplar Street, Oakland, California, 94608.

quality of life, and even to their own profitability, by turning over the handling of their by-products to the sales and marketing division instead of the purchasing department; and by properly emphasizing the possible usefulness rather than the nuisance aspect of the side streams of the system. From the viewpoint of society as a whole, perhaps we should re-examine our present, unspoken agreement to accept the responsibility and burden of disposing anything anyone chooses to define as "waste," irrespective of its possible utility to someone else.

New directions for higher quality of life for ourselves and our descendants here on Earth lie in our agricultural systems, our energy systems, and our manufacturing systems, if we focus on understanding and improving the structure and organization of the flows in the living systems we call the biosphere and human civilization.

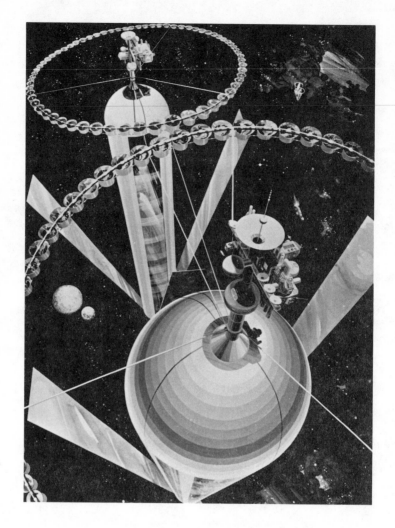

Two cylindrical, solar-powered space colonies,
orbiting between the Earth and Moon, 19 miles long and
4 miles in diameter, which could potentially
house several million people. The small
containers ringing the colony are agricultural
stations and the cylindrical living area is capped by a
manufacturing and power station.

IV.
Sundark Streaming

*North America as seen by
Apollo 16 astronauts on April 16, 1972.*

18. Terrestrial Chauvinism

The earliest pictures of the whole Earth seen from deep space were taken by the crew of Apollo 8 in December of 1968. These pictures suddenly made the environmentalist movement in the United States respectable to the general public, which had previously ignored the warnings of environmental activists, as a tempest in a teapot. Such pictures make it perfectly clear that the biosphere of Earth is a single, integrated system, and that the use of DDT in North America could indeed affect penguins in Antarctica. Economists with strong environmentalist sympathies began to elaborate on Buckminster Fuller's metaphor "Spaceship Earth," pointing out that the biosphere is as essential to the survival of humanity on Earth as the life support system of a spaceship like Apollo.

The metaphor was carried still further. A tiny capsule like Apollo depends entirely on the initial stock of materials, fuel, equipment, food, and oxygen placed aboard. Apollo had no mechanisms on board for converting used materials (carbon dioxide, urine, and feces) back into usable resources (oxygen, fresh water, and food), or for obtaining new resources from outside. Apollo did not even have solar panels to obtain new energy from the Sun; it relied on chemically powered fuel cells. We were solemnly admonished, "We have only the Earth. Once we use up the initial supply of resources, no more will be available."

The unspoken assumption of these economists and environmentalists may be explicitly stated as follows: Due to physical constraints beyond our control, the only material and energy resources available to the human race for the foreseeable future are just those of the planet Earth. I will refer to this assumption as *terrestrial chauvinism*. This assumption places a rigid Aristotelian boundary around the Earth, divorcing it from its proper environment in the solar system and in the universe. It also places a rigid boundary around our knowledge and capabilities to overcome the gravitational barrier between the surface of the Earth and free space. Both of these boundaries are inappropriate, and doubly dangerous because they have been drawn unconsciously. Since not even the atmosphere of the Earth has any well-defined limit, just where can we draw an intrinsic boundary between the Earth and space? Our daily human activities, involving communications and weather satellites, already extend out to geosynchronous orbit, 22,800 miles above the equator.

Doomsday Has Been Cancelled

A handful of space critics have raised the question: whether we could ever hope to use space for anything more than scientific exploration or expensive displays of national power; but have then used fundamentally specious arguments to "prove" that terrestrial chauvinism is justified, pointing out, for example, that the Apollo program cost about $50 billion (in 1978 dollars) and succeeded in bringing back only 875 pounds of rock and soil samples from the Moon, for an average price per pound exceeding $57 million. Since no natural resource, not even high quality drugs on the black market, is worth that much money, it is inconceivable that mining the Moon, for example, could ever be profitable.

I could argue equally well that it is impossible to have an air transportation industry in North America. If I wanted to travel from San Francisco to New York by airplane, I would first have to spend about a billion dollars to build an airport at the edge of San Francisco Bay and an airport near New York, say in the marshes by Jamaica Bay on Long Island, and I would somehow have to amortize that investment or convince the taxpayers to absorb that cost. Next, I would have to buy a Boeing 747 for approximately $40 million at today's prices. After loading up perhaps three hundred passengers, sardine-style, at San Francisco airport, we would all fly to New York, climb off the airplane, and scrap the jumbo jet. Since the ticket price would have to exceed $133,000 per person, we can safely conclude that airlines linking the major cities of North America will never be possible.

Thus far, the space program has been largely developmental. Since only a limited number of flights to the Moon were planned in the Apollo program, it was far cheaper to use the existing state of rocket technology of the early 1960s than to develop a far more sophisticated type of vehicle, which could be used many times, amortizing the high costs of the hardware, just as airlines do. The rocket technology available at that time was based on the military rockets of World War II and on the developments of ICBM technology during the 1950s and early 1960s. The purpose of a military rocket is to deliver a warhead to a target, not to complete one or more roundtrips. In that context only throw-away boosters make economic sense.

But if we are to contemplate larger scale operations in space, it pays to spend more money to develop and build reusable launch vehicles; because the additional costs can be amortized over greater total payloads, leading to reduced costs per pound. To argue that the Saturn rocket, used to launch Apollo to the Moon, represents the ultimate limits in space technology, is comparable to claiming that Ford's Model T, the Spirit of St. Louis, or Robert Fulton's steamboat represent the ultimate development of ground, air, or water transportation, respectively.

NASA's next generation of launch vehicle for putting humans into orbit is the *Space Shuttle*, designed to carry up to 35 tons of payload to low-Earth-orbit (LEO), roughly 150 to 500 miles above the surface. Because the Space

Shuttle will be reusable, and because of its sizeable payload capacity, equivalent to a fully loaded semitrailer truck or railroad boxcar, costs per pound for the Shuttle will be about $325, instead of about $10,000 characteristic of the Saturn rocket.

The Space Shuttle system consists basically of three pieces of hardware: the *Shuttle Orbiter*, the spacecraft itself, which is shaped like a delta-winged airplane; an *External Tank*, which contains liquid oxygen and liquid hydrogen to burn in the main engines aboard the Shuttle Orbiter; and two *Solid-propellant Rocket Boosters* (SRB's) strapped onto either side of the External Tank.

For liftoff the SRB's ignite simultaneously with the three main engines. At an altitude of about ten miles the propellants in the SRB's are completely exhausted and the SRB's separate from the External Tank, to fall into the ocean with parachutes, to be retrieved and reused with another launch. The Orbiter and External Tank continue their flight for about ten minutes after liftoff, when the liquids in the External Tank have all been burned up. If the launch site is Cape Canaveral, Florida, the Orbiter and External Tank, at this point, are high above Africa, just a tiny bit short of orbital speed. The Orbiter and External Tank separate, the Orbiter fires its engines again, using a small supply of fuel onboard, to insert itself into orbit. The External Tank, in the meanwhile, reenters the Earth's atmosphere, to burn up and disintegrate over the Indian Ocean. This tank is thus the only part of the system which is thrown away; everything else is reusable. Although the Shuttle system is far cheaper than its predecessors, it is clear from this description that further savings in launch costs are possible in the near future, by making everything reusable.

What is the significance of this major reduction in the costs of transportation to LEO? This will be the subject of the next few chapters, but before discussing specific possibilities for profits in space, I want to develop a larger framework for considering the economic uses of space.

If we consider a primitive society of hunters and gatherers, we find that most of their time is spent in two categories of activities: first, obtaining food and a few other essentials of life; and then, when sustenance is assured, enjoying themselves in socializing or playing games. In simple agricultural or pastoral societies, besides procuring their basic survival needs, significant time and effort are spent on processing and fabricating artifacts (tools, clothing, furniture, and buildings) before time is devoted to recreational activities. Extensive division of labor appears in such societies. In more complex societies, such as our own, still another category of activities is inserted, before time is taken for pleasure — service activities such as mail delivery, repairing of artifacts, and professional entertainment.

Thus a kind of hierarchy of activities in human societies is suggested:

- Primary activities: The extractive industries, which obtain basic material requirements for society, including hunting, fishing, agriculture, forestry, and mining.
- Secondary activities: The processing and fabricating industries, which process raw materials into artifacts and more sophisticated products, including manufacturing, construction, meat packing, and printing.
- Tertiary activities: The service industries, including education, transportation, communications, defense, and entertainment.
- Quarternary activities: The activities we do for their own sake, including socializing, dancing, playing games, amateur sports, hobbies, and scientific research.

In the final analysis, the quarternary activities motivate all the others: we work, eat, and sleep in order to enjoy our favorite pastimes.

Serious plans to launch an artificial satellite of the Earth for the first time were made in the United States and in the Soviet Union as part of each country's participation in the International Geophysical Year (1956–1957). If we consider what has been done in space in the two decades since, we can see a pattern emerging which underscores the fundamental significance of reductions in the cost of transportation to and from orbit. The first Earth satellites, the long series of lunar and planetary instrument probes, and the manned space programs of both nations were undertaken as quarternary activities, in the name of scientific research and of national prestige. In that context, the usual economic considerations of costs and revenues are inappropriate, so that these programs could be carried out despite exorbitant cost per pound.

By the mid-1960s, the success of experiments such as Echo I and Telstar I showed that communications satellites could be highly profitable. Since information transmitted by electromagnetic waves weighs nothing, no launch costs would be incurred in the relaying of millions of bits of information by way of a satellite high above the surface of the Earth. While the cost of launching a two-ton satellite, providing four thousand telephone circuits between any two continents, may be a few million dollars, modest charges for use of the telephone circuits can amortize that cost and return reasonable profits to the investors in the space of a few years. The first commercial uses of space, consequently, were tertiary activities, communications and information services.

During the 1980s, when the Space Shuttle will be the basic workhorse for working in space, materials processing in weightlessness, and the construction of very large structures in orbit, to facilitate the expansion of communications and other information services, will be erected, beginning several secondary activities in space for the first time.

Terrestrial Chauvinism

The primary industries — extracting minerals and energy — may follow by the end of the 1980s. But their full exploitation, as I will discuss later, will require development of the next generation of launch vehicle, with further steps in reducing costs per pound to orbit. That next level of launch vehicle technology, already on the drawing boards in conceptual design stages, will also make possible the rapid humanization of space and the birth of Gaia's first children, the first independent biospheres in space.

Not later than the first or second decade of the next century, when many of us alive today will still be here, terrestrial chauvinism will have died completely. It is not true that "we have only the Earth;" what is true is that we have only one Earth, forever unique and sacred in the universe, our original home — but only the first of many Gaian biospheres to be nurtured and inhabited by *Homo sapiens*.

Nearly five centuries ago Columbus sought a new trade route to Cathay; he discovered instead a whole New World. By 1992 we may be building new worlds in space from the material resources of the solar system, using the abundant energy of the Sun we orbit. We are no more confined and limited to this planet than the Earth stands still.

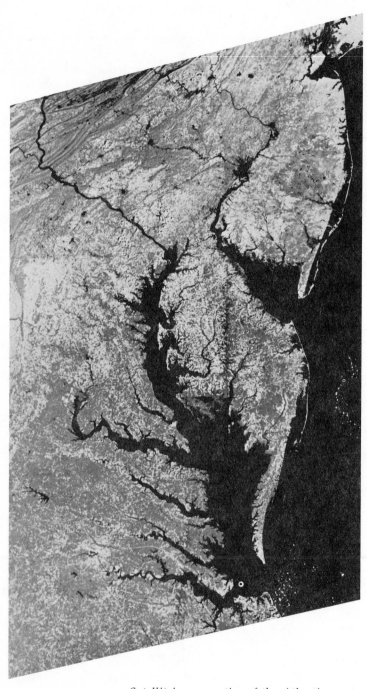

Satellite's perspective of the Atlantic coast,
New York City to Norfolk, 1972.

19. The View From Above

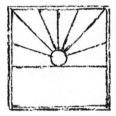

With the emergence of *Homo sapiens*, Gaia acquired, for the first time, a significant level of consciousness. This development has major potentials for improving the survivability of the biosphere as a whole. Presently we need the development of an extensive and elaborate network of sensory organs and systems; together with the means to interpret signals from the sensory system, in order to provide the whole organism with current information, on a continuing basis, about the status of the organism and its external environment. Without these additional systems, consciousness by itself will be of little practical benefit to Gaia.

Until early in the twentieth century, weather forecasting was very much a hit-or-miss proposition, because forecasters had only local weather information available. From the type of clouds and their direction of motion, from the trends of the barometer and thermometer, it was possible in a general way to anticipate major changes by twelve to twenty-four hours. Developing telegraph and telephone lines provided some additional information about major changes, making it possible to predict within just a few hours, when a hurricane would arrive in New York, if it had already hit Norfolk, Washington, and Philadelphia. But if a hurricane came from sea, the art of forecasting was completely inadequate.

Early in this century systematic weather observation systems were finally developed in many of the industrialized countries. The collection of temperature, humidity, barometric pressure, wind speed, direction, and cloud-cover information, from a large number of observation stations several times a day, finally provided a sufficiently large data base to permit meteorologists to recognize that weather systems were characterized by large masses of air, extending over a few hundred miles, having more or less homogeneous temperature and humidity. Boundaries between masses of warm, moist air, and masses of cold, dry air were discovered to be the primary locations of bad weather, with the "fronts" between masses behaving in different ways, depending on which type of air mass was pushing the front forward and which type was retreating.

The art of forecasting advanced slowly through the rest of this century until the advent of weather satellites, which enabled us to see the whole pattern of frontal systems, vortices, tropical storms, cyclones, anticyclones, and watch the pattern evolve over days and weeks. Never having had a network of weather stations over the major oceans, it was difficult to forecast the arrival of fronts from the Pacific Ocean on the West Coast of the United States and Mexico; this has now become routine and reliable.

Satellites are just beginning to be used to monitor the kinds of information we will need to project climactic trends as well as daily and weekly weather. The entire planetary weather machine is driven by the solar energy impinging on the Earth. We do not know whether the Sun shines with constant brightness or varies by a few percent every few weeks or months. Measurements of the albedo of the Earth (the fraction of sunlight falling on the Earth which is immediately reflected back into space), will play an important role in long range weather forecasting and in understanding the determinants of global climate. Constant monitoring of surface water temperatures and wave heights on the oceans will be made, in the next few years, by the Seasat series of satellites. These satellites will provide new data for weather forecasting as well as important information on the relationship between ocean conditions and biological productivity of the sea.

Satellites designed to look at land areas of the world, in several different wavelength bands, in the visible, infrared, and ultraviolet portions of the electromagnetic spectrum, have already revealed more details about fault systems, volcano chains, and mineral deposits than could have been pieced together by thousands of geologists working in the field for centuries. Such information can help in the development of earthquake prediction techniques, land use planning (to avoid the development of cities on fault lines), agricultural yield forecasts, and efficient prospecting for ores and fossil fuels.[1]

As wondrous as these applications seem, we have barely begun to scratch the surface of information services in space. The cost advantages of the Space Shuttle will open up whole new horizons in the 1980s. The communications satellites launched by COMSAT (Communications Satellite Corporation) have all been rather small (not more than about two tons total mass). This has limited the number of channels (telephone circuits) each satellite can accomodate, the power available in the transmitters, and the sensitivity of the receiver antennas aboard the satellite. Thus the transceiver stations on the ground which relay messages to and from the satellites in geosynchronous orbit are necessarily large, with high power required for the signals sent up to the satellite, and large receiver antennas to catch the faint signals transmitted by the satellite. Such transceiver installations today typically have a twelve-foot diameter, parabolic dish antenna, with electronic equipment heavy enough to require a small truck to transport it all.

The advent of the Space Shuttle will enable somewhat heavier satellites to be launched into geosynchronous orbit, and much larger structures to be

[1]Lloyd Darden, *The Earth in the Looking Glass*, Garden City: Anchor Press and Doubleday, 1974). An excellent discussion of the opportunities for Earth observation from orbit.

116

accomodated. As we develop the techniques to erect very large truss-like structures in orbit during the early and mid 1980s, it will become possible to reduce the size, scale, and power requirements for the transceivers on the ground. By about 1987 or 1988 we can expect the development of a personal telephone about the size of a wristwatch which will be able to transmit to, and receive from, a large satellite in geosynchronous orbit. Such a wristphone might initially sell for a few hundred dollars, and then decline in cost over five or ten years to perhaps $10 or $15, since the device is comparable in complexity to pocket calculators. Each personal wristphone could be dialed direct, anywhere on Earth, and the cost for a three-minute telephone conversation with someone on the opposite side of the world, should cost the user ten to fifty cents.

The initial market for such devices will likely be in the business and professional communities, replacing the pocket pagers used today by salesmen, lawyers, and doctors to keep in touch with their offices. Within a few years, as the capacity of the system increases, people who need emergency communications capabilities would begin to use wristphones. These would include hikers in remote wilderness areas, forest rangers, ambulance personnel in rural areas, and people working at night in urban areas who are exposed to higher risks of assault. For some additional cost the wristphone could also include a navigation receiver, capable of determining the user's position within ten to thirty meters anywhere on Earth. At about the same time use of wristphones would also begin among hobbyists like the "CB" enthusiasts of the 1970s. Finally, perhaps fifteen years after initial implementation of the system, a large fraction of the general population would begin to use the wristphone as a supplement to, or replacement for, conventional telephones. According to one analysis of this type of communications system, annual revenues for this single service would amount to $600 million to $6 billion near the turn of the century, earning 10 to 20% return on investment annually, after inflation.

The total potential revenues of a wide variety of information and communications services, made possible by the view of Earth from above, are staggering. Communications satellites; navigation satellites; satellites which collect measurements from thousands of unmanned instrument packages in remote locations around the globe for processing at a central location; direct television broadcast satellites; and dozens of other services will be commercialized in the next decade or two, and are likely to earn $20 to $100 billion (1978 dollars) each year, near the turn of the century, with improved quality of life for millions, even billions, of people, as we improve and extend the flows of information throughout the global system.[2]

[2]"Space Industrialization 1980 to 2010," *NASA Contract NAS 8-32197*, Huntsville, Alabama, Science Applications, 15 March 1978.

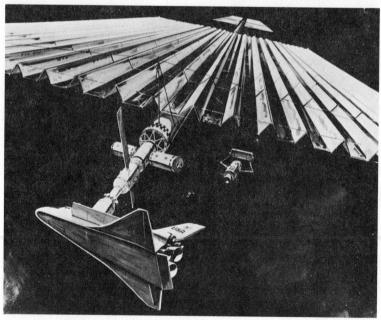

Above. *Artist's conception of a Solar Power Satellite under construction.* Below. *One of several configurations of Space-Based Power Conversion Systems now under study by NASA.*

20. Factories in Orbit

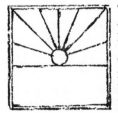The Space Shuttle promises access to space with transportation costs in the vicinity of $325 per pound during the 1980s. The cargo bay of the Shuttle Orbitor has cylindrical volume of about 4.8 meters in diameter by 18.5 meters in length (15 feet by 60 feet) equipped with large hatches to permit objects which completely fill the bay to be ejected into space, if desired. Many of the Shuttle's planned missions will be the launches of large satellites into orbit, or of planetary exploration probes (such as the Mariner, Pioneer, and Viking series of probes) deep into space. But the Shuttle will be used to carry various experimental packages into orbit as well; many of which will be returned to Earth in the Shuttle Orbiter.

The European Space Agency (ESA) has been developing an orbital laboratory called Spacelab to fly in the Shuttle. Spacelab comes in several different configurations, including modules for performing experiments in zero-gravity in a shirt-sleeve environment. The flight crew for the Shuttle will normally consist of two pilots and a mission specialist, an engineer or scientist who will have overall responsibility for carrying out the launch of payloads from the cargo bay and projects on orbit (requiring extensive use of the Orbiter itself). In addition, the Shuttle can accomodate four payload specialists, engineers or scientists who will operate experimental packages or other payloads in the cargo bay, while the Shuttle Orbiter remains in space for a few days to a month.

The Spacelab experimental program will include a large number of experiments in astronomy, biology, Earth sensing and surveying, and zero-gravity materials processing. Initially, most of these experiments will be scientific rather than developmental in nature, but commercial possibilities are already being considered. If some product can be manufactured more easily in weightlessness than here on the ground, or have superior properties, it will be profitable to manufacture it in space—but only if the value of the product here on the Earth is higher than the cost of transporting the raw materials into orbit and bringing the finished products back down.

The essential question, then, is what products in the world economy today are worth a few hundred dollars a pound or more? Most of the goods sold in the United States economy today cost about $1 to $2 a pound. Most meats in the supermarket fall in this range; fruits and vegetables generally run $0.25 to $1 a pound; automobiles from Detroit typically cost $6,000 and weigh about 3,000 pounds for a cost per pound of $2. Transistorized radios and pocket calculators are available in department stores for about $5 to $10 each, weighing about four ounces, for a cost per pound of $20 to $50. For the pocket calculators most of the cost of the device is in the integrated circuit chip, which weighs a fraction of an ounce, having a value of perhaps $1,000 a pound or more. High grade optical components are also in this range, while industrial diamonds (used for grinding and polishing) cost about $10,000 per pound. Perhaps the most expensive materials on Earth today are pharmaceutical products, including vaccines, which may cost $10,000 to $100,000 per pound but are used in such tiny quantities in clinical use that the cost to the patient of a single dose may be only a few dollars.

The total value of retail goods sold in the United States economy each year is roughly $1,000 billion; perhaps $5 billion of this has a value in excess of $1,000 per pound. The total value of goods with a value in excess of $50 per pound, on the other hand, may be $100 billion. Reducing the cost of space transportation from $325 per pound to $10 or $25 a pound would thus open up vast new possibilities for materials processing in orbit.[1] Several hundred materials or products having a high value per pound have been examined to see whether they could be made cheaper, faster, or better in weightlessness, and several dozen things for which we can see an economic need or use, but which do not presently exist commercially, have been considered as possible candidates.

No specific possibilities are considered sure-fire bets for profitable orbital manufacture as yet, but the candidates are numerous and very interesting. High quality optical glass is very difficult to make here on the ground, because the molten glass must, necessarily, be mixed in a container of a different material which stays solid under much higher temperatures. Some of the container material, nonetheless, is dissolved by the molten glass, contaminating the mixture, with the result that the optical components have numerous tiny defects sprinkled though them, which scatter light, thereby degrading performance. In orbit pure ingredients, for high quality glasses, can be melted in special furnaces which suspend the mixture electromagnetically or acoustically without touching any container walls, resulting, hopefully, in very high quality components.[2]

As commercially profitable products are identified during the mid-1980s, processing will step up, from small, laboratory scale experiments aboard Spacelab, to larger scale pilot plants in the Shuttle cargo bay, to full scale production facilities in free-flying space stations. Several different

[1]David R. Criswell, "Space Industrialization: Rationales and Key Technologies," *Lunar Utilization: Special Session of the Seventh Annual Lunar Science Conference*, (Houston: Lunar Science Institute, March 1976).

[2]G. Harry Stine, *The Third Industrial Revolution*, (New York: G.P. Putnam's Sons, 1975). Discusses a wide variety of materials processing and research possibilities in weightlessness.

corporations may find it advantageous to combine efforts to establish an "industrial park" in orbit, which would provide life support systems for workers, basic structures and pressure vessels for factories, and basic utility services such as communications and energy. The actual manufacturing equipment would be provided by each user, who would rent the services for each manufacturing operation.

In a manufacturing operation of any real complexity some amount of human labor is necessary for economic reasons. As yet no manufacturing facility on Earth is totally automated; it is too expensive to develop and build automatic machinery or robots equipped to take care of all the likely eventualities. By about 1990 it is likely that dozens of workers in space will be engaged in manufacturing operations, returning finished products to the Earth aboard the Shuttle Orbiter. The Shuttle Orbiter closes its hatches after loading and securing the cargo; it briefly fires the main engines to transfer from its mission orbit around the Earth to a reentry trajectory; turns its nose forward, slightly elevated, to absorb the heat of reentry in the ceramic tiles lining its belly; and glides to a landing on a long runway, just like an airplane, lowering its landing gear moments before touchdown. Workers could be rotated between the Earth and the orbital factories aboard the Shuttle, riding in the main cabin in seats designed for mission and payload specialists.

We need not be disturbed by the fact that we cannot point with certainty to a particular product which will be a profitable investment in five or ten years to come. The Virginia Colony in North America was chartered as a profit-making corporation. The original investors and speculators had a long list of ideas about how to make money in the New World, but none were successful; yet the Virginia Company flourished. The economic success of the company came from the discovery of tobacco, a completely unexpected surprise that could not have been anticipated before the settlers actually arrived in Virginia. We, also, may be surprised by whatever turns out to be profitable to manufacture in orbital factories.

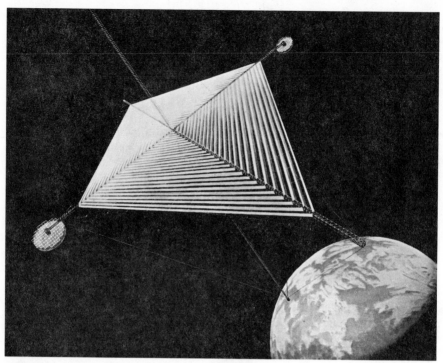

Above. *Future Solar Power Satellite collects and transmits microwave energy while in geosynchronous orbit some 36,000 miles from Earth. Below. Off-shore Power Station Antenna (rectenna) receives energy from SPS and converts it to conventional electrical power.*

21. Catch the Sundark

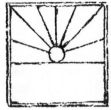The remarkable Apollo photographs of the Earth, seen from space, have brought about enormous changes in our perceptions of the Earth and its biosphere. They gave many people a sense of the barrenness and lifelessness of outer space. But we can get another, important, perception from those pictures, as well. Consider again the cover painting of this book, focussing your attention — not on the Earth itself, nor on the astronauts and space hardware in close view — on the rest of the picture. What is there to see in the darkness of space surrounding the Earth, except for a light, sprinkling of stardust? What can we see in the night sky when we look at the darkness surrounding the Moon?

The new perception is that *the entire picture is flooded with sunshine.* If I want to know whether I will be bathed in sunlight when I step out of my house in the morning, I do not have to look out an east window to see if the Sun itself is visible. I can look out of any window to see that the sky is bright blue or that the grass is sparkling with light, and know that the air is suffused with sunshine. In space we do not see sunlight except where it is reflected by the Earth, the Moon, astronauts, or artifacts; instead, we perceive sundark streaming by. It is clear to the mind's eye that the radiant energy f the Sun flows through all of the Apollo pictures. Every cubic meter of space is flooded with it, but it remains invisible to our eyes, permitting us to look through it and past it, to behold the stark darknes of the interstellar void.

The pictures of the Earth rising above the lunar horizon contain this same all-pervading sunshine, but they also remind us that outer space contains materials as well as abundant and long-lasting solar energy. Outer space can be an excellent culture-medium for life, but as yet the vast resources of the solar system are as inaccessible as were the vast quantities of pre-biotic molecules scattered across the open oceans and continents, before photosynthesis. The rapid development of space transportation technology tolls the death-knell for terrestrial chauvinism. The only question to be settled is the exact date of the funeral, and many are at work trying to schedule it at an early date.

Can we catch the sundark and tame it to our needs? Can we harvest the continual flow of solar energy streaming past our planet for the use of civilization on Earth as well as in orbit?

Sunlight consists of electromagnetic waves of varying wavelengths which transport energy without mass. Energy, like information, could be transmitted from space to the Earth or from the Earth into space without paying space transportation costs. Two important possibilities for harvesting solar energy from space have been considered with increasing interest during the past few years. The first basic concept is to place large reflectors in orbit, to redirect raw sunlight to the ground. The second concept is to place large satellites in space to convert sunlight into other kinds of electromagnetic waves, which are then transmitted to the Earth for conversion into other forms of power.

Raw sunlight, reflected from space, could be used in many different ways. At low levels of intensity, it could be used to light the streets of urban areas during the night. At levels equivalent to several full Moons, sunlight could be used for round-the-clock rescue and relief operations in areas devastated by major disasters such as hurricanes and typhoons, floods, or earthquakes, or for round-the-clock harvesting of crops about to be destroyed by approaching tropical storms. If the intensity of the reflected sunlight were greater than one-tenth of full daylight brightness, it could be used to accelerate the growth and ripening of most crops in prime agricultural areas of the world. Finally, if the intensity of reflected sunlight were comparable to or greater than normal noonday sunlight at the surface of the Earth, a vast number of new possibilities would arise, including less expensive generation of electrical power from solar cells, covering larger areas of land. Such systems do not appear to be economically practical at the present because of the need to provide energy storage or a backup energy source for the night hours.

Other applications of reflectors in orbit might include deliberate modification of local weather (e.g., to dissipate fog, prevent damaging frosts, or break up hurricanes). Thawing out frozen waterways, desalinizing water for irrigation, drying crops, and producing fertilizers are but a few more possibilities.[1] All of these applications, however, would have to be considered in view of the potential disturbance to the day-night cycles of animals and plants living within the illuminated areas.

Smaller satellites of this type, capable of providing illumination for disaster relief, might be launched during the latter part of the 1980s. Such satellites, placed in relatively low orbits, might require a few Space Shuttle flights to deliver the parts for assembly in space. Experimental use of these reflectors in limited target areas could provide the information necessary to determine whether local ecosystems in various parts of the world could

[1]Kenneth W. Billman, William P. Gilbreath, and Stuart W. Bowen, "Satellite Mirror Systems for Providing Terrestrial Power: System Concept," in Richard A. Van Patten, Paul Siegler, and E.V.B. Stearns, eds., *The Industrialization of Space*, Vol. 36, (San Diego: Advances in the Astronautical Sciences, American Astronautical Society, 1978). Provides a fairly comprehensive discussion of these and other possibilities.

tolerate continuous sunlight. Were we to be confronted with the rapid onset of a new ice age, implementation of a very extensive system of reflector satellites could provide the leverage needed to reverse the climactic shift, helping Gaia maintain the planetary equilibrium. (While the thought of intervening in the workings of the biosphere on such a massive scale is awesome indeed, it is perhaps more horrifying to consider what it might be like to read an Environmental Impact Statement for an ice age.)

The alternative to reflecting raw sunlight from space is transmitting "processed" sunlight. In 1968 Dr. Peter E. Glaser of the Arthur D. Little Company proposed building large satellites to collect solar energy in space, twenty-four hours a day, convert it into electricity, and transmit the power to Earth by a microwave beam.[2] On the ground a large array of antennas would capture the microwaves and convert them back into electricity. Such Solar Power Satellites (SPS) could be placed in geosynchronous orbit, 22,800 miles above the Earth's equator, where a satellite takes exactly twenty-four hours to orbit the Earth once, while the Earth below turns on its axis just once. Geosynchronous satellites thus appear to hover above a fixed spot on the equator, day and night.

An SPS, at that distance from the Earth, would be bathed in sunlight twenty-four hours a day, all year long, except for a few weeks in the spring and fall, when the satellite would be eclipsed by the Earth for a brief period each day, losing about 2% of the solar energy it could otherwise collect in a year. These power "outages," however, would occur near local midnight, in the vicinity of the receiver antenna on the ground, and would occur on schedule, permitting previous arrangements for the substitution of electricity from other sources or other satellites.

A number of alternative designs for the SPS exist and are being studied, as have a number of different orbits besides geosynchronous. Each of these alternatives has major advantages and liabilities. At the present time, it is probably premature to restrict attention to any particular variant. Glaser has discussed primarily photovoltaic cells for the conversion of sunlight into electricity aboard the satellite, anticipating major improvements in both the cost and the weight of solar cells during the next few decades; but his patent on the SPS concept covers any means of conversion.

Gordon R. Woodcock and Daniel L. Gregory at the Boeing Company have been studying SPS designs based on a thermal cycle since the late 1960s. In their approach huge, bowl-shaped mirrors, made of thin plastic film and coated with aluminum, would focus sunlight into a cavity, to heat helium gas to very high temperatures, to drive turbogenerators; just the way nuclear reactors or fossil fuel boilers produce very hot steam, at high pressure, to turn turbogenerators here on Earth.

[2]Peter E. Glaser, "Solar Power from Satellites," *Physics Today*, February 1977, p. 30. Presents a very readable description of the Solar Power Satellite concept.

Another approach receiving some attention is the possibility of transmitting power from orbit to the ground by high energy laser beams instead of microwaves. At the present time, however, the technology for generating microwaves, and for converting them back into electricity, is already well developed. Experiments by the Jet Propulsion Laboratory in the California desert have already demonstrated an overall efficiency of about 60% in converting electricity into microwaves, transmitting the microwaves over several kilometers, and converting the microwaves back into electrical power. The technologies for generating laser beams and converting them into electricity are far less advanced, and it would be risky to predict that twenty years from now the two technologies would be within comparable development.

Solar Power Satellites, based on microwave transmission, would be enormous structures, perhaps five kilometers in width and twenty kilometers in length (somewhat larger than Manhattan Island). Because of the advantages of the space environment, however, such a satellite would be no more massive than a supertanker, about 100,000 metric tons (220 million pounds). This is possible because the structure does not have to support its own weight; it need only be strong enough to remain stiff in an environment where the principal stresses are those due to rapid cooling and heating of the structure as it passes into and out of the Earth's shadow.

A typical SPS design would provide ten million kilowatts of power at the receiver antenna farm which would cover a patch of land about five miles across and eight miles in length. The farm would be sufficient to provide the total electrical needs for a city of about a million people, including heavy industry, office buildings, and street lighting. Large nuclear power plants today provide about one million kilowatts. Grand Coulee Dam, on the Columbia River in Washington State, is the largest hydroelectric powerplant in the world; it produces about 2.2 million kilowatts. About two hundred Solar Power Satellites would meet the total electrical energy needs for the United States in about 2025. If we were to supply, electrical power equal to that produced by one SPS of this size, by burning coal, we would have to mine, transport, and burn 100,000 metric tons of coal every day (a mass equal to that of the power satellite itself).

While the receiver antenna farm covers a large area, the antenna array itself is lightweight and can be made 80% — 90% transparent to rain and sunlight. If the array were suported by a trusswork structure, ten or twenty feet above the surface, the land beneath could be used for a variety of other purposes at the same time, including cattle grazing, fodder production, or raising major staple grain crops such as wheat. Wire mesh screening, hung below the antenna array, could completely shield the microwaves.

Both the Department of Energy and NASA are presently examining the SPS concept from a variety of viewpoints. Environmental concerns loom large in the picture. It is unclear to what extent, if any, the microwave beam, passing through the atmosphere, would affect local weather and global climate; or just what impact rocket traffic through the atmosphere (especially the stratosphere and ionosphere) may have. The question of people being exposed to microwaves, in the vicinity of the receiver antenna farm, is very important.

The projected costs for Solar Power Satellites are, as yet, uncertain, but it is likely that electricity from SPS will not be a great deal more expensive than nuclear power in the 1990s, and may turn out to be much cheaper than nuclear power or coal. We may be willing to pay somewhat more for electricity from an SPS, if it decreases our balance of payments deficit due to petroleum imports, or if it proves to be environmentally preferable to nuclear powerplants or coal-burning generator plants.

The major socioeconomic benefits of Solar Power Satellites, I think, will be found in the Third World, but I want to postpone that discussion until later. Present considerations by DOE and NASA are based on the assumption that only a modest fraction of U.S. electrical needs will be supplied by SPS, with the first satellite completed in about 1996 to 2000.

The Space Shuttle itself is inadequate to support a major program of launching SPS parts into orbit for assembly by hundreds of workers; to deliver the parts for a single SPS would require 3,450 Space Shuttle flights, and NASA anticipates a maximum of only sixty flights a year, when the Shuttle system reaches maturity in the mid-1980s. A number of newer, larger, launch vehicles are on the drawing board in preliminary conceptual design studies. Projections of the effects of newer and stronger materials, better aerodynamic and structural design, and the development of more efficient engines, combine to suggest that the next generation launch vehicle, which may be a Single-Stage-to-Orbit (SSTO), winged rocket, could deliver 220 metric tons or more, to orbit as early as 1990, with a lift cost of about $10 a pound, instead of $325 a pound as in the Shuttle—a development which would have far-reaching implications.

The cost of doing the necessary research, design, and testing of hardware for a commercially viable Solar Power Satellite program may total several tens of billions of dollars over the next decade or two. The risk of finding out that the SPS concept is not an attractive energy system is significant, but not overwhelming. In the meanwhile, the expansion of communications and information services in orbit will itself require greater and greater amounts of electrical power in space. Developing the SPS technologies in such a way as to be responsive to the needs of the information services for large arrays of solar energy collection and conversion will minimize the chances of wasting our time, effort, and money *in toto*.

It seems likely that in the 1980s we will begin extractive industries (primary activities) in space, with the deployment of one or more small reflector satellites, to test the use of augmented, raw sunlight here on the ground. By the 1990s we are likely to have taken significant steps toward Solar Power Satellites, because of their intrinsic advantages of nearly perpetual sundark and minimal environmental disturbance. As we will see in the next chapter, however, the rapid and effective development of an SPS program will likely come with the extension of extractive industries in space — for raw materials as well as energy. The funeral for terrestrial chauvinism may occur in the 1980s.

22. Planetary Chauvinism

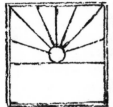Given the reasonable expectation of major advances in space technology, speculative writers, including many sober and reputable scientists, have considered it inevitable that at some time in the future vast numbers of people would leave Earth for jobs and adventures elsewhere in the universe. Most speculators, however, assume that the principal arena for human civilization will always be the surfaces of the planets. Grandiose schemes, some of them technically feasible, have been outlined for "terraforming" other planets (modifying the atmosphere of a whole planet in order to make climactological conditions suitable for terrestrial lifeforms, including people). Gaia, as we have seen, has done just that to the planet Earth which was once barren and inhospitable. Terraforming the Moon, Venus, or Mars would be expensive and slow, requiring decades or centuries to achieve.

Even if these projects could be carried out, the total land area available in the solar system would be rather limited. The total surface area of the Moon is slightly more than the land area of Africa. The area of Mars is about equal to that of North and South America plus Australia. Venus, however, would contribute a land area about three times that of all the continents of Earth, since it is only a bit smaller in diameter than the Earth but has no oceans. Some of the larger moons of Jupiter and Saturn are comparable in size to our own Moon and might likewise be candidates for terraforming, although their distance from the Sun would make it very difficult to sustain reasonable temperatures even with rather thick atmospheres. Still, the real estate available in the solar system would be rather limited.

If we restrict our consideration of living places to planets, we are unconsciously erecting another Aristotelian boundary, and placing virtually all of the cosmos beyond the pale; such narrow-mindedness is, in brief, planetary chauvinism. Widening our perspective, we can pose a fundamental question: *Is the surface of a planet really the best place possible for a technological, industrial, and, perhaps, rapidly expanding society to live?*

Dr. Gerard K. O'Neill posed just this question for his freshman physics class at Princeton University in the fall of 1969. O'Neill is an elementary particles physicist with a solid reputation as an experimenter and designer of high energy particle accelerators. Like many professional scientists, he was deeply troubled by the antitechnological bias so common among college students in the late 1960s. On campuses across the country students denounced the first Apollo landing on the Moon on July 20, 1969, as a waste of money, inspired solely by jingoistic pride, contributing nothing to the desperate social needs here on Earth. O'Neill decided to spend part of his course examining just what could be done in space to respond to the Earth's pressing needs, if we really decided to make that concerted effort.

A technological society, living on its planet of origin, will inevitably find conflicts between the extraction of raw materials and the fabric of the biosphere. Mining cannot be done without some disruption, however temporary, of the immediate vicinity. No matter how carefully designed an industrial process can be, an occasional spill of biotoxic materials will occur. All the goodwill in the universe cannot guarantee zero adverse impact on the biosphere. The waters impounded by beaver dams kill off large areas of vegetation and provide breeding grounds for a variety of insects which are noxious to many mammals, including humans.

Aside from ecological problems, an industrial society is constantly confronted by the difficulties of gravity, which cannot be turned off for more than a few seconds at a time, as in parabolic flight in jet planes. If more intense gravitational effects are desired, we can simulate them only by very cumbersome centrifuges whose bearings are also constantly fighting gravity.

Because we have always lived with Earth's gravity, we tend to overlook what a nuisance it can be. On an automobile assembly line, for example, a completed engine, ready to be mounted on a partly assembled chassis, must be lifted up by a hoist. The hoist and engine are dragged over to the chassis, fighting the friction induced by the weight of the engine and hoist. The engine is then lowered slowly into place and bolted onto the chassis, which is dragged over to the next assembly station . . . and so on, always struggling against the adverse effects of gravity.

Although the sundark streams past all the planets continually, the body of each planet shades half its own surface at any instant, making it very difficult (as we know here on Earth) to tap this flow of energy efficiently while remaining planetbound.

Given all the disadvantages of living on a planet, O'Neill's students convinced themselves that if a civilization had once mastered the skills to climb up out of the gravitational pit of its home planet, it would be foolish to descend into another gravitational pit to conduct its basic activities, if it is at all possible to carry out those activities in free space itself.

Besides a steady supply of abundant and inexpensive energy, which is provided in free space by the streaming sundark, any civilization needs raw materials. Hauling these up out of the gravitational pit of the Earth is somewhat difficult and expensive. But raw materials can be found in the solar system in far more accessible locations than the surface of the Earth. The Apollo expeditions to the Moon, originally conceived as scientific explorations of no practical importance, have proven to be geological prospecting surveys: the rock and soil samples returned by the astronauts showed that the Moon is an excellent source for most of the materials needed for a viable industrial society in free space. On a weight basis average lunar soils consist of about 40% oxygen, 20% silicon, and 30% metals, including up to 15% iron with the balance about evenly divided between aluminum, titanium, and magnesium. The gravitational pit of the Moon is only one-twentieth as deep as Earth—twenty times less energy is needed to launch a pound of materials from the surface of the Moon into free space than to launch a pound of materials from the surface of the Earth.

A number of important materials, however, appear to be scarce on the Moon, including hydrogen, carbon, and nitrogen—all of them essential for life. These elements may yet be found on the Moon, possibly frozen underground in the polar regions or on the floors of craters near the poles, where the Sun never shines. This is a distinct possibility because the Moon's axis is tipped less than one degree to the orbit of the Earth and Moon around the Sun, in sharp contrast to the Earth whose axial inclination of 23° produces six months of total darkness, alternating with six months of constant daylight in its polar regions. The perpetual night in some of the lunar craters would result in temperatures rather close to absolute zero, so that the slightest puff of gas arriving in one of these craters would be instantly frozen, and trapped to accumulate for many millions of years.

The mineral resources of the Moon have been poorly mapped. For some years now, NASA has requested funding from Congress for a Lunar Polar Orbiter which could adequately survey all of the Moon, from North Pole to South Pole. This would provide evidence for the existence (or lack) of such frozen deposits near the poles, as well as a comprehensive atlas of the principal metallic contents of the surface rocks and soils. Thus far, NASA has not been successful in convincing Congress of the value of such a survey; perhaps because NASA has spoken only of the scientific benefits of the program with no mention of its potential economic value.

Besides the Moon, numerous other sources of raw materials are available in the solar system, including vast numbers of asteroids, all of them with minute gravitational fields. The largest known asteroid, Ceres, was discovered on the evening of January 1, 1801, by the Italian astronomer G. Piazzi, for whom a lunar crater 130 kilometers in diameter (80 miles) is named. Ceres is about 770 kilometers across (480 miles). Since 1801 more than 50,000 asteroids have been discovered, ranging in size from a few giants, comparable to Ceres, down to objects about one or two kilometers across. In all likelihood, the population of smaller asteroids number in the hundreds of thousands. Most of these Lilliputian members of the solar system orbit the Sun in a wide band between Mars and Jupiter, but since 1975, two families of asteroids have been discovered whose orbits regularly pass within a few million miles of Earth. These asteroids, named the Apollo and Amor asteroids, after the first member of each family to be discovered, are in somewhat precarious orbits, astronomically speaking. Within the next ten or twenty million years, they are likely to impact the Earth or the Moon.

Based on chemical analyses of meteorites and spectroscopic studies of the light reflected from asteroids, it is considered likely that many of the asteroids contain fair amounts of carbon, nitrogen, and water, as well as a variety of light elements such as sulfur, phosphorus, and potassium, which are also rare on the Moon. Some of the asteroids are composed largely of nickel, cobalt, and iron, in proportions comparable to those of very high grade stainless steel.

Free space seems very well suited to industrial, technological societies. O'Neill and his students wondered whether reasonable and pleasant living conditions could be provided for people. Much to everyone's surprise, they found that normal Earth gravity, sea level atmospheric pressure and climate, day/night cycles of sunlight, seasonal variations, and shielding from cosmic rays and solar flares could all be provided in very large scale habitats, using present day strengths of materials. The most startling discovery was that habitats in free space were feasible in this century, with as much as 98% of the raw materials required for construction obtainable from the Moon. Feasibility explains the current interest in space colonies or space settlements, as such habitats came to be called.[1]

O'Neill continued to study these ideas for several more years, and finally got an article accepted for publication in a physics journal (*Physics Today*, published by the American Institute of Physics) in 1974. He worked out reasonable schemes for self-sufficient agriculture in space, taking advantage of the unique new environment of constant sunlight; for launching raw materials from the Moon by an electromagnetic catapult; and for providing day and night and seasonal cycles. Materials available today are apparently strong enough to allow the construction of space colonies in cylindrical shapes, with an interior land area comparable to the entire San Francisco peninsula (which has a population of about 1.3 million people on its 230 square kilometers—90 square miles). Such a space city would not be a submarine in any sense, but a whole world in itself.

To build such colonies in space would cost tens of billions of dollars, and we are not prepared to spend that much money just to provide a new place for ten or a hundred thousand people to live. While materials-processing industries in space may become very profitable by the 1990s, and information services in space will be certainly profitable, these two industries are unlikely to require more than a few hundred people working on a regular

[1]Gerard K. O'Neill, *The High Frontier: Human Colonies in Space*, (New York: William Morrow, 1977). Discusses the concept of space colonization extensively with a personal account of the evolution of the idea since 1969.

basis — hardly sufficient to justify building a colony. Deployment of many large reflector satellites would not require numerous workers, either, since the total mass of even the largest reflectors proposed (perhaps a few kilometers across), is small enough to be manageable by a few dozen space construction workers.

Early in 1975, however, the idea of human colonies in space built from lunar materials came together with the Solar Power Satellite concept, and a great many nascent ideas crystallized rapidly in a remarkable fusion of radical concepts. The assembly of an SPS, launched piecemeal from the Earth, is estimated to require some 800 to 1,000 workers in space to complete the job in one year. If we wanted to build several such satellites a year, in order to make a really significant contribution to the Earth's energy needs, we would need several thousand workers living in space for long periods of time. At this scale of space habitation, space colonies become very interesting. If we propose to mine the Moon for the raw materials needed to build space colonies, then surely we could mine the Moon for the materials needed to build Solar Power Satellites.

During the summers of 1975, 1976, and 1977, NASA's Ames Research Center, just south of San Francisco, California, sponsored intensive workshops to examine these ideas to see whether engineering solutions are practical and possible for the manufacture of Solar Power Satellites and space colonies from lunar or asteroidal materials. These workshops have involved physicists and aerospace engineers, chemists and architects, geologists and mining engineers, biologists and physiologists, psychologists and anthropologists, industrial designers and artists. Design problems tackled in these workshops have included electromagnetic catapults (mass drivers) for launching raw materials into space from the surface of the Moon; a lunar mining system; refining equipment to extract useful metals, semiconductor grade silicon, glass, and oxygen from lunar soils; space farms to feed the workers an Earth-like diet of fresh foods raised in minimum areas; and factories to produce component parts for Solar Power Satellites and space colonies. I had the pleasure of participating in the 1977 workshop, working through the requirements of equipment, living quarters, people, and transportation systems, to initiate such a large scale venture in space during the 1980s and 1990s.

Surprisingly enough, it now appears that a focussed effort to implement such a system could be undertaken in the 1980s, with rapid proliferation of Solar Power Satellites in the 1990s, for a total investment of about $75 or $80 billion before delivery of the first power satellite. Thereafter, the system could build about two and a half SPS's each year, with three thousand workers in space, earning about $8 to $20 billion annually after expenses. The total investment would thus be less than twice the cost of the entire Apollo program (corrected for inflation). Electricity from SPS's built from nonterrestrial materials would be significantly cheaper than electricity today, and much cheaper than electricity produced by more conventional powerplants in the 1990s. The first space colony proper would then be constructed sometime in the 1990s, to permit expansion of the workforce, so that SPS's could be built in greater numbers. The total mass launched into orbit, until the system begins to pay off its debts, is about 80,000 metric tons, somewhat less than the total mass of just one SPS.

These results should not, perhaps, be very surprising. When Europeans began to colonize the New World in the sixteenth century, they did not bring houses with them. They brought only the tools and equipment with which to build homes, churches, shops, and fortifications, from the raw materials available in the new land; that equipment weighed far less than even a single house adequate to shelter a shipload of colonists. By 1992, the 500th anniversary of Christopher Columbus' first voyage, the first "new worlds" in space may very likely be under construction, burying both our terrestrial and planetary chauvinisms forever.[2]

[2]Although the concept of space colonization first became a topic for serious public discussion as recently as May 1974, the literature available has grown explosively. The best source of current information on technical and political developments in the fields of space colonization, solar power satellites, and space industrialization is the *L-5 News*, the monthly publication of the L-5 Society, 1620 North Park Avenue, Tucson, Arizona, 85719. Annual membership dues in this non-profit citizens' group, supporting a major thrust into space in the near future, are $20 ($15 for students), including a subscription to the *L-5 News*. Besides O'Neill's book, some of the other basic references in that field are included in the bibliography.

23. Catch a Falling Star

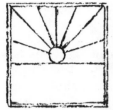 At the present moment, in the summer of 1978, it appears that the Moon is the most likely source of raw materials for large scale construction projects in space; because we have more information about the composition of lunar materials than materials from any other source off the Earth. Yet the disadvantages of working on the surface of a planet, even one as small as the Moon, are sufficiently great to warrant serious attention to the asteroids. NASA is studying several possible mid-1980s missions in which instrument probes would rendezvous with one or more near-Earth asteroids, take rock samples, and send back information on detailed chemical analyses. It may be quite feasible to base a Solar Power Satellite program on asteroidal materials in about the same time scale as a program based on lunar mines.

During the 1977 summer workshop at NASA's Ames Research Laboratory this possibility was examined in detail. While the lunar approach would place a mass driver on the surface of the Moon, to launch raw materials into space for processing at an orbital factory complex, the asteroidal approach would use a mass driver as a kind of rocket engine to propel most of a small asteroid to the factory. If mining equipment, landed on a small asteroid, is used to grind up part of the asteroid, sorting out useful and desirable materials such as carbon, water, nitrogen, and metals, the residual matter can be fired off at high speed with an electromagnetic catapult to provide weak but steady thrust over a period of many months. For certain asteroids, it would be possible to alter their orbit around the Sun in such a way as to pass close by Venus, for example, and use Venus's gravitational field to make a major change in the asteroid's trajectory. Using such gravity-assisted maneuvers past Venus, the Earth, and the Moon, several known asteroids (or large chunks of them) could be brought into high orbits around the Earth in total mission times of less than five years.

Although transporting crews to an asteroid, at distances as great as Venus, is more difficult and more risky than transporting them to the surface of the Moon, it is far easier to establish a mining base on (or inside) a small asteroid (with continuous solar power available), than on the Moon. Substantial cost reductions might be attained with this approach. Since asteroids offer a wider variety of raw materials than the Moon, it is difficult to forecast which approach will be implemented first.

The asteroidal approach has important implications beyond those of establishing space colonies and harvesting solar energy from space. A small nickel-iron asteroid, perhaps a hundred meters in diameter, could be retrieved in a mission time of less than five years. Once retrieved to high Earth orbit, an orbital factory could carve off chunks of the asteroid; melt them in solar furnaces; refine the metals to yield pure nickel or high grade stainless steel; inject tiny bubbles of an inert gas, such as helium or nitrogen, to make a liquid metal froth; and let it cool in zero-gravity to form a foamed metal with a density less than that of water. This material could then be machined into large aerodynamically-shaped structures (about the size of a large jetliner) with movable ballasts inside, controlled by autopilot-like computers and "dropped" into the Earth's atmosphere. Because of their low density, such lifting bodies would not be heated to very high temperatures during reentry, and could be guided to splash down in the ocean, completely intact. Because of the low density of the foamed metal, the lifting body would float, and could then be towed into harbor for use in conventional metallurgy, or carved up for use as a new, exotic construction material of high strength, high corrosion resistance, and low density.

Delivery of raw materials to the Earth in this manner might become economically feasible by the turn of the century. A mission to fetch such an asteroid might cost a few tens of billions of dollars, but the economic value of that much nickel would be roughly five trillion dollars, providing enough nickel to meet the global demand for nickel for a century, at present consumption rates. The cost, per pound, for the delivery of raw materials to the Earth in this fashion could be as low as 20¢ — far below present nickel prices of about $5 a pound.[1]

While this proposal may seem outrageously speculative, it is appropriate to note that one of the principal sources of nickel on Earth today is the Sudbury deposit in Ontario, Canada, which geologists now believe is an asteroid which collided with the Earth about one and a half billion years ago. Capturing asteroids in near-Earth orbits and carving them up for the purposes of Gaian life, will have a beneficial long term effect on the health of the biosphere of Earth, since many of these asteroids are destined to collide with the Earth. Given the vast resources of our solar system, the entire debate over Earth's limited mineral resources will soon be forgotten.

[1]Michael J. Gaffey and Thomas B. McCord, "Mining Outer Space," *Technology Review*, June 1977, p. 50.

24. Fly Me to the Moon

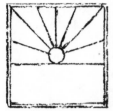

In 1969 my wife, Helen, and I went to see the movie *2001: A Space Odyssey*, just a few months after the first Apollo landing on the Moon. It seemed entirely reasonable at the time that continued advances in space technology would make commercial passenger service into space possible by the turn of the century. Pan American Airlines, whose insignia was shown in the movie on a Single-Stage-to-Orbit (SSTO) passenger rocket, had announced that it had started a waiting list for reservations aboard its first space flight, whenever that might occur. Helen and I agreed that, if it became possible in our lifetime, we would visit the Moon.

Most of the industries likely to flourish in space in the next few decades indicate a clear need for the development of space transportation systems considerably less expensive per pound than the Space Shuttle. Aerospace engineers at NASA and some of the major aerospace companies express confidence that the cost per pound to get to low Earth orbit may be $10 to $20 by the early 1990s, with the next generation vehicle operating in a mixed cargo/passenger mode.

What are the implications of such a breakthrough in price? Inexpensive spaceships will provide a new global transportation system and space tourism. At the cost per pound estimated for the launch of these new vehicles, the price of a ticket for an average adult would be $5,000 to $10,000 to go into Earth orbit and return. While this may still seem like a great deal of money, it is a very reasonable price for a large multinational corporation or for a government to spend for transporting key executives or senior diplomatic personnel halfway around the globe for critical negotiations—especially if the flight time for an SSTO, between any two places on the surface of the globe, were less than two or three hours. Round trips between Washington and Moscow, between New York and Calcutta, or between London and Sydney could be completed in a single day, with four to eight hours to transact business at the destination. Burning liquid oxygen and liquid hydrogen, it is likely that the environmental impacts of such vehicles on the atmosphere would be less than those of conventional and supersonic jet aircraft.

If ticket prices, for each adult going into orbit for a few days to a week, were indeed $5,000 to $10,000, a few thousand North Americans each year could be expected to take vacations in space in the 1990s, since five to ten thousand of them spend that much money today on South Seas cruises aboard luxury liners or on week-long tours of Antarctica. Besides a magnificent view of all of Gaia from a hotel in orbit, such a vacation would offer the experience of weightlessness, which most astronauts found exhilirating after an initial period of a day or two's vertigo.

New sports will doubtlessly be developed for zero-gravity conditions by space workers, and tourists will most likely have a chance to participate in or watch such games. Since rates for an orbital hotel are likely to be high initially, the basic rate may include special entertainment features, such as zero or low-gravity ballet, gymnastics, and wrestling, all of which would assume new dimensions of grace and complexity in the new environment of space. Lastly, space tourists before the turn of the century may have the opportunity to experience the stark vision of a myriad of untwinkling stars sprinkled across the voids of the universe, while suspended in weightlessness on a tether from the orbiting hotel.

Touring the Moon may become possible sometime after the turn of the century; it will depend on the development of the SPS program; for only that will, in turn, justify the development of inexpensive transportation to the surface of the Moon. I'm starting to save my pennies.

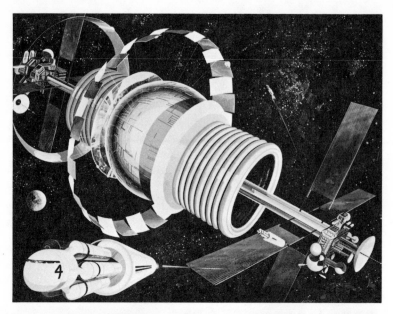

Exterior and interior renderings of the projected Bernal Sphere space habitat. This rotating manufacturing complex would have a one mile circumference and could house 10,000 people. Shields made of lunar surface material would provide protection from cosmic rays.

25. Living and Working in Space

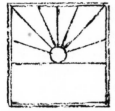Once the beachhead in space, for the manufacture of Solar Power Satellites from nonterrestrial raw materials, has been established, every economic consideration urges the rapid expansion of the capacity of the system to produce SPS's. In contrast to a system in which SPS's are manufactured on the Earth for assembly in orbit, the system based on nonterrestrial materials has a number of built-in features, allowing it to expand rapidly. The essential reason for this is the weightless, energy-rich environment of space. The refining and manufacturing plants in orbit, which convert raw materials into Solar Power Satellites, are themselves relatively lightweight structures, just like the SPS's they produce. It is feasible for these orbital factories to build additional orbital factories as well as power satellites.

Under these circumstances, the number of factories and their output will grow exponentially in time. It would be possible, by the mid- to late-1990s, to phase out the construction of fossil fuel and nuclear powerplants, and to shut down all such powerplants on Earth by about 2010, and still expand the total electrical generating capacity for the world at a rapid rate. If the operation of Solar Power Satellites were in the hands of the countries receiving power from each satellite, we would have little reason to fear the possibility of someone else blackmailing us by threatening to cut off our only source of energy.

The consequences of such a scenario will be enormous for terrestrial economics and politics (which I will take up in the next chapter). First I want to discuss some of the implications of such rapid growth for the lives of space colonists. The living quarters for the workers who build the first power satellites must necessarily come from Earth. If an SPS program is undertaken in the 1980s, these living quarters may well be built into expended External Tanks from the Space Shuttle system. These tanks, presently planned to be thrown away by re-entering the Earth's atmosphere and burning up over the Indian Ocean, could be refurbished into rather comfortable accommodations. The liquid hydrogen tank, the larger of the two tanks making up the External Tank set, is a sausage-shaped vessel, 8.5 meters (27½ feet) in diameter and 31 meters (96 feet) in length — in effect, standing on its end, it is a eleven-story high apartment tower. By inserting flooring, walls, airconditioning ducts, plumbing and wiring, and furnishings, into an expended tank, a relatively inexpensive housing unit for up to twenty-one people can be provided. Each floor could have three single-person, studio apartments, with about 18 square meters (180 square feet) per person of private space, and standard 2.3 meter (8 foot) ceiling heights. Several converted tanks, connected together with cables and passageways, could be rotated to provide near-Earth-normal weight throughout the living quarters. Some floors could be used for communal facilities such as a laundryroom, bathrooms, galleys, dining rooms, library and music rooms, a gymnasium, and general recreation room.[1]

Living accommodations of this type would be solely transitional, because the next generation of launch vehicle, after the Space Shuttle, will have no disposable External Tank. The second full-capacity refining and manufacturing facility would have to have its habitat built from nonterrestrial materials to reduce construction costs and time—and that habitat would become the first real space colony. It should be possible to build a space colony for about 6,000 people in a period of a few months to two years, while building two or more SPS's each year, with a total workforce of 3,000 to 6,000 people. The doubling time for the number of space colonies and the new land area in space may be less than two years.

Just how far could the total land area in space colonies grow? Very early in his studies of the space colony idea, O'Neill asked just this question. Considering only the raw materials available in a few of the largest asteroids, such as Ceres, Vesta, Pallas, and Juno, he found the total land area inside space colonies, which could be built from these asteroids, was more than 3,000 times the total land area of the planet Earth. Using additional raw materials from the rest of the asteroids, and from the moons of the outer planets of the solar system, the total possible land area would be many times greater still.

The proliferation of space colonies would be assured for at least a few decades, by the energy requirements of terrestrial civilization from Solar Power Satellites. While the human population of space colonies grows from a few thousands to a few million, new technological advances in space manufacturing would combine with the development of a diversified internal economy, to create new purposes and rationales for the continued growth of space colonies, perhaps at a more moderate rate. It would not be inconceivable, fifty years from now, for the population of the Earth to be completely stabilized by the emigration of several million people annually into space. The fleet of Single-Stage-to-Orbit vehicles, required to transport such numbers of people, is comparable to the present-day fleet of jet planes operated by the airline companies of the United States, where 2,700 planes transport annually more than two hundred million people.

[1] J.P. Vajk, J.H. Engel, and J.A. Shettler, "Habitat and Logistics Support Requirements for the Initiation of a Space Manufacturing Enterprise," Third NASA Ames Research Center Summer Study on Space Manufacturing, 1978.

In the earliest stages of power satellite construction from nonterrestrial materials, food would be imported from the Earth. If launch costs are about $10 per pound, it would cost about $10,000 annually to provide 500 kilograms (1,100 pounds) of freeze-dried foods per person. The economic value of having a worker in space, helping build SPS's, would be $5 to 20 million annually. The space colonists' desire for fresh food would motivate agriculture. We will bring with us, into space, other species of Gaian life including leafy vegetables, staple grains, rabbits, poultry, goats, and even cattle. Early colonists will probably bring pets with them as well.

An agricultural system will necessarily require recycling of all human and farm wastes. Rather than tying up a large fraction of the organic materials in compost piles, it is likely that high-temperature, oxygen-rich digestion of wastes will be used to accelerate the return of these materials into the living biomass of the space colony. Since the selection of lifeforms brought into the space colonies will be conscious and deliberate, we can leave behind pests such as nematodes and snails, blights and rusts, and economically and medically significant animal diseases such as trichinosis, Newcastle's disease, and hoof-and-mouth disease.

In the industrial sectors of the space colonies, which would be physically isolated from the residential and the agricultural sectors, virtually total recycling would be the rule, from the start, for two fundamentally economic reasons. Since the raw materials will come from truly astronomical distances, and since energy for recycling will be cheap and abundant (especially thermal energy provided by concentrating mirrors), it will be far more economical to recycle chemical catalysts and snippings of finished metals, than to import fresh materials. Secondly, if the colonists were to dump their garbage overboard, the wastes would hang around the colonies themselves indefinitely, interfering with sunlight and travel in the vicinity. Ejecting garbage at sufficient speeds to remove it from the colonies would create reaction forces on the colonies, eventually perturbing their orbits enough to require importing more material for reaction mass to put the colonies back in their proper orbits.

Similar considerations will also apply to personal belongings. While energy will be available in sufficient abundance to support rather affluent lifestyles, conspicuous consumption and planned obsolescence will have little place in the internal economies of the colonies, since it would be economically preferable to minimize the fraction of total effort expended on recycling and maximize more creative efforts. Strong pressures toward durable personal goods and multi-purpose furnishings will provide incentive for quality craftsmanship in apparel and furnishings. It is possible that the first generation of space colonists may behave like the *nouveau riche* of the Industrial Revolution, but a sense of proportion will reassert itself, leading to the development of an ethic of elegant frugality.

Doomsday Has Been Cancelled

Enormous space colonies, large enough to support even twenty million people with several acres of land per person, will be technically feasible; but it is more likely that colonies will be built for communities no larger than 50,000 to 100,000 people. If the population density of a colony were comparable to that of cities as pleasant and attractive as San Francisco or New Orleans, the entire residential sector of the colony would be no more than three or four kilometers in circumference. In a community built on this scale, where no point is more than two kilometers distant from any other point, roller skates, unicycles, bicycles, and tricycles, supplemented by small electric cars if necessary, would suffice for personal transportation. Since streets and parking spaces for automobiles typically take up 30-40% of the land area of cities like San Francisco, the available green space and living space per capita would be much larger than in terrestrial cities with the same total population density. Community design and architecture for such cities would be far more human-centered than has been possible for our Earth-bound cities.

For psychological and aesthetic reasons, the residential and community areas of even the first space habitats are likely to have an abundance of potted plants, flowers, and trees, and some workers are likely to indulge in some container gardening of fresh foods such as lettuce, tomatoes, or cucumbers. The first colony proper may include free-flying songbirds as well as trees and lawns in the community areas.

Regardless of the adopted geometries of space colonies (a large variety of configurations have already been considered from engineering, architectural, and psychological points of view), some recreational facilities will be provided near the axis of rotation, where low gravity and even zero-gravity are available. At one-tenth normal gravity, for example, human-powered flight would be possible. Diving into a swimming pool at one-tenth gravity from a high, diving board, even an amateur diver could perform a routine of fifteen to thirty flips and turns before knifing into the water. Most people involved in studies of space colonies have let their imaginations run wild with new possibilities for love-making in zero-gravity.

Since the number of space colonies will grow very rapidly once the first one is complete, diversification of habitat designs, interior climates and landscapes, and architectural styles will be possible. More important, perhaps, will be the opportunity for diversification, innovation, and experimentation in political and economic systems, community lifestyles, cultures, and languages. Internal political autonomy will be a fact for even the first colony, because of self-sufficiency in life-supporting necessities. Cultural systems and patterns of behavior will no longer need to be constrained to fit externally given conditions of climate, terrain, or architecture. It will be possible to design the conditions, diet, and even the length of day, to fit whatever human systems a community chooses. Each new colony will soon develop a unique character and flavor, just as communities on Earth have always done.

Transportation between colonies will be a simple affair, since free space is not a resistant medium like the Earth's atmosphere. Freed from the constraints of streamlining, spaceliners, equivalent to today's jetliners (but far more spacious inside), will ply regular routes among the growing number of colonies, using solar energy for power and liquid oxygen (available in excess quantities from refining lunar or asteroidal ores) for reaction mass. Smaller space vehicles will provide the opportunity for an individual, or small group of friends, to go out into the star-studded sky, for a few hours, or a few days at a time, to contemplate the enormity of the universe, or the unobstructed glories of the Earth, the Moon, and the streaming sundark. Just as the oceans, the deserts, the mountains, and the forests have provided poetic and transcendant insights throughout recorded history, space itself will provide new poetry, music, literature, and metaphors for the mystical experience. Nature no longer means just the biosphere of Earth; it encompasses all of the cosmos.

Until the population in space reaches about a million people, sufficient to sustain enough full-time artists for a resident orchestra, corps de ballet, repertoire dramatic theater, and so forth, live performers from Earth will be much in demand. Soloists will certainly be invited to perform in space, since the SSTO ticket price will be comparable to the performer's fees; but whether such luxuries as a space colony tour by the Metropolitan Opera Company, the Bolshoi Ballet, or the London Philharmonic Orchestra will be feasible by the turn of the century is, as yet, unclear.

Much of the descriptions of living conditions in the space colonies may strike you as idyllic and utopian, but it is necessary business to provide living conditions conducive to personal satisfaction of the work force. To finance such a large enterprise it is likely that the workers will receive a portion of their earnings in the form of shares. Under these conditions, space workers would have a great deal of influence in the design of new colonies, reflecting their personal tastes as well as their practical experience in the space environment.

Many features of life will be very pleasant and attractive; but the space environment is not one which easily forgives carelessness. Industrial workers and members of their families will have accidents, and many will die, some of them in new and horrible ways. It has always been thus, from prehistoric times to the present century, when explorers in the Arctic and Antarctic, in the depths of the ocean, atop the Himalayas, or even backpackers in the Sierra Nevadas have met untimely deaths in environments very different from the Serengeti Plain of eastern Africa, where our early ancestors were biologically at home. But human cultures have developed means of surviving such extreme environments as the North Slope of Alaska, the high valleys of the Andes and the Himalayas, the rain forests of the Amazon, and the scorching sands of the Sinai and the Sahara. In the new environment of space, we shall again survive, make our way, and then thrive.

26. Beyond the Global Village

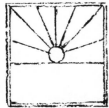 During the latter half of the twentieth century, the extension of commerce, communications, and transportation into worldwide networks, combined with the frightening increase in the capacity of nuclear weaponry, has indeed created a global village. The four billion humans on Earth today are as interdependent as were the inhabitants of a Neolithic agrarian village.

In view of these complex interdependences, it seems absurd that we continue in the 1970s to organize our economic and political systems according to rules formulated more than three centuries ago:

> The basic coordinates of the present world order system are contained in the Peace of Westphalia which brought the Thirty Years War to an end in 1648. According to Westphalia logic, the world order system is constituted *exclusively* by the governments of sovereign states. These governments have complete discretion to rule *national space* (or territory), and can also enter into voluntary arrangements (e.g., treaties) to regulate external relations and interconnections of various sorts. But these governments are *sovereign* and *equal* by juridical fiat, rather than by virtue of some higher authority within the world order system. No one government is entitled to greater formal status than another by reasons of wealth or power or size. In such circumstances, "law and order" rests upon the volition of governments and upon their perception of common interests.[1]

More than fifty corporations have annual sales exceeding the Gross National Products of two-thirds of the sovereign states belonging to the United Nations. The People's Republic of China, a country of eight hundred million people, has the same voice as the Seychelles Republic, a government representing sixty thousand people. Minor political subdivisions — such as the city of New York or the state of California — have annual governmental budgets greater than those of all but a handful of nations.

Perhaps it is no wonder that the "logic of Westphalia" seems to be unworkable and obsolete — it focusses on boundaries in the system rather than on the flows of goods, services, information, wealth, people, or even political power. Yet no government is willing to surrender its sovereignty to a World Government, nor would the citizens of most large nations tolerate deliberate and positive steps, by their governments, in that direction.

[1]Richard A. Falk, *A Study of Future Worlds*, (New York: Macmillan Publishing Company, 1975).

Doomsday Has Been Cancelled

The transglobal perspective, afforded by the large scale extension of human economic activities and habitation into space, offers real hope for circumventing these dilemmas. The proper role of the sovereign nation-state in the post-terrestrial era would then be to serve as a convenient administrative unit of historical and cultural origins, rather than to be a legal actor in the Westphalian zero-sum game. From an orbital perspective, international relations look very different:

> Up there you go around every hour and a half, time after time after time . . . you wake up over the Mid-East, over North Africa. As you eat breakfast you look out the window as you're going past and there's the Mediterranean area, and Greece, and Rome, and North Africa, and the Sinai, the whole area. And you realize that in one glance that what you're seeing is what was the whole history of man for years — the cradle of civilization . . .
>
> And you finally come up across the coast of California and look for those friendly things: Los Angeles and Phoenix and on across El Paso and there's Houston, there's home, and you look and sure enough there's the Astrodome. And you identify with that . . . you identify with Houston and then you identify with Los Angeles and Phoenix and New Orleans and everything. And the next thing you recognize in yourself, is you're identifying with North Africa. You look forward to that, you anticipate it . . . .
>
> You look down there and you can't imagine how many borders and boundaries you've crossed again and again and again. And you don't even see them. At that wake-up scene — the mid-East — you know there are hundreds of people killing each other over some imaginary line that you can't see. From where you see it, the thing is a whole and it's so beautiful. And you wish you could take one from each side in hand and say, "Look at it from this perspective. Look at that. What's important?"[2]

Relocating the United Nations headquarters into Earth orbit in the 1990s might be worth considering. Surrounded by material wealth, produced from lunar or asteroidal resources, using solar energy, any delegate attempting to justify aggression or belligerence on the basis of a national need would be ludicrous, in the extreme. Even the most cynical diplomats might find it difficult to bicker over the location of a political boundary line, with the living Earth in full view. With large numbers of people living in a multitude of space colonies, each under the nominal control of some nation on Earth, just as ships at sea are governed by the laws of the state of registry, the significance of national borders will be further diminished in importance. World government is likely to become an irrelevant notion, but international law and universal public opinion will certainly continue to play important roles in the affairs of nations.

[2]Russell L. Schweickart, *CoEvolution Quarterly*, Summer 1975, pp. 42-45. The Apollo 9 astronaut spoke at the Lindisfarne Association, Box 1395, Southhampton, N.Y. 11968, in 1974.

One major recurrent problem in the global economic system is that of instabilities in the world monetary system. The ability of any given nation to borrow funds for economic development is based on the strength of that country's currency in relation to hard currencies (such as the Deutschmark, the Swiss Franc, the United States dollar, or the Japanese yen). The strength of each nation's currency is gauged subjectively on the basis of the net flow of money into and out of each country and on comparative inflation rates in various countries (as if the accumulation of money within the borders of a state had anything real to do with wealth).

Once space colonies have made the human economic system patently open-ended, it will become far clearer that *the real basis of wealth is knowledge and cooperative efforts.* The entire matter of balance of payments between space colonies and nations on Earth will highlight the contradictions and inequities of the present monetary system, encouraging positive steps toward meaningful reform; obviously, no one will be shipping bars of gold bullion or bundles of Treasury Notes between Fort Knox and the space colonies in order to maintain international balances of currencies and import/export payments. Just how such reforms might be carried out is a problem requiring a great deal of meticulous study and inspiration.

Now I would like to examine how a major space colonization program can contribute positively to three important problems confronting the international order today: the threat of a nuclear holocaust; the continued expansion of agricultural production to feed a growing population a more adequate diet; and acceleration of the economic development of the poorest nations without massive ecological distruption or severe social upheaval.

At the present time the principal risk of holocaust appears to be the possibility of errors in judgment in a crisis situation by one or more members of the "nuclear club," which now includes the United States, the Soviet Union, the United Kingdom, France, India, and the People's Republic of China. Some reports have suggested that Israel is already a member of the club. The Union of South Africa, reported recently to be on the verge of carrying out a nuclear test shot, was persuaded by the United States and the Soviet Union (whose reconnaissance satellites first reported the preparations for the test) not to carry out the test.

A number of other nations, whose international relations or domestic politics are somewhat volatile, probably could develop nuclear weapons rapidly if they chose to do so. These include (besides Israel and the Union of South Africa) South Korea, the Republic of China (Taiwan), Pakistan, Argentina, and Brazil. Several of the more industrialized, and internally stable nations could do likewise, including Canada, Japan, Sweden, Switzerland, West Germany, Spain, and Iran.

Thus far, we have been most fortunate: the present members of the nuclear club seem to understand the profound and critical difference between conventional weapons and nuclear weapons. Most governments which have nuclear capability seem to have a very healthy fear of crossing that critical line into an entirely different class of violence. Despite multiple opportunities and provocations, not a single tactical nuclear weapon has been used since the end of World War II. Possibly history has forgiven the United States for its use of nuclear weapons at Hiroshima and Nagasaki, on the grounds that we did not, at that time, comprehend the enormity of our deeds. In hindsight it is easy to pass judgment; but hopefully we are all wiser for that experience.

But we cannot continue to rely indefinitely on the governments of a steadily growing nuclear club to behave prudently in every emergency, especially if the logic of the zero-sum game exerts pressures to seize whatever resources are believed to be necessary for survival. It is unfortunate — but entirely predictable from the mentality of the zero-sum game — that serious consideration was given to the idea of military intervention by the United States during the OPEC petroleum boycott in 1973 and 1974 to secure the continued flow of petroleum to North America and Europe. Breaking out of the zero-sum game mentality would be a major benefit of the thrust into space.

The spread of nuclear power plants has received a great deal of attention in recent years as a contributing factor in the proliferation of nuclear weapons. Critics of nuclear power argue that stringent security measures, to keep fissionable materials out of the hands of unstable governments, terrorist groups, or guerrilla insurgents, would bring the world closer to a univeral police state. Nuclear power proponents, on the other hand, argue that the construction of a nuclear weapon from such materials would be enormously difficult to do in a clandestine manner, and that it is relatively simple to devise and implement adequate safeguards for fissionable materials.

The exponential increase in the number of Solar Power Satellites available from a space colonization program, building satellites from nonterrestrial materials, would allow the whole world to meet a rapidly growing portion of its energy needs as early as the 1990s, without extensive deployment of nuclear powerplants — curtailing the potential risks of nuclear blackmail, terrorism, and sabotage.

A decision to carry out a major space colonization program, with the construction of Solar Power Satellites for global use, could make an additional contribution to global disarmament. In the fiscal year 1975 the United States spent $92.8 billion (about 6% of its Gross National Product) for defense, while the Soviet Union spent $103.8 billion[3] (about 10.6% of its

---

[3]The Military Balance, (London: International Institute for Strategic Studies, 1976); Ervin Laszlo, Goals for Mankind: A Report to the Club of Rome on the New Horizons of Global Community, (New York: E.P. Dutton, 1977), p. 261.

GNP). Because of the significance of defense in the national economies of the superpowers, abrupt changes in the levels of expenditure for defense would be difficult to achieve without significant disruption of the domestic economy, unless both the U.S. and the U.S.S.R. were to shift simultaneously their military hardware procurement funds into procurement of space hardware produced by the same segments of the respective economies. A joint American-Soviet venture to establish large scale industrial bases in space could provide the overarching goal (which appears to be necessary) to transcend the zero-sum mentality of the present standoff between these superpowers.

Can space industrialization contribute to the improvement of agricultural productivity in Third World countries? The problems of agriculture in these countries are inextricably interwoven with those of rural underdevelopment: widespread unemployment due to major inequities in land distribution; high rates of adult illiteracy; poor public hygiene resulting in high infant mortality and debilitation of adults; and poor transportation which keeps the costs of farm supplies high, and the prices farmers receive for their produce, low. Space industrialization can do nothing for the problems of land distribution. Land reform must be achieved by an internal political process; it cannot be imposed from outside.

Advanced communications satellites, available during the latter part of the 1980s, will be able to provide direct television broadcasts to village-owned TV receivers in the hinterlands. During experiments, a few years ago, with NASA's ATS-6 communications satellite, the Indian government found that villagers were eager to watch public education programming in their own language, dealing with public hygiene, infant care, and agricultural techniques suitable for their respective climate and crops. Each country could develop an inexpensive, wide variety of programs, produced in central recording studios, in the principal languages of the country, to bring this kind of service to its villages, far more effectively and inexpensively than by attempting to expand the conventional school system. In many Latin American countries only a tiny fraction of the population attends schools past the sixth or seventh grade, but the schools still soak up more than twenty percent of total government spending.

Earth resources satellites can be used for large scale land use planning, assuring the preservation of prime agricultural lands for agriculture; surveying large irrigation, water catchment, and flood control projects; locating new mineral resources for foreign export and domestic consumption; and surveying new highway and railroad alignments for the most rapid and inexpensive construction. Weather satellites can play a vital role in water resource management. In the monsoon belt, farmers vitally need to know when the monsoons will arrive if they are to maximize their productivity. If they plant their crop too soon, the seeds will germinate days before the rains arrive, and a large fraction of the seedlings will wither and die from lack of moisture. If the farmers wait too long, the rains will come before the fields have been fully sown, and a large fraction of the seeds, planted after the ground is sopping wet, will rot in the ground. The combination of satellite-based weather observation, with direct television broadcast to the farming villages, would help more farmers determine the optimum planting time.

One of the most critical factors confronting agriculture in the Third World is a severe shortage of inexpensive energy. Because the transportation systems are so poorly developed in the poorest countries, liquid fuels derived from petroleum (gasoline and kerosene, for example) are far more expensive in villages in the interior of India than in the most remote hamlets of Appalachia or the Rocky Mountains in the United States, while personal incomes may be as much as twenty to forty times lower. The high price of energy affects agriculture by making irrigation and fertilizers extravagantly expensive for most small farmers. The worst effects of these high prices are indirect.

In recent decades, progress in economic development of many of the poorest countries had brought about a gradual, but steadily accelerating, shift from the use of firewood for cooking and heating purposes toward the use of kerosene. This trend was viewed as very hopeful and positive by foresters around the world, since population growth and rising consumption of firewood spelled disaster for natural woodlands in the absence of vigorous and effective programs for the management of sustained yields. Just as enormous areas of Europe and North America have been deforested in historical times, it was expected that vast areas of Africa, Asia, and South America would suffer these effects in the next fifty or a hundred years. But the trend toward substitution of kerosene for firewood was halted and sharply reversed by the sudden rise in the world prices of petroleum early in the 1970s. Deforestation is now proceeding much more rapidly in much of the Third World than during the 1950s and 1960s; the government of India now projects total deforestation of the country by 1996.

In the temperate climate of Europe and the eastern portion of North America, deforestation permanently alters the landscape but does not destroy the land itself. New ecological relationships emerge, as in most of England, which has gone from dense hardwood forests to open fields of family farms, to enclosed farms surrounded by hedges of diverse plants and animals—all in the space of a few centuries. But in tropical climates, deforestation can be deadly, especially if rainfall is highly seasonal, for the soil is exposed to rapid erosion from the heavy seasonal rains. Since the living and decaying biomass per acre is reduced, the capacity of the soil to retain water over long periods is reduced, making the entire landscape far more vulnerable to drought conditions.

A major factor in the steady expansion of the Sahara Desert, southward into the Sahel region of Africa, has been the deforestation of this area. An extreme example of the severity of this problem is the city of Ouagadougou, the capital of Upper Volta, a city of some 75,000 residents, each of whom requires nearly one ton of firewood each year just for cooking purposes. For a distance of about forty kilometers in all directions from the city, not a single tree or large shrub is to be found standing. The average manual laborer's family spends 25-30% of its income for fuel, which grows more and more expensive as the distance to available firewood grows longer.

Progressive deforestation of the Himalayan foothills of Nepal accelerates erosion of local agricultural areas while producing severe flooding downstream—in the prime agricultural areas of India, Bangladesh, and Pakistan. The useful lifetime of expensive dams, built in Pakistan for hydroelectric power and for irrigation, has already been shortened by decades, due to rapid siltation from erosion in the Himalayan foothills.

An ominous effect of the steep rise in the prices of kerosene and firewood is the increasing diversion of animal manures from the fields to the fireplace. An entirely new industry has arisen in India; cow dung is collected, shaped by hand into patties to dry in the sun, and sold for fuel. This practice, once rare, is becoming widespread. In 1975, an estimated eighty million tons of dried cow dung went up in smoke, with the loss of agricultural nutrients equivalent to one-third of India's total fertilizer needs.

Massive infusions of energy, at prices well below that of kerosene in the Third World today, could provide the sword needed to sever the Gordian knot of interconnected adversities and increase food production. Solar Power Satellites appear to be a very attractice possibility, and a number of agencies of the Indian government have already expressed interest in the SPS concept. With electricity from space available at the prices projected for the nonterrestrial-materials-approach, it would be economically feasible to use the electricity to synthesize liquid fuels (such as methanol–wood alcohol) and fertilizers (such as ammonia) from air and water.

Liquid fuels such as methanol can be used for heating and cooking without expensive or elaborate high-technology equipment. Small liquid fuel stoves can be designed for much higher efficiency than wood stoves and can be mass-produced for sale at low prices. Methanol has twice the energy content per kilogram as firewood, and can be easily transported in glass, ceramic, or plastic containers. The existing infrastructure, which presently distributes firewood and animal manure for fuel, could readily assume the task of distributing the new liquid fuels from SPS-powered chemical synthesis plants scattered through the hinterlands. One ten million kilowatt SPS could synthesize enough methanol to provide the cooking fuel for about sixteen million people, neglecting the improved efficiency of the liquid fuel stoves, while freeing up millions of tons of cow dung and firewood, with major ecological benefits to those parts of the world most severely threatened today.[4] Were India to rely solely on biomass sources for its energy needs, the total natural biomass production of 20% of India's land area would be required annually by the turn of the century for its projected population of 1,100 million. Carefully managed village woodlots of a few acres each, planted densely with fast-growing trees, would be a viable alternative to SPS.

An important problem for the economic development of the Third World is the high cost of fuels and raw materials, due to poorly developed — and thus expensive — transportation systems. The importation of raw materials (especially metals) from space and the delivery of solar power from power satellites, however, can be done at the same price for virtually any location on Earth, reducing this discrepancy between the developed and the underdeveloped countries. Space industrialization also offers a number of possibilities for direct participation by Third World nations. One of the more intriguing ideas is an international launch and recovery site, with freeport status, to be located on or near the Earth's equator.

Equatorial launch sites offer a number of important technical advantages for rockets. Since the equator bulges farthest out from the Earth's axis of rotation, a rocket launched from the equator begins with a few hundred miles an hour more velocity toward the east than a rocket launched at Cape Canaveral or Tyuratam (the principal Soviet launch site). Because this additional velocity is available at the beginning of the flight, when the rocket is heaviest with fuel, the payload which can be placed in a given orbit is dramatically increased by equatorial launch. For satellites destined to go into geosynchronous orbit above the equator, major savings in the fuel otherwise needed to change the inclination of the orbital plane can be realized as well. Payloads launched into an equatorial orbit, provide multiple opportunities, every day, for rendezvous with subsequent flights, or for return to the launch site: in sharp contrast to launch sites at high latitudes, where the rotation of the Earth permits, at most, two chances a day, and sometimes only one chance every few days, or weeks, for rendezvous or return.

Combined with an industrial park, focussed on high-technology industries and industries directly involved in space activities, such an Earthport on the equator, if given duty-free status as a freeport, would provide major economic benefits and a strong spur to economic development of the host country.[5] Several equatorial nations have already formally expressed interest in such possibilities; some of these nations include Indonesia, Liberia, the

---

[4]Eric Eckholm, *Losing Ground: Environmental Stress and World Food Prospects*, (New York: W.W. Norton, 1976). Discusses the environmental damage in the Third World resulting from the "firewood crisis."

[5]The Sabre Foundation, 221 West Carillo Street, Santa Barbara, California 93101, began a long-term "Earthport Project" in 1976, to lay the foundations for such an international spaceport and free trade zone, and publishes a newsletter on the progress of this concept.

Sudan, Sierra Leone, Panama, and Rwanda.

The development of the countless opportunities of space industrialization in the next few decades, just beginning to be explored systematically, offers significant hope for economic development of the Third World, in ways which are highly synergistic with low-technology, small scale activities in villages and cities. In an age when our mutual interdependence is just becoming widely recognized, we may solve some of our most urgent problems by stepping outside the existing Westphalian system, beyond the global village.

On a mission in the future,
the reusable Space Shuttle deposits a
satellite in Earth orbit.

27. Earth and Space, War and Peace

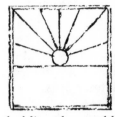 With very few exceptions in the history of the world, expansion of economic activity into a new territory has soon been followed by expansion of military activities into that territory as well. Critics of the space programs have argued that a major thrust into space will bring about the militarization of space with new weapon systems more horrible than any yet witnessed on Earth, holding the world hostage to the military minds of the superpowers.

Is this really what the future might hold? Does *Star Wars*, with its total destruction of entire planets, describe our own future? Couldn't we just declare space to be strictly off-limits to any kind of military activity?

Thus far, the principal activities in space by the military forces of the United States and the Soviet Union have been reconnaissance and surveillance. Satellites equipped with specialized sensors monitor the Earth, and the space environment of the Earth-Moon system, for signs of nuclear test explosions in violation of the treaty prohibiting such tests in the Earth's atmosphere, in the oceans, or in outer space. "Spy satellites," equpped with high-resolution cameras, routinely photograph military installations, movements of troops, military equipment, and major construction projects of possible military significance. The availability of such satellites to both the U.S. and the U.S.S.R. played an important role in making the first Strategic Arms Limitation Treaty (SALT-I) possible since each of the parties to the treaty could verify, by means of its own satellites, that the other party was in compliance with the terms of the treaty.

Spy satellites can make major contributions to peace by reducing uncertainties about the capabilities and intentions of other nations or by exposing clandestine operations to international scrutiny. According to news accounts in the late 1970s, Soviet spy satellites first detected extensive construction operations in the desert in the Union of South Africa. On the basis of satellite photographs of the area, combined with intelligence information from more conventional sources, Soviet photointerpreters concluded that South Africa was preparing a test site for nuclear explosives. According to these accounts, the Kremlin then forwarded this information to the White House. U.S. Air Force reconnaissance satellites photographed the area, and American photointerpreters confirmed the Soviet interpretation. Under international pressure from the United States and other nations who were informed of the situation, South Africa halted the nuclear test program amid strong denials that it had any intention of developing nuclear explosives.

Other military space systems currently in operation by the major powers include dedicated, military communications satellites, navigation satellites, and weather satellites. The communications satellite network provide secure, and nearly instantaneous, communications between armed forces around the world and their respective high commands, contributing to stability, by minimizing the chances of distant units losing touch with higher authority in crisis situations. These have also been used, at least occasionally, by the diplomatic services of each country.

At the present time reconnaissance and surveillance satellites are government monopolies. The civilian Landsat program, for reasons of military security, has limited the resolution of its camera systems far below what is technically feasible today. But it is interesting to speculate what might happen if a private company were to launch a high-resolution-Earth-resources satellite from the launch site of a neutral Third World country, and were willing to sell photographs of any spot on Earth to any customer on Earth. The principal revenues for such a service would come from mining and drilling companies searching for new mineral deposits, and from governments planning hydraulic projects or major transportation systems; but photographs of military installations in adjacent countries would also find a sizeable market. Such an "open skies" system would, I think, promote peace by making it much more difficult for a would-be aggressor to launch a surprise attack.

International humanitarian organizations, such as the Red Cross or Amnesty International, might be able to mobilize international opinion by documenting, with high-resolution photographs, inadequate conditions in prisoner-of-war camps and the existence of forced-labor prison camps for political prisoners. The dramatic display of aerial reconnaisance pictures of Soviet missiles in Cuba validated the charge of Soviet belligerency by the United States in the U.N. General Assembly in October, 1962. News photographs showing the Soviet ambassador steadfastly refusing to look at the pictures exhibited in the Assembly, rallied international pressure on the Soviet Union, bringing about the prompt withdrawal of these weapons from the Western hemisphere.

Naturally, nations which are up to no good will try desperately to conceal new military developments, either by going underground (at substantial increase in cost) or by attempting to interfere with the operation of spy satellites. Such interference is presently prohibited by the first Strategic Arms Limitation Treaty (SALT-1), which relies on "national technical means of verification" to monitor compliance with the limitations on numbers of ICBM's, ABM's, and other advanced strategic weapons: this means that both the U.S. and the U.S.S.R. will use spy satellites and will not interfere with each other's satellites.

These activities in space seem to be accepted as reasonable arenas for military activity, given the present terrestrial postures of the major powers. But some signs of escalation have been viewed with alarm. On at least one occasion, the Soviets are believed to have temporarily blinded a U.S. spy satellite by beaming enough laser light at it from the ground, to overload its infrared sensors, which were designed to detect the exhaust flames of ICBM's during launch. It is generally accepted that the U.S.S.R. is rapidly developing "killer satellites" capable of rendezvous with other satellites in order to disable or destroy them in a variety of ways, and the U.S. has responded by initiating killer satellite development as well.

Perhaps the prospect of killer satellites raiding various types of military satellites, or fighting duels in orbit with laser beams, or particle beams, should be viewed with no more alarm than naval engagements between patrol boats in the Pacific Ocean during World War II: neither action involves major forces of either side, and the action is remote from civilian populations. The real concern, I think, is that such smallscale military activities will lead to development of major systems in orbit capable of devastating the Earth itself.

The 1967 *Treaty on Principles Governing the Activities in the Exploration and Use of Outer Space, Including the Moon and Other Celestial Bodies*, negotiated principally between the U.S. and the U.S.S.R., before anyone realized the major economic potentialities of outer space, explicitly prohibits the placement of nuclear weapons or other weapons of mass destruction in space. The remaining concern, then, can only be the possibility of some kind of death ray in orbit, capable of burning up cities and their inhabitants. The microwave beams of Solar Power Satellites cannot do that, for a variety of fundamental, physical reasons. Should anyone attempt to modify an SPS to produce a beam of dangerously high powered densities, the necessary modifications to the satellite would be readily visible from the ground with modest telescopes. (Either the collector area of the satellite or the transmitting antennae array would have to be increased enormously to raise the power density to dangerous levels).

But a power satellite could readily serve as a platform for a battery of high energy lasers. With advanced optical systems, capable of controlling hundreds of individual mirror facets with precisions of a few millionths of a degree in direction, perhaps one or two million kilowatts of laser light could be directed to a spot on the Earth perhaps a few meters across. In a few seconds such a laser beam could severely damage ICBM's or aircraft or even tanks. Surely such a system would be a very dangerous weapon in the wrong hands.

Viewed more dispassionately, such a weapon cannot be used for burning up whole cities; rather than being like a sledgehammer (like a nuclear weapon), it is a surgically precise scalpel — far too expensive to use except on very selected targets of very high importance — such as ICBM's. A space-based, high energy laser, anti-ballistic-missile-defense system may be desirable to reduce the risks of nuclear holocaust, by making the present reign of nuclear terror permanently obsolete.

The present nuclear statemate is dangerous, because of the energy concentration in nuclear warheads, and because of the very short time available for human decisions when ICBM's have been launched. Typical flight times from Soviet launch sites to American cities (or vice versa) are twenty to thirty minutes. The present strategy of Mutual Assured Destruction (MAD) is based on a number of pre-programmed responses to detection of a salvo of ICBM's approaching the United States; responses designed to ensure that any foreign power which initiates a first strike will be severely damaged or destroyed by a retaliatory strike. The short time available for reaction provides very little flexibility in deciding which of the programmed responses to use, and thus the major powers hold each other's civilian populations in hostage under a cloud of terror.

A space-based laser ABM system could react almost instantaneously to the launch of an ICBM from any spot on Earth, identifying, tracking, and destroying the missile and its warhead in a period of ten or twenty seconds, while the missile is still climbing up through the atmosphere. Such a system would be highly effective, unlike ground-based ABM missiles, and would render ICBM's totally obsolete. Such a technological shift in the balance between offensive and defensive capabilities would disrupt the perilous combination of missiles with nuclear warheads. Either ICBM's would have to be abandoned as the primary delivery system for nuclear weapons, or nuclear weapons themselves would have to be abandoned. Switching over from ICBM's to bombers would considerably lengthen the reaction time available to nuclear attack, giving greater stability to the standoff, while preserving the option of destroying the bombers in the same way. Either response, it seems to me, would be far preferable to the present madness.

Assuming such a system were deployed in conjunction with a Solar Power Satellite system, either under international auspices or bilaterally by the U.S. and NATO, and by the Soviet Union and the Warsaw Pact, we may well see Armageddon becoming far less likely by the late 1990s. Even the risk of occasional misuse of laser beams to strike small targets on the ground (like a thunderbolt from Zeus) would be a small price to pay for the purpose of ridding ourselves of the deadly cloud we have lived under for more than two decades. With proper international accords, even such misuse could be made unlikely.

Ideally the world would find some way to escape from the risks of nuclear holocaust, other than the deployment of a new and different weapon system, even if the new system is closer to a purely defensive system. The long term significance of the human thrust into space may be to rid us of the zero-sum game mentality and provide a more enduring basis for world peace.

28. The Universal Laboratory

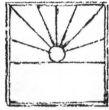Permanent habitation in space will result from the requirements of space industries for large numbers of workers in orbit. The largest number of space colony residents in the early years will be foundry workers and skilled construction workers involved in the extraction of useful materials from nonterrestrial ores and in the construction of Solar Power Satellites. A modest number of people will be needed to support the space communities themselves, providing basic goods and services for the colonists. These will include maintenance workers, farmers, physicians, nurses, and medical technicians, administrators, teachers, and clergy.

The opportunities for scientific research and development will not be overlooked in the new environment of space. Areas of research which will obviously benefit from these new opportunities include astronomy, low-temperature physics, meteorology and climatology, and fusion-energy research. Another area of enormous potential is *genetic engineering*, which may become a powerful tool for the development of new strains of plants and animals, for understanding and perhaps reversing the aging process, and for the breeding of new strains of special-purpose miocroorganisms. Such microbes might be developed to digest specific chemical pollutants, to synthesize insulin and other pharmaceutical products, and, perhaps, to cure metabolic diseases due to errors in the genetic code.

One of the principal methods available for research on genetic engineering is recombinant DNA experimentation, in which fragments of genes from one type of organism are "spliced" into the genes of a recipient organism, perhaps of an entirely different species. The differences in the biochemical repertoire of an altered cell culture then provides information on the roles various pieces of the genes play in controlling the biochemical factory inside those cells.

During the 1970s considerable controversy has been raised over the safety of this line of research. One of the favorite recipient organisms used in these experiments is *Escherichia coli*, a bacterium which normally inhabits the human intestinal tract, and does no harm to us under normal conditions. The reason *E. coli* is so popular is because it is a very simple biochemical factory, having a total repertoire of only a thousand or so chemical processes, all of which have been catalogued. A great many of these reactions have been correlated with specific pieces of the single chromosome of *E. coli*, making it an almost ideal organism for such experiments.

The controversy over these experiments arises from the possibility that gene fragments, inserted into *E. coli* and other benign host organisms, might change them into virulent pathogens, producing serious epidemics if any of them were to escape from the laboratory, into the human intestinal tract or other habitats where these organisms are able to flourish. In the face of an unknowable risk potential, many critics have questioned whether laboratory procedures are adequate to prevent such an escape. Some have argued that such experiments should be performed only in a few laboratories, where very stringent confinement measures can be rigorously applied (such as the Army's bacteriological research laboratories). Others have insisted that all such research should be postponed until we somehow learn enough to gauge the risks involved in this kind of research. A few have urged the use of alternative, recipient microorganisms, which are not adapted to living in humans, instead of *E. coli*. Whatever the interim decisions are, it is clear that recombinant DNA research could be carried on more safely in orbiting laboratories which could guarantee *total* quarantine from the general human population.

One area of astronomical research deserves special mention here — the search for planets of other stars and intelligent life elsewhere in the universe. Large telescopes on the surface of the Earth or Moon are not feasible because of gravity. On the Earth, atmospheric turbulence limits the resolution achievable even with large telescopes. In free space, however, it is not necessary to support a telescope against its own weight. Instead of building telescopes only 200 inches in diameter (like the instrument at Mount Palomar which has produced such profound changes in our perceptions and understanding of the cosmos), it will be practical to build telescopes 200 meters in diameter. Such a telescope could detect Earth-sized planets, orbiting stars ten light years away; directed at objects within our own solar system, such a telescope would provide resolution of surface details, only twenty kilometers in size, on Pluto.

Still larger telescopes up to two kilometers in diameter (about the presently forseeable limit due to the necessity of keeping different parts of the mirror precisely aligned within a fraction of a wavelength of the light gathered) could also be built by space, industrial facilities. Capable of detecting Earth-sized planets up to one hundred light-years distant, such an instrument would simplify the task of searching for technological civilizations about other stars, allowing us to concentrate our radio listening efforts on such planetary systems. Whether such distant civilizations would have anything to say to us (or we to them) remains, as yet, a matter for speculation.

Perhaps the biggest winners in research opportunities will be the "soft sciences." Once the number of space colonies has increased sufficiently to permit real cultural diversification, sociologists, anthropologists, psychologists, political scientists and economists will have a field day. Some communities in space may decide to eliminate money completely in internal transactions; others may decide to try pure communism. One community may choose near-total isolationism; while others will maintain completely unrestricted, free trade among themselves. Even Plato's philosopher-kings may appear someday. The parameters of human interactions may thus be explored in ways which have never really been possible here on Earth. But I think one thing can be stated with a high degree of certainty: although many space communities may be organized along utopian lines, none is more likely to achieve the desired utopian goals than any such attempts here on Earth.

Saturn and her rings.

29. The Endless Horizon

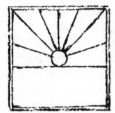 Once the first self-sufficient and self-reproducing human settlement in space has been established, every economic consideration will favor rapid growth of the human population living in the Earth's atmosphere. Most of the increase in numbers will be due to emigration for better jobs, just as in the early history of the Americas and Australia, when the European population grew more by immigration than by births. In previous chapters, I have discussed the types of activities in space which are likely to be profitable in the next few decades; now I would like to indulge in some longer range speculations about the next few centuries.

Once asteroid mining begins in earnest, one or more space colonies of a few thousand people each are likely to be equipped with low-thrust propulsion systems (such as mass drivers, ion engines, or solar sails) to wander among the near-Earth asteroids as prospecting and mining bases. These early wandering cities, dipping as close to the Sun as the orbit of Venus, soaring as far out as the orbit of Mars, would significantly reduce the costs of nonterrestrial mining.

Not long after that, other human settlements of several thousands of people would fan out to orbit around several or all of the planets of the solar system, providing bases for the systematic long term scientific study and exploration of these alien worlds. In the past plans for the human exploration of Mars assumed the launch from the Earth's surface: a handful of astronauts crowded into cramped spaceships barely larger than Apollo for two to three years, with only a few months spent on the surface of Mars, unable to explore more than a tiny vicinity of a single landing spot.

From an orbiting space colony, with access to abundant and inexpensive hydrogen and oxygen from asteroid mining, small expeditions could venture down to the surface of Mars, the polar regions of Mercury, or the surfaces of the moons of Jupiter, Saturn, Uranus, and Neptune, as desired. Small, chemically powered rockets would allow numerous expeditions over a period of many years, at a far less total cost than for a single Earth-based expedition to Mars.

Small-sized cities may ply the solar system like ocean liners, cruising tropical seas. With advanced propulsion systems (such as high-energy lasers on the ground, or in orbit around the Earth, beaming energy to heat a gas aboard a rocket to provide high-performance propulsion), one or two year cruises to see Jupiter's Red Spot or to view the rings of Saturn and Uranus from close-up, would become feasible, without being prohibitively expensive, especially if these cruising cities provided university-level educational programs enroute.

(A friend who is actively involved in laser propulsion concepts turned forty in December of 1977. Just a few weeks later, while we exchanged notes over a few beers, he told me he was really motivated by the desire to visit Saturn's rings for his sixtieth birthday—he just might make it!)

Early in the next century, several instrumented probes are likely to be built in space using nonterrestrial raw materials and launched toward the nearer stars. Equipped with sensors and computers, of a sophistication unbelievable to us today, such probes will be capable of searching the vicinity of another star for planets, for signs of life, and for indications of civilization, including space industries. Travel times for such probes destined to the nearest stars would be a few decades to a few centuries.

As the human population of the solar system grows, and as the total economy of the space communities expands and becomes more intricate and complex, small groups of people will have the opportunity to set out on their own, homesteading the asteroid belt or various orbits around other planets, to pursue whatever visions or lifestyles they may choose. In less than a hundred years human settlements will be found in most parts of the solar system, with no possibility of crowding—after all, more than just a little bit of space is available out there.

Propulsion systems we can consider for use in space are based on chemical energy, solar energy, or nuclear energy. None of these is really adequate for efficient travel to interstellar distances. Up until the discovery of radioactivity by Henri Becquerel in 1895, the most concentrated energy sources known were chemical. Chemical energy is associated with the molecular level of physical structure, in the electromagnetic interactions between two or more atoms. Typically, the chemical bond between two atoms in a molecule involves a few electron volts. (An electron volt is a very tiny unit of energy. It is the energy acquired by an electron, freely accelerated between two metallic plates hooked up with batteries, providing one volt of potential difference between the plates. The chemical energy released in metabolizing one day's food—about 3,000 calories—is 7.8×10^{25} electron volts.)

In contrast to chemical energy, the release of nuclear energy is far more concentrated, since it involves rearrangements in the structure of the atomic nucleus, some 10,000 times smaller in dimensions than the atom. The interactions between the protons and the neutrons of a nucleus involve a few million electron volts for each nucleus involved in a nuclear reaction of some kind. Because of this factor of a million greater concentration in energy release per atom involved, a pound of uranium used in a nuclear reactor is equivalent in energy content to hundreds of tons of coal.

During the twentieth century, advances in the study of radioactivity, nuclear physics, cosmic rays, and elementary particles have shown that atomic nuclei consist of protons and neutrons. But besides these two types of particles and electrons — which had been recognized as distinct entities late in the last century — an enormous bestiary of subnuclear particles have been identified and studied. Reactions and transmutations among these particles involve the release of a few thousand million electron volts, a thousand times greater than energies involved in nuclear reactions.

It is unlikely that we have reached the deepest levels of physical structure. A great deal of effort has been expended since the 1920s in attempting to gain a unified understanding of physics from the very smallest scale to the very largest. The most thorough understanding of small scale structures and phenomena has come in this century, through the development of quantum mechanics; while the most comprehensive understanding of the large scale behavior of the universe and the behavior of very massive objects, has been attained through the theory of general relativity. These two branches of modern theoretical physics have transformed science and technology, with drastic revisions in our worldview. At first sight, the underlying philosophical foundations of these two branches of physics appear drastically different from each other and from the foundations of the classical physics of the nineteenth century. Attempts to merge these two theories into a single, unified theory have thus far had limited success, and results to date have been very primitive. Yet these results already suggest that several more layers of physical structure remain to be discovered below the level of structure of elementary particles — each level having energy concentrations a factor of a thousand or a million greater than the level above.

Should these speculations prove to be correct, and if we learn how to tap these far more concentrated enrgies, to provide new flows of entropy, then at some time in the future — perhaps only decades, but more likely a few centuries away — the possibility of a few thousand people and their supporting ecosystem leaving the solar system aboard a large space colony, bound for other solar systems, will become real, and Gaian life will have become galactic.

Why is outer space so fascinating and so attractive to so many people? Is this merely a Western-Aristotelian-expansionist infatuation, thoroughly opposed to human spiritual values? Is it just an adolescent, escapist fantasy?

Long before Western science and technology began, a fascination with the heavens above could be found in almost every human culture. The Roman poet Ovid, nearly two thousand years ago, described the emergence of human consciousness in an image based on this fascination with the heavens:

Doomsday Has Been Cancelled

God elevated the forehead of Man
And ordered him to contemplate the stars.

Among some of the peoples of Gambia in West Africa, an infant was given its name under the starry sky, as the father held the naked newborn in his uplifted arms, facing the heavens, to whisper in the infant's ear, "Behold the only thing greater than yourself!"[1]

Even if the desire to go into space is an adolescent escapist fantasy, we might do well not to dismiss it lightly, for a society which cannot participate in the dreams and fantasies of children and adolescents is surely a sad and melancholy place.

Oceanographer Jacques-Yves Cousteau argues persuasively that our curiosity and outward movement, wherever we are capable of going, is biological in origin:

> The more time I spend in observing nature, the more I believe that man's motivation for exploration is but the sophistication of a universal, instinctive drive deeply ingrained in all living creatures.
>
> Life is growth: individuals and species grow in size, number, in territorial appetite. The peripheral manifestation of growing is exploring the outside world.
>
> Plants develop in the most favorable direction, which implies that they have explored the others and found them less adequate. Some plants send shoots — that is, feelers — great distances before they claim the space that has been acknowledged propitious.
>
> For individual animals the world is to be explored and discovered from birth on, and for them, until they die, the wilderness is infinite; and infinity, for a tuna, is the vast ocean. In the animal world the physical need for exploration develops in collectivities as well: tribes, schools, packs — all reach out for new horizons...
>
> When the *impulse to explore*, built into each individual human being, is confined or antagonized by a rigid social or familial structure, it may be bent into unnatural drives—alcoholism, drug abuse, or sexual perversions.[2]

We can certainly survive indefinitely into the future with just the material resources of the Earth, but I think we would be crippled in our spirit, perhaps fatally damaged, if we were to be arbitrarily confined on this planet long after we have achieved the capability of transcending its gravitational hold on us. The step into space, which will happen in the next few decades, inevitably leads to an endless horizon. Our descendants—and many of us now living — will have limitless possibilities for living, learning, exploring,

[1]Alex Haley, *Roots: The Saga of an American Family*, (New York: Doubleday Books, 1976), pp. 1–2.
[2]J.Y. Cousteau, "The Pulse of the Sea," *Saturday Review*, 4 September 1976 pp. 60–61.

and loving freely and joyously. Life will have taken another step toward transforming more of the mute, lifeless matter of the universe into sentience and intelligent consciousness; more and more of the substance of the universe will come awake to see and appreciate itself, participating ever more fully in the never-ending process of Creation.

V.

The Human Element

30. Original Sin

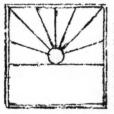

At first glance it may seem that the discussion in the preceding two parts about Earth-based and space-based systems for improving the human condition if just about technology. But the subject is really people, ranging from the people who first dream these ideas, to the people who turn them into reality, to the people who eventually benefit from their applications. In this part I want to examine some questions and potentialities which explicitly concern the human animal, and to explore some of the purely human aspects of the newly emerging technological capabilities discussed in earlier chapters.

Are we a flawed species? This question has fascinated philosophers, theologians, and mystics for centuries. The Judaic and Christian traditions have taught that humanity fell from a preternatural state of innocence and sinlessness in the Garden of Eden, and that ever since that time in the remote past, we have borne the burden of "original sin." The Christian apostle, Paul, described this condition as the perennial personal dilemma: "The good that I would, that I do not; but the evil which I would not, that I do." (Letter to the Romans, 7:19.)

With the Age of Enlightenment and the subsequent secularization of most of Western society, these religious views were discarded as pious superstitions with no relevance to public policy. The dominant political philosophy throughout most of the Western world today is liberalism — which first became a visible force in society during the French Revolution. Liberalism adopted a different world view based on the premise that men and women are inherently good. If only everyone could be freed from ignorance, fear, poverty, hunger, disease, and slavery, everyone will certainly do right, and the just and perfect society will result.

But the actual results of such an assumption about human nature are constant disillusionment. Every year, in every city and county hospital across the United States, the same pattern of disillusionment can be seen among young residents and social workers. The resident works very hard and diligently to "dry out" a derelict, human wretch on the detoxification ward. Before discharging the patient, the resident instructs the patient about the dangers of too much alcohol and too little good food, attempting to remedy possible deficiencies in the patient's education. Meanwhile, the social worker has found housing, clothing, and some income for the patient, perhaps from a job the patient is capable of carrying out. The patient is referred to various counseling services available at the hospital or through public assistance agencies.

The patient, profusely and genuinely grateful to the resident and the social worker, vows never again to touch the stuff. But when the same derelict shows up again two or three weeks later, half-dead from another binge on rotgut wine, the resident and the social worker become angry. After two or three rounds with the same patient, they may become openly impatient, and occasionally become verbally abusive toward the patient. At the same time, they become angry at themselves for treating their beneficiary with such contempt, and further resent having been made to feel guilty. This whole cycle of disillusionment is the inevitable consequence of believing the liberal premise that people are inherently good.

This same denial of original sin, the denial of the capacity in all of us to do evil, leads inexorably to the conviction in the political arena that all of the evils of the world result from the actions and conspiracies of a handful of villains in the system. If only we could identify the particular people who are so corrupt and get them out of office or in jail, everything will be fine, since you and I, of course, are moral and decent and can be counted on to do what is right and good.

Marxist Communism is also a philosophical heir of the French Revolution. In a fully Marxist society, fear, hunger, poverty, disease, and slavery have been eliminated. The correct treatment for evildoers, then, is political reeducation to fill the gaps in the wayward individual's liberal education, or to correct errors in his or her interpretation of that education.

In the United States, as business enterprises and government bureaucracies have grown larger, efficiency of the organization has become a greater and greater concern. One response to this concern has been the development of formal programs for the periodic evaluation of an employee's performance by his or her superiors. Given the liberal premise, such evaluations have frequently focussed on identifying, for the benefit of the employee, those areas of his or her performance which are considered deficient. Once the employee has thus been "educated," it is assumed that he or she will subsequently do the right and good thing.

The actual result of this approach has, all too often, been to focus the supervisor's attention so strongly on the personal weaknesses and deficiencies of the employee that his or her strengths become invisible and unrewarded. Besides leaving the employee's self-esteem very low, this system leads to the phenomenon humorously described as "Peter's Principle:" in any hierarchical organization, each person rises to his or her level of incompetence and is frozen in that position for the remainder of his or her career.[1]

While the liberal premise about human nature leads to enormous dif-

---

[1] Laurence J. Peter and Raymond Hull, *The Peter Principle: Why Things Always Go Wrong*, (New York: William Morrow and Company, 1969).

Original Sin

ficulties, so does its logical opposite, perhaps most purely embodied in the theology of Manichaeism, a syncretistic religion founded in the third century by a Persian named Manes (also called Mani or Manicheus). Manes claimed to be the last and greatest of the prophets, completing the revelations of Gautama Buddha, Zoroaster, and Jesus Christ. His theology, designed to appeal to the masses, incorporated elements of Buddhism, Zoroastrianism, and Gnostic Christianity. The religion was highly successful for nearly two centuries, winning converts through much of Europe, North Africa, and Asia as far as India. (Perhaps its most famous adherent was Augustine, until he returned to orthodox Christianity to become one of its most notable theologians of all time.)

Manichaean theology held that in the beginning, there was Light (identified with goodness and truth) and Darkness (identified with evil and discord), each unaware of the other. When the Light discovered the Darkness just beyond its boundaries, it created a divine being — Primal Man — to probe the Darkness, accompanied by lesser, personified fragments of Light. The Darkness overwhelmed the Primal Man and he fled back to the Light; but countless fragments of Light were captured by the Darkness. Threatened by the very existence of the Light, the Darkness created all of the material world to use in its onslaught against the Light. All of material creation, is, thus, inherently evil. Human beings were created in the ultimate act of mockery, in the image and likeness of the Primal Man, with tiny fragments of Light imprisoned in each human being. While these imprisoned bits of the Light struggle to escape from the realm of the Darkness, to rejoin the untainted light from which they were separated so long ago, they are defiled and mocked by the corrupt human flesh they are forced to inhabit, flesh which prolongs the imprisonment of these bits of Light, by reproducing itself.[2]

Although Manichaeism as an organized religion died out by the fifth century under intense pressure from Christianity, the central ideas – that material creation is inherently evil and that we human beings have very limited, if any, free will — continued to reappear in various forms and degrees down to the sixteenth and seventeenth centuries in the teachings of Martin Luther, John Calvin, and Cornelis Otto Jansen. They have thus entered modern secular attitudes as a forgotten, but submerged and powerful, current. The result is a deep pessimism about humanity's capacity to achieve anything good; its most extreme form appears in the slogan "People are pollution."

While philosophers and theologians may have rejected the formal ideas of Manichaeism, such ideas and attitudes can survive in the general population without conscious awareness or recognition of their origin from a

[2]Hans Jonas, *The Gnostic Religion: The Message of the Alien God and the Beginnings of Christianity*, (Boston: Beacon Press, 1963).

popular religion which was once widespread. Despite the near-universality of Roman Catholicism in Italy for centuries, shrines to pagan fertility gods are still found near many Italian villages, showing signs of recent maintenance and frequent offerings. It would be very difficult to prove that Manichaean attitudes have been transmitted intact through dozens of generations; yet our use of the handshake in Western cultures as a social greeting suggests such a possibility. In ancient times the handshake was used only on rare, ceremonial occasions, except by the Manichees who used it as a gesture of recognition, symbolizing the fragments of the Light groping to rejoin each other and to return to the realm of Light.

Neither the liberal premise nor the Manichaean worldview can provide a viable approach to a humane and positive future. During the Constitutional Convention in Philadelphia in 1787, the founding fathers of the United Staes had some of their most heated debates over the question of how to deal with the realities of human nature. From their extensive and profound knowledge of human history, they saw how so many different systems of government had foundered because of imperfect men and women. Yet they desired to create a system of government which would not become oppressive to moral and decent people.

The result was the first deliberately designed government in history, whose unique characteristic was the innovative system of checks and balances with which we are so familiar today. The bicameral congress balanced the interests of the people against the interests of the states; the three branches of the federal government balanced the political ambitions of presidents and legislators against the impartiality of appointed judges with lifelong tenure; the risks inherent in lifelong tenure were offset by the possibility of removal from office for misconduct or malfeasance. Events in recent years have again proven the wisdom of designing a system to work despite the imperfections of the real human beings who would actually operate the system.

The problem of periodic evaluations of employees, which end up focussing on deficient behavior to the exclusion of personal strengths, can be countered by recognizing and accepting the imperfections of human beings. As management theorist Peter F. Drucker has pointed out, the emphasis in Japanese corporations is quite different. The usual pattern in Japan is for a company to hire a worker for life. While this practice has numerous pitfalls of its own, it leads to an approach of managing people which is much more humane and satisfying to everyone concerned. The emphasis in this approach is to seek out each employee's strongest points and to find for each employee that position in the company in which those strengths can be utilized and in which the known weaknesses become irrelevant.[3]

[3]Peter F. Drucker, *The Effective Executive*, (New York: Harper & Row, 1966).

Original Sin

When we accept that we are not perfect beings, yet are capable of doing good, we can stop wasting time and effort in frustration and disillusionment with ourselves and each other; we can stop paralyzing ourselves with despair and a sense of futility. Then we can proceed to work together in an atmosphere of mutual assistance and positive reinforcement to turn our visions and dreams of Quality into reality.

31. Human Needs and the Goals of Society

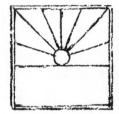 Each one of us perceives Quality differently. In a group as diverse as the residents of a modern industrialized nation, it is very difficult to find common ground on which to base positive goals which everyone would find desirable and attractive. A diversity of positive goals will be found instead, with support for each goal coming from different segments or groupings within the country. It is possible, in view of this natural fragmentation, to identify the types of positive goals which large fractions of the population would support?

The basic needs of human beings seem to be more universal than their perceptions of Quality. The survival of a society depends on its ability to fulfill the needs of its people. Consideration of these basic human needs thus provides a useful point of departure for thinking about positive goals for society.

The modern understanding of human nature and human needs is based on psychology and allied disciplines. Psychoanalysis and psychotherapy first began to explore the motivations of human behavior in response to the medical need to understand and treat people who were so emotionally disturbed as to be incapable of functioning in society. Pioneering work in analysis around the beginning of the twentieth century by Freud, Adler, Jung, and others, has thus had a profound effect on not only methods of treatment for emotional illness, but also social and political thinking in Western societies during this century.

Unfortunately, many of the resulting speculations were based upon behavior patterns and bizarre motivations of obsessive-compulsive neurotics, manic-depressives, or schizophrenics — taken to be representative of human nature itself. Such a distorted perception of human nature must surely have contributed to the mood of despair in the West in recent times. It is clearly as inappropriate to adopt a pessimistic view of human nature from these mental aberrations, as it would be to define the natural condition of the digestive tract in terms of the nausea and diarrhea of cholera patients.

Abraham H. Maslow was one of the first people in the fields of psychology and psychoanalysis to examine what constitutes mental health — rather than mental illness. He deliberately set out to study the behavior and the motivations of people who were most fully human, both by available psychometric norms and by everyday commonsense standards. By contrasting these healthy individuals to the emotionally disturbed, Maslow identified a hierarchy of human needs which play a major role in motivating behavior. While these needs motivate behavior, behavior remains subject to deliberate choice and is thus not determinable from those needs. But just as surely as a deficiency of Vitamin C in our daily diet will produce scurvy, deprivation of these basic needs will, in time, produce mental dysfunction and illness.

The explicit forms in which these basic needs are consciously perceived may be highly variable between cultures, but Maslow argued that careful examination would reveal an underlying unity:

> Certainly in any particular culture an individual's conscious motivational content will usually be extremely different from the conscious motivational content of an individual in another society. However, it is the common experience of anthropologists that people, even in different societies, are much more alike than we would think from our first contact with them, and that as we know them better we seem to find more and more of this commonness .... Our classification of basic needs is in part an attempt to account for this unity behind the apparent diversity from culture to culture. No claim is made yet that it is ultimate or universal for all cultures. The claim is made only that it is relatively *more* ultimate, *more* universal, *more* basic than the superficial conscious desires, and makes a closer approach to common human characteristics.[1]

Our first and most basic needs are our physiological and survival needs. The most mature and well-balanced person, deprived of food and drink, will gradually come to be obsessed with his or her craving for something to eat and drink. The behavior of newborn infants appears to be overwhelmingly motivated by their need for food, warmth, support against falling, sleep, and physical contact with their mothers.

Once these needs have been largely satisfied, Maslow found, a person becomes more strongly motivated by the need for safety and security. We seem to have a need for a reasonable degree of predictability in our daily environment. In early childhood, these needs appear as a very keen awareness of the presence or absence of parents. Later in life these needs are expressed as a concern for job security or material possessions.

When living conditions provide a reasonable degree of stability, in addition to adequate means for fulfilling survival needs, behavior becomes motivated primarily by the need to belong and to love. On the basis of the clinical experience of numerous psychoanalysts beginning with Freud, Maslow was convinced that deprivation of these needs was the most common source of maladjustments, at least in Western cultures.

The need for self-esteem and recognition by others come next in Maslow's hierarchy; gratification tends to be short-lived, however, unless the

[1] A.H. Maslow, *Motivation and Personality*, (New York: Harper & Row, 1954), pp. 54–55.

esteem is perceived to be justifiable and deserved. In contrast to Maslow, the pioneer psychoanalyst Alfred Adler held that the basic source of most emotional disorders was a lack of self-esteem and feelings of inadequacy. (The difference in views between Adler and Maslow may simply reflect an error on Maslow's part in distinguishing esteem as something separate from love and belongingness. Self-esteem is a prerequisite for the non-judgmental acceptance of another—which is called love; being loved by another makes it possible to love and respect oneself.)

After all of the more basic needs have been gratified, then we begin to be motivated by the need for self-actualization — the need to make actual all of one's potentialities—"to become more and more what one . . . is, to become everything . . . one is capable of becoming."[2]

As our needs at each stage in this hierarchy are met, Maslow found, we become oblivious of the existence of these needs. While we have specific names for many of the feelings of deprivation (hunger, thirst, loneliness), we have no specific names for the feelings of fulfillment of these needs—only very general terms (satisfied, contented, comfortable). Once our needs at any particular stage in the hierarchy have been met, we soon become dissatisfied and restless again. We may feel bored and lethargic; we may even come to hold in contempt the means of gratification we so recently struggled to obtain. This malaise continues until we begin to fulfill the needs of the next stage in the hierarchy, whether or not we have been consciously aware of those needs.

The ordering of needs in this hierarchy, Maslow claimed, reflects the relative priorities and urgencies which healthy people assign to the fulfillment of unsatiated or thwarted needs. Since this ordering appears to be the same among all the healthy and mature adults studied, Maslow argued that it was intrinsic to human nature. As we grow in maturity, we are all impelled to advance toward the later stages, as the needs of each stage become satisfied. The hierarchical ordering of needs, however, does not imply that specific behavior patterns at any moment are motivated exclusively by needs at a single stage. Conversely, a single need can motivate many different elements of behavior at the same time.

In addition to the basic, universal needs described above, Maslow singled out two other categories of needs which were clearly recognizable in some of his subjects. These are the cognitive needs — the need to know and to understand—and the aesthetic needs—the need for art or natural beauty. Among the subjects in whom these needs were clearly identifiable, these needs sometimes assumed a force and strength comparable to the universal, basic needs found in all his subjects. Frequently, in intellectually or artistically gifted people, these needs overlapped the need for self-actualization.

[1]A. H. Maslow, *Motivation and Personality*, p. 46.

Doomsday Has Been Cancelled

What implications does Maslow's theory of basic needs have for society and for the future? If a country is very poor and the bulk of its population has difficulty in meeting basic physiological and survival needs, then the focus of most government and business activity must be directed toward meeting those needs, if that society is to continue to function.

In wealthier nations in which the basic needs for survival, safety, and security have been met, the social focus has to be more and more directed toward the expansion of opportunities, for individuals to fulfill their personal needs for love, esteem, and self-actualization. It is no accident that such currents as the women's liberation movement first began in the most highly industrialized nations, where the earlier stages of basic needs have been amply fulfilled.

It would be suicidal for a country in which poverty and famine flourish, to channel the lion's share of national resources into projects which fulfill the self-actualization needs of well-fed civil servants. The conquest of hunger, poverty, disease, and ignorance must remain the top priorities in such nations. But it would be equally destructive for the government of a highly developed nation to pour all of its resources into efforts to ensure the complete fulfillment of the survival and security needs of every last citizen of the country, and of everyone in the Third World. The health and viability of such societies require the allocation of a significant portion of its resources for the fulfillment of the later stage needs of the bulk of the population, for whom the earlier, more fundamental needs have been satisfied.

If we label as immoral an interest in anything beyond adequate food, housing, medical care, education, and job security for everyone, we will cripple society's ability to fulfill the later stage, basic needs of the majority in the wealthier countries, and make it far more difficult to help poorer nations meet their basic needs. The allocation of resources for low-income housing and medical clinics; for educational enrichment programs for pre-school children in urban slums; and for economic developmental aid to Third World nations is certainly legitimate and humane. It is equally humane, and socially desirable, for a wealthy nation to allocate social resources for music, drama, and art; for adult education programs in affluent suburbs; for space exploration; and for scientific research having no immediately obvious economic benefits.

32. Transforming the Roots

During the nineteenth century, the material standard of living in Western societies made such rapid and obvious advances, that many people expected the human race to move further and further away from the "bestiality" of primitive societies with each generation. With the continued growth of affluence, social inequities would be reduced, drudgery and poverty would vanish, and the just and perfect society would soon arrive. This naive idea of Progress, however, ignored the capacity of each one of us to do evil as well as good. The idea of Progress, as the natural direction of human history, has been discarded by most people, and it is generally believed that human nature is constant through the ages, or changes very slowly with biological evolution. Many find in this idea a cause for despair, seeing little hope for improvements in the ways we mistreat one another.

It may indeed be true that human nature has not progressed significantly since the beginnings of recorded history, but Princeton University psychologist Julian Jaynes disputes this contention persuasively in discussing his theory on the origin of modern human consciousness.[1] Jaynes makes the startling claim that consciousness, as we know it, emerged as recently as the earlier half of the first millenium B.C., shortly before the times of the first Greek philosophers, Lao Tzu and Confucius. Whatever the truth of this matter may be, the mere fact that our human nature has the capacity to commit evil as well as good, does not mean we are doomed to failure in our attempts to deal with that imperfect nature. I want to discuss some of the techniques which have begun to emerge in recent years, which offer real hope that we can overcome some of the obstacles our own personalities can create for us.

Human consciousness, of course, depends on the physiological functioning of the human brain, which is the product of a lengthy evolutionary process extending back more than half a billion years. At about that time four related groups of animals are believed to have parted ways on their evolutionary journey through time. These four groups—the annelids (segmented worms, including the common earthworm), the echinoderms (starfish and sea urchins), the arthropods (crustaceans, myriapods, arachnids, and insects), and the chordates (lancelets, tunicates, and vertebrates) — all

[1]Julian Jaynes, *The Origin of Consciousness in the Breakdown of the Bicameral Mind*, (Boston: Houghton Mifflin,1976).

have a nervous system organized around a central bundle of neurons which extends along nearly the entire length of the animal. At intervals along this central bundle, major bundles of nerves branch off to innervate a segment of the animal with sensory and motor fibers. An enlargement of the central nerve bundle, at each of these major branching points, serves both as a local control center for each segment of the body, and as a communications center, coordinating activities of that segment with whatever is happening in other segments.

The chordates introduced a very important modification in this basic design, surrounding the central nerve bundle with a protective tube, the notochord. In the vertebrates, the notochord evolved into the spinal column which later allowed land-going vertebrates to grow to much larger sizes than invertebrates could ever achieve, and which, still later, allowed human beings to walk upright, freeing their hands and stimulating the development of hand-eye-brain coordination.

Another important development occurred in the evolution of the vertebrates. The first ganglion along the spinal cord assumed a more and more important role in the entire nervous system at the expense of the lower ganglia. In the evolutionary progression of the vertebrates, from jawless fishes up to the mammals, the brain has become more differentiated, taking over more and more of the sensory and motor control functions of the entire system, leaving various reflexes, and the control of such involuntary functions as digestion, under the control of lower ganglia. In mammals, the foremost lobe of the brain, the cerebrum, has taken over virtually all of the voluntary motor control functions.

This "new brain," especially the cerebral cortex with its familiar convolutions of gray matter, is the locus of intellectual processes, speech, vision, hearing, and motor control of the hands, eyes, and larynx in *Homo sapiens*. It would thus seem to be the locus of the activities we consider conscious. But not all of consciousness resides in the new brain: much of our pre-intellectual, experiential awareness takes place in the "old brain," the parts of the brain just below the cerebrum, including the hypothalamus, the limbic system, the pons, the medulla, and the brain stem. It is in these parts, much more prominent in reptiles than the cerebrum, that the neural activities we experience as emotions take place, closely coupled to the parts of the brain controlling the hormone-secreting endocrine system.

For centuries the Western world has cherished our intellect and rationality as our best and highest faculties. Indeed, all of our technological and scientific advances depend on the manipulation of symbols by the cerebral cortex. But our emotions and our direct, pre-intellectual awareness of experience itself, have been denigrated or ignored, for the most part, in a kind of cerebral chauvinism.

Thus our feelings, our emotions, are as fully, legitimately, and objectively parts of us as our intellectual thoughts. Feelings do not happen to us; rather, they are parts of the very core of personality; my feelings are part of the "me" which consciously experiences life. While I can accept some of your intellectual ideas and concepts, and integrate them into my intellectual world view, I cannot in this manner absorb your feelings into my personality. Your emotional responses will probably be different from mine in any given situation. In a discussion of theoretical physics, art history, constitutional law, you and I may come to the same intellectual conclusions, and still come away with radically different feelings about the matters discussed.

This distinction between thoughts and feelings is profoundly important, but common English usage has unfortunately obscured it. We say, for example, "I *feel* that the price of coffee has reached the limit consumers will tolerate," when we really mean, "On the basis of insufficient information, my intellectual judgment is that consumers will not pay higher prices."

The perception of Quality of life depends on our feelings, not on our thoughts. In an absolute material sense, most welfare recipients in the United States today are far better off than most of the nobility of Europe were, just a few centuries ago; they have softer beds, better health and public sanitation, more and better clothing, and far more entertainment. To point out these facts to the welfare recipient, however, does nothing to dispel his or her feelings of dissatisfaction, even if the facts are accepted as perfectly true. For this reason massive governmental programs, which attempt to decrease the objective material gap between the wealthy and the impoverished, are of little value, since they are nearly impossible to structure and administer in a way that would enable the poor to feel their frustrations and dissatisfactions are considered or even recognized. Local philanthropic organizations which deal personally with the poor, contribute far more to improving quality of life for the unfortunate, even if the objective material assistance they provide is miniscule in comparison with welfare or unemployment checks.

The ancient Greek Sophists urged their followers, "Know thyself." We are intellectually prepared to become more intimately acquainted with ourselves, when we recognize that our feelings are intrinsic parts of ourselves, and that no one else is responsible for the fact that certain stimuli make us feel this way or that. If I become sad or angry or happy in response to what someone else says, that feeling provides a clue to my own motivations and values, to my deeper memories of significant experiences, and to my personality. No one else can make me weep or laugh or shudder, but if I pay attention to my own feelings, I can discover what things trigger these feelings in me, and I can learn more precisely what constitutes Quality for me.

The focus on feelings is also the key to interpersonal communications and close relationships. Intimacy does not come from exchanging intellectual concepts; ideas are not uniquely yours or mine. I can only share myself with you, letting you know who I really am, by showing you my feelings and my emotional reactions to ideas, circumstances, and people. When I hide my feelings from you or suppress feelings, which I judge to be evil or inappropriate for me to have, then I thwart the possibility of genuine intimacy between us.

Conversely, we can draw closer together only if I respect the inner feelings you confide with me, if I accept them as a valid part of you just as I accept the color of your eyes or your height. Acceptance of our own emotions and each other's feelings requires a suspension of judgment, a refusal to think, "You have no right to feel that way;" "It is despicable of me to feel annoyed;" "But surely she wouldn't feel that way about it if she really cared."

Few people naturally and instinctively suspend judgment in this manner; those who are able to do so can form friendships easily, and in their presence even strangers often feel warm and loved. For others, this suspension of judgment and this acceptance of feelings has to be learned consciously and deliberately and practiced until these become as natural as table manners. A number of techniques and approaches for teaching people how to do this have emerged, in a variety of forms. Some of the better known among these are Transactional Analysis (TA),[2] encounter groups, Erhard Seminar Training (est),[3] Marriage Encounter,[4] and Parent Effectiveness Training (PET).[5]

As yet, some of these methods are fairly primitive in their development and refinement. In some cases, they can be traumatic rather than helpful. Yet it seems very significant to me that all of these new approaches have emerged from diverse sources in a very short period of time, just when the social fabric seems to have imposed newer levels of stress on individuals and families. The focus on feelings, which is the common element in these methods, seems to mark the beginnings of an important transformation at the very roots of our consciousness, as we extend our awareness deeper and deeper into the riches of the old brain.

Many would suggest that all this is foolishness; that in an earlier, less technological and less alienated world, people were more in touch with their feelings and required no such deliberate and artificial techniques to assist human communication. Surely people would have been more in touch with their feelings and emotions before industrialization, when individual roles

[2]Eric Berne, *Games People Play*, (New York: Grove Press, 1964); Thomas Harris, *I'm Okay – You're OK*, (New York: Harper & Row, 1967); Jut Meininger, *Success Through Transactional Analysis*, (New York: Grosset and Dunlop, 1973).

[3]Adelaide Bry, *est: Sixty Hours That Transform Your Life*, (New York: Harper & Row, 1967).

[4]John Powell, *The Secret of Staying in Love*, (Niles, Ill.: Argus Communications, 1974); John Powell, *Why Am I Afraid To Tell You Who I Am?*, (Niles: Argus Communications, 1975).

[5]Thomas Gordon, *PET: Parent Effectiveness Training*, (New York: Peter H. Wyden, 1970).

in society were less complex, when everyone worked near home, when everyone knew everyone else in the village — would they not?

It is far from clear that earlier societies were so idyllic, from an emotional point of view. Jaynes points out that the earliest written literatures of Greece, Egypt, Sumer, India, and Israel show no awareness of personal emotions at all; the language speaks only of externally visible activity.[6] Moreover, since individual roles were more rigidly defined, individual personalities may have been more readily overlooked. A young adult, with his personal joys and sorrows, might be dismissed with a remark such as, "Oh, that's just John Carver's second boy," in which the person has become invisible; only the role is seen. While rigid roles may have provided adequately for the security needs of each individual, it seems difficult to argue that needs of love and esteem would have been fulfilled any more easily than in present societies.

The underlying message of the new approaches to awareness of our emotions is that we can take charge of our emotional lives as much as our material lives. Society can thus be transformed in the direction of greater cooperation and love, as more and more of us get in touch with our feelings, share them with others deliberately, and begin to accept one another's emotions, whatever they may be, without judgment. Perhaps human nature can change in historical time scales.

[6]Jaynes, *Origin of Consciousness*, Chapter 5.

Rose Briones on her 96th birthday,
Pt. Reyes Station, California, 1978.

33. Methuselah's Children

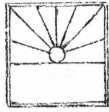 When a single-celled organism grows sufficiently large, it splits into two genetically identical cells, and each goes it separate way. Unless such a cell dies by mishap (eaten by another creature, lethally infected by a virus; or exposed to radiation, toxic chemicals, or adverse conditions of temperature and humidity), it is immortal. *Every amoeba alive today is the descendant of billions of generations of ancestors who never died.*

About 600 to 800 million years ago, complex multicellular animals and plants first appeared on Earth, with the new sexual reproduction replacing fissioning. The survival of an interbreeding community of such complex organisms then required the development of a genetic program to kill the individual, once the reproductive period had been completed. Over geological timespans, the total number of individuals of a given species must remain more or less constant in the absence of major perturbations or conscious intervention, which could enlarge the carrying capacity of a given area for that species. The total number of births each millenium must be very nearly equal to the total number of deaths in that millenium.

If most individuals in a gene pool have lifespans comparable to time scales in which the environment can change significantly, the rate of appearance of genetic variations might be too low to permit the group as a whole to coevolve with its environment. Probably for this reason, multicelled animals and plants, which reproduce sexually, appear to have a time-bomb built into their genetic heritage.

We humans also suffer from this genetic disease called death. The earliest burial sites of human cave-dwellers show signs of belief in immortality, perhaps a yearning for it. Such a desire is perhaps a result of self-awareness — if I am aware of an "I" within me, then I can recognize that "I" will die as a mortal piece of flesh. Human culture itself is one form of escaping total personal annihilation: though my body will not survive in this world, at least the memory of my identity and of my contributions of ideas or artifacts may survive for later generations.

Ever since Western society at large discarded the transcendant ideas of traditional religions from our daily lives, we have been very uncomfortable with reminders of personal mortality. In the United States, especially, the aged are put away in rest homes or convalescent hospitals; we expect them to die, not in their own beds at home, surrounded by their families and friends, among their personal mementoes, but in a sterile hospital, attended to by strangers whom we pay to take care of this unpleasant task for us. Otherwise, we would feel intense frustration when confronted with these vivid reminders, as we refuse to admit our need for self-transcendance.

Although the cult of youthfulness has been carried to an extreme in the United States, it is still very surprising to be reminded in the twentieth century, by philosopher Eric Hoffer, that "we can hardly know how things happened in history unless we keep in mind that much of the time it was juveniles who made them happen." Alexander the Great carried out his conquest of the Persian Empire during his early twenties; Joan of Arc was seventeen when she recaptured Orleans from the English, and only nineteen when she was burned at the stake.[1] The preeminence of such youths was due in part to the high mortality rates of earlier times, when famine, disease, and infection following injuries forced universal awareness of the mortality of the flesh.

Despite major advances in the life expectancy of newborn children, since the beginning of the Industrial Revolution, few people today actually live to greater ages than our ancestors. The conquest of infectious diseases, improvements in diet, and public sanitation have all contributed to longer life expectancy, with the greatest contributions from reduction of mortality in infancy. If we are lucky enough not to be killed by accidents; if we obtain reasonable medical care for infectious diseases or wound infections; if we do not die of postpartum hemorrhage; if we escape famine; our intrinsic longevity is still near the Biblical three-score-and-ten years.

Virtually all of the deaths in old age fall into two, possibly three, categories of degenerative disorders. The first category is degeneration of the circulatory system: myocardial infarctions, strokes, aneurisms, and congestive heart failure are typical terminal events in this process. The second category of deaths are those due to degeneration of the immune system; some manifestations of this process are the failure of lymphocytes to manufacture antibodies against invading microbes, failure of the lymphocytes to attack and devour foreign cells or dead cells of our own bodies, or aberrant behavior by the lymphocytes which begin to attack healthy, normal cells of our own bodies. Cancer may prove to be a third, distinct category of degenerative process, although many believe it may be another form of immune system disorder in which the lymphocytes fail to attack cancer cells.[2]

Gerontology, the study of the aging process, has begun to unravel the details of the biochemical pathways by which the genetic code directs our senility and commands our death. At least three mechanisms have been identified, but the relationships among them are as yet very unclear. They

[1]Eric Hoffer, *The Temper of Our Time*, (New York: Harper & Row, 1967), Chapter 1.
[2]Albert Rosenfeld, *Prolongevity*, (New York: Alfred A. Knopf, 1976). Presents a fairly comprehensive and very readable account of the status of research on aging.

may prove to be completely independent systems, the redundancy serving to guarantee that each individual will die even if one or another of the programmed self-destruction systems should fail to operate.

One of these systems operates within each cell of the body. With the exception of a few types of cells which do not multiply after infancy, we grow in size by the regular multiplication of cells within each growing organ. An individual cell grows until reaching a critical size; then the marvelous chromosomal dance of mitosis unfolds, splitting the cell into two copies with identical sets of chromosomes. In adults, this process continues at a very low rate to replace cells which have died from disease, trauma, or wear and tear. (Brain neurons and heart muscle cells cannot undergo mitosis after infancy and thus cannot be replaced; we never have more brain cells than we did as infants.)

When the ovum is fertilized by a sperm cell and mitosis begins, some kind of clock is set, at least in mammals, and the time-bomb is armed. In the 1960s Dr. Leonard Hayflick showed that human cells grown in cultures, even if originally taken from tissues capable of mitosis throughout life, stop dividing about fifty generations after the union of the original ovum and sperm. It was possible to prove definitely that this time-bomb is in the nucleus of the cell and has nothing to do with "wearing out" the cytoplasm — "flesh" of the cell.

In laboratory cell cultures a number of chemicals have been shown to extend the "Hayflick limit" from about fifty generations of mitosis to at least one hundred generations. Some of these chemicals include cortisone and Vitamin C. The experiment was terminated before the cell culture showed any signs of self-destruction, so the full potential of such chemical intervention is unknown, both for laboratory cell cultures and for living flesh. Such long term experiments, terminated for lack of funding, remind me of a cartoon I saw a few years ago in which a biochemist is explaining to a visitor in his laboratory, "I think I've found a potion for immortality, but it will take forever to prove it."

A second mechanism has been postulated to kill us, by way of the endocrine system, which produces the hormones regulating biochemical processes throughout the body. Thyroid hormones control the rate of metabolism in cells, in which the oxidation of complex organic substances (sugars, fats, proteins) releases energy for use by the cell. If the thyroid gland does not release enough of these metabolic hormones (hypothyroidism), the reduced levels of cellular metabolism result in symptoms remarkably similar to those of aging: hair loses its pigmentation, the skin loses its elasticity and becomes wrinkled, joints become immobilized by arthritis, and so forth.

Thyroid hormones extracts are readily available today in the industrialized countries, so we seldom see untreated cases of hypothyroidism.

But when treatment for this disorder first became available, the effect of treating an advanced case was an incredible rejuvenation: hair color returned, wrinkles disappeared, and long-immobilized joints were once again free. These results stimulated some attempts to treat the symptoms of normal aging by thyroid hormone supplements, but these were generally unsuccessful, occasinally ending in disaster by killing a patient.

Such clues strongly suggest that the aging process involves a derangement of cellular metabolism and may be controlled by hormones. Pursuing this line of reasoning, Dr. W. Donner Denckla at the Roche Institute of Molecular Biology (among others) is trying to isolate a hormone believed to be secreted by the pituitary gland, the "master" gland of the endocrine system. Denckla calls this postulated hormone DECO, an acronym for "decreasing oxygen consumption." Its action would be to block normal metabolic oxidation in the cells of the body despite the presence of adequate levels of thyroid hormones, oxygen, and nutrients. The effect would be the gradual starvation of our cells, just as in hypothyroidism.

If DECO exists and can be isolated, this mechanism for death could eventually be controlled by at least two approaches. We might learn to produce a chemical antagonist for DECO itself, or the hypothetical "releasing factor" for DECO. The release of most pituitary hormones — perhaps all of them — is controlled by chemicals called releasing factors, produced in the hypothalamus, a part of the old brain near the pituitary. If we succeed in synthesizing an antagonist for DECO, or for its releasing factor, the effects of DECO on the cells could be reduced or completely halted. The body's cells should then be able to repair much of the damage already done, just as was the case with advanced hypothyroidism, offering the exciting prospect of significant rejuvenation as well as retardation of the aging process.

A third possible mechanism for aging may be cumulative damage to our cells by free oxygen atoms and by other oxidizing agents. Oxygen is essential to our metabolism, but it is a dangerous and toxic substance, producing cross-linkages between protein molecule chains. The modern eukaryotic cell, of all multicelled animals and higher plants, it has recently been discovered, protects itself to some extent against the ravages of free oxygen by means of tiny organelles called peroxisomes. These tiny bodies in the cell catalyze the reaction of free oxygen with amino acids, effectively losing the chemical energy of this reaction; but that is a small price to pay for the benefits of even partial protection.

If a DNA chain molecule were thus cross-linked to another protein molecule or to another part of itself, then linked portions of the DNA helix could no longer function as templates for the synthesis of some particular protein or enzyme. Without access to these genetic instructions, the cell would die if the protein specified by the blocked portion of the helix were essential to the functioning of that particular cell. Oxidants can also induce cross-linkages in the proteins elastin and collagen, which make up much of the connective tissue of our bodies. These long-chain molecules would thus lose their elasticity, resulting in hardening of the arteries, stiffening of cartilage, loss of flexibility in the skin, and other symptoms of aging.

Gerontologist Dr. Johan Bjorksten is convinced that the cross-linking of our genes is a major villain in the death program, and he has concentrated his efforts on a search for chemicals which inhibit nonmetabolic oxidation in our bodies. Vitamins C and E both appear to have some antioxidant effects, but they are far from the definitive answer. At the Fall, 1976 meeting of the American Chemical Society, Bjorksten summarized the status of gerontological research and stated that no intrinsic biological reason has been found which would prevent us from extending human longevity to about eight hundred years. He is no longer interested in paltry increments of five or ten years in lifespan; he aims for an increase in longevity of about eighty years, in the near future.

Just as Edward Jenner did not need to know and understand the germ theory of disease in order to develop a highly successful vaccine against smallpox, we do not need to fully understand the aging process in order to develop effective therapies to halt, or even reverse, aging. Bjorksten believes that, with adequate funding, a breakthrough of some eighty years in functional lifespan could come as early as the mid-1980s. While other, less optimistic gerontologists would estimate closer to forty or fifty years for such an advance, many of us today would live to see it happen and perhaps partake in its benefits.

Following Bjorksten's lecture, one newspaper denounced the idea of such a breakthough as frightening. The Social Security System is already going broke; if people were to live to eight hundred, they would either starve after retirement at age sixty-five, or they would have to go on working until the age of 750. Moreover, the editorial asked in one of the most age-discriminatory statements I have ever seen, who could stand the sight of 200-year-old nude bathers on the California beaches? "Who needs it?" the editorial concluded. "By the time most of us have made our way through the first century of progress, we're ready to rest. Right to life is one thing, but this is carrying things too far. Remove from us a few wrinkles or a few pounds, but please don't expect us to be here in 2776."[3]

It seems to me that only those who do not enjoy their work, to whom life itself is a loathsome burden, would recoil in such horror from the thought of active work until the age of 750. Those who can delight in learning, loving, and experiencing the wonders of the universe, feel no weariness or desire to lie down to rest. As Andrew Marvel observed long ago,

> The grave's a fine and private place,
> But none, I think, do there embrace.

[3]Editorial, *The Oakland Tribune*, 4 September 1976.

Are the objections raised by the editorial reasonable? Would enormous prolongation of lifespans create misery or multiply opportunities for joy and happiness?

Confronted with a breakthrough in longevity, many of our present tacit assumptions would need to be dusted off and reexamined; many features of the present system would become glaringly unjust. Prior to the Great Depression, people generally continued to work as long as they chose to do so. But when the Social Security System was being drafted, the age of sixty-five was arbitrarily selected as the minimum age for collection of benefits, and that soon became adopted as the universal (and often compulsory) age for retirement, without benefit of public debate or Congressional hearing. In attempting to bail out the Social Secuity System, Congress, in 1978, relaxed the retirement age, forbidding most employers from requiring retirement before age seventy. A more fundamental reform would be forced upon us by a major breakthrough in human lifespan, and I will take up the economic issues in the next chapter.

Today, upon reaching the age of forty, becoming more mindful of the uncertainty of life, many people review their careers to date. Seeing how little of what they once dreamed of doing has actually been done, seeing how little time remains, and knowing that society does not readily allow them to change careers at this late stage in life, many are crushed down with the burden of "middle age." Many turn bitter and rigid, trying to stop time itself by resisting all change. Others turn apathetic; a few turn suicidal. But why should anyone, at any age, be trapped for the rest of their lifetime — however long or short it may be — in a single career or single profession? Is that not just another form of slavery?

Certainly many will not welcome longer life for themselves, and it would be cruel to compel them to accept antiaging treatments. Perhaps we already have too many laws and regulations to protect us from ourselves; sometimes it seems to me we should be grateful that attempted suicide has not been made a capital offense. The decision of whether or not to deliberately postpone one's own aging and death is so fundamentally tied to individual values and visions of Quality that each person must be left free to choose or reject these treatments.

According to the Genesis account of humanity's early history, we are all descended from Noah, who was the grandson of Methuselah. "And all the days of Methuselah were nine hundred and sixty nine years, and he died." (Genesis 5:27). Perhaps in the near future we may all have the chance to claim our proper inheritance as Methuselah's children.

34. In the Sweat of Your Brow

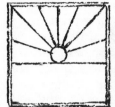 A dramatic breakthrough in human longevity would soon require extensive reforms in our economic systems. I want to explore some possibilities for such reforms, reforms which seem to me to be desirable in any case. Hunting and gathering peoples use no money and have no need for it. The few material possessions necessary for survival or personal adornment are most commonly made by the user. In a few instances such goods are obtained from someone else, either in the same or a neighboring group, as gifts or in exchange. The exchange is seldom bartering, in which the goods or services are explicitly identified by both parties to the transaction. The usual arrangement is based on an implicit understanding that if I give you a bowl or some arrows today, then some other day when I have need for body pigments or for a knife, you will remember your obligation to me and provide what I need from what you have. The equivalency between different kinds of goods and services is thus arbitrary and it is determined without the action of a marketplace.

Even in more complicated societies, having fixed villages and far greater specialization of occupations, money in many cases is still not necessary. But many more features of industrialized systems become recognizable. One case in point is the economic system prevalent in Tikopia, an island in the Solomon Islands of western Polynesia, prior to extensive cultural influence by Westerners. The Tikopian culture was extensively studied by anthropologist Raymond Firth, 1928-1929, and again in 1952, providing an early classic in the field of economic anthropology.[1]

Tikopia at that time had no money and little bartering. Most economic trade was based on borrowing goods and services against obligations to provide for unspecified future needs. The bulk of economic activity is directly related to acquiring and preparing food for the one principal meal of the day, which is usually eaten in the middle of the afternoon. The diet is primarily vegetarian, supplemented by fish. Staples include taro, a root crop similar to yams, and coconuts. Fishing is done either from canoes at sea or with nets in the shallow waters of the coral reefs. Land is owned privately, but another's land may be farmed for annual crops with the consent of the owner.

Most farming activities can be done by individuals or by individual households, but some important activities require the cooperation of many

[1]Raymond Firth, *Primitive Polynesian Economy*, (New York: W.W. Norton & Company, 1975).

people. In such cases, some individual takes the initiative to act as an entrepreneur, organizing the necessary work force and arranging to borrow the necessary capital equipment from the owner. For a day of deep-sea fishing, for example, the entrepreneur will ask various friends and relatives to come with him to fish. If he does not own a canoe, he will borrow one for the day from a relative or friend.

Occasionally, a portion of the catch is set aside as a ritual offering, in a ceremonial rededication of the canoe to ancestral spirits, or is presented to the local chieftain as a periodic gift of courtesy and respect. Usually, only those who participate in the fishing share in the distribution of the catch at the end of the day. All of the crew members receive more or less equal shares of the catch, including the entrepreneur and the owner of the canoe, whether or not the owner went to sea that day, in recognition of the owner's participation by means of the capital equipment. The relative valuation of labor and capital is necessarily arbitrary: neither the crew alone nor the canoe alone could yield any catch at all; doubling the crew would not necessarily double the catch; using a larger canoe would not necessarily increase the catch. That the owner of the canoe receive a share of the catch is viewed as a matter of simple justice.

As societies become more complex, it becomes increasingly difficult to maintain a system of borrowing goods and services against unspecified future demands on one's own property and talents. Bartering affords some opportunities to keep the balance of obligations current, but the social invention which allowed economic activities to expand, beyond transactions among villagers who have known each other all of their lives, was money. Modern economists describe money as a medium of exchange and as a store of economic value, but its real significance is far deeper. If someone else provides us with certain goods or services, money allows us to discharge our future obligations to him or her immediately, in the form which is transferable, even to total strangers or enemies. Thus the sphere of economic activities is considerably broadened. But the essential arbitrariness in the relative values of different goods and services remains unaltered.

In agrarian communities which use money, the arbitrariness of prices remains apparent in the haggling over each purchase: depending on the personal interaction between buyer and seller, the price for identical goods varies from one transaction to the next. In highly industrialized countries such as the United States, we have agreed to accept fixed pricing of goods in our supermarkets and department stores, recognizing the absurdity, under these conditions, of haggling. We have chosen not to haggle over items of little economic significance and, as a result, we seem to have forgotten the extent to which relative prices of different kinds of goods and services are arbitrary; we feel uncomfortable on those rare occasions (such as buying a house or a car) when we are expected to bargain with total strangers.

In the Sweat of Your Brow

We have also forgotten the arbitrariness of the distribution of benefits from the production of wealth. If an entrepreneur raises the capital to build a factory and hires workers to manufacture chair legs, how shall the value added be divided up? If one man can till one-sixth of an acre in a day, using only hand tools, while another man can till five acres in the same day, using a tractor, then it is clear that the increased productivity of the human plus equipment is thirty times greater for the man with a tractor than for the man with the shovel and hoe. The tractor is equivalent in productivity to twenty-nine men with shovels and hoes. If the man who uses the tractor also owns the tractor, no problem of equity is apparent in the distribution of the proceeds. But if a lathe in a factory allows a lathe operator to make chair legs a hundred times faster than skilled woodcarvers using only hand tools, how shall the proceeds be distributed equitably between the lathe operator and the owner of the lathe?

For various historical reasons, including our agricultural heritage and the excesses of the early industrial period, we seem to have adopted the notion that labor is the only significant factor in industrial production, ignoring the contribution of capital equipment. We distribute more and more of the proceeds to the owner of the living labor (the worker), despite the fact that more and more of the productivity is attributable to the nonliving labor (the machinery). We conceal this distortion by speaking of increased productivity per hour of each worker's time, instead of increased productivity per hour of worker-and-machinery time.

By admitting only labor as valid input in production, we have enslaved ourselves to toil. A fundamental principle in economic theory is Say's law: the total value of goods and services produced is exactly equal to the total value of wages and dividends. If you cannot participate in the economy by receiving wages, dividends, or welfare (redistributed wages and dividends), you cannot purchase goods or services, no matter how large the Gross National Product per person. Yet all our social institutions seem to assume that only income derived from selling our labor is honorable. In election years politicians speak pejoratively of dividends as "unearned income;" were they legislating the economy of Tikopia, it is easy enough to believe that the canoe owner would be subjected to nearly confiscatory taxation on his share of the catch of the fish.

Among some primitive societies the elderly who are no longer strong enough to contribute to food production are cast out to die alone. We generally view this practice with horror, yet we do virtually the same thing to our elderly and incapacitated by denying them legitimate participation in the economy if they are unable to sell their labor. Although more and more of our wealth comes from machines, we continue to call for "full employment," instead of universal participation in the ownership of capital machinery.

Doomsday Has Been Cancelled

Attorney Louis Kelso has advocated a number of reforms and new institutional arrangements which would allow wider and wider distribution of ownership of capital.[2] One of these concepts was implemented by Congress in 1976 in legislation authorizing Employee Stock Ownership Plans (ESOP). Employees of a company may now form an ESOP which may borrow money to purchase newly issued shares from the company. The company then makes tax-deductible contributions to the ESOP, and these contributions are used to pay off the principal and the interest on the loan. Over a period of a few years participating employees become part owners of the company; and the company has a new source of cheaper capitalization for the purchase of new equipment. The employees obtain a second income from their shares of capital, and the company pays off the borrowed money with tax-free dollars, thereby reducing its costs.

While ESOP is an important first step, it does not address the needs of those who do not have a job. Kelso points out that a government-sponsored program to purchase shares in the names of present welfare recipients would be feasible at little cost to taxpayers. It is possible to finance the purchase of consumer goods such as vacation trips, refrigerators, recreational vehicles, and even homes on borrowed money, although none of these goods can produce wealth. The purchase of equity in productive machinery should be similarly financeable, especially since few businesses invest in equipment which will not pay for itself in about five years or less. Kelso suggests that shares of General Motors or AT&T could be purchased on behalf of welfare recipients (or taxpayers in general) by borrowing money from banks and other lending institutions, held in escrow until the income from the shares has paid off the loan, and then turned over to the individuals in whose names they were purchased. The role of the government would be simply to guarantee the loans.

But this plan would only work if some tax reforms were also implemented. Although capital machinery pays for itself within about five years, dividends on shares would generally take ten years to pay off a loan for the purchase of the shares, due to the present "double taxation" of dividends. After a corporation adds up its total revenues, its taxes (in the United States, at least) are based on net income, which is the remainder after interest expenses, utility bills, insurance premiums, the costs of raw materials, and wages have been subtracted from revenues. Only after taxes (amounting to 49% of net income) have been paid, are dividends distributed to the shareholders (the people who own the capital assets of the corporation), who must then pay personal income taxes on these dividends.

Suppose the same principle were applied to labor. Suppose each corporation had to pay 49% taxes on the total revenue, less interest expenses,

[2]Louis O. Kelso and Patricia Hetter, *How to Turn Eighty Million Workers Into Capitalists on Borrowed Money*, (New York: Random House, 1967).

198

utility bills, insurance premiums, and the costs of raw materials. Wages would then be 30-45% lower. Changing the tax laws, so that dividends could be distributed before paying taxes, would then make it much more feasible for everyone to become a participant in the economy, through dividend income, as well as wages, reversing the trend toward ever greater concentration of new capital investments in fewer and fewer hands.

Automation would no longer be viewed as a threat to income; it is only a threat to jobs, most of which are inherently distasteful and mind-destroying toil. Eventually, everyone would receive most of their income and purchasing power from the ownership of stocks. Those who chose to sell their own labor would receive additional monetary rewards. In such an economy, the problem of slaving away until the age of 750 in order to save the Social Security System from going bankrupt would vanish. Artists would no longer have to starve. We could all work at whatever we find satisfying and fulfilling, instead of accepting drudgery or humiliation as the exchange for our daily bread.

When Adam and Eve were expelled from the Garden of Eden, Adam was placed under a curse: "In the sweat of your brow shall you eat your bread." (Genesis 3:19). During the last few decades, we have outgrown the attitude, once widely held, that the use of anaesthetics in childbirth is immoral, because it seemed to defy the curse placed on Eve: "In sorrow shall you bear your children." (Genesis 3:16). Yet we still accept the curse on Adam as a moral and economic necessity. Once we outgrow the attitude that income derived only from labor is honorable, society can become vastly richer, both spiritually and materially. Dramatic breakthroughs in longevity may be the catalyst we need to bring about change in our institutions and attitudes.

One-hundred-thousand mile view
of Africa, Europe and the Middle East,
Apollo 10, 1969.

35. The Consciousness of Solar Citizens

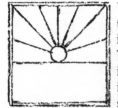 What kinds of changes in world view might result from the extension of Gaian life (including *Homo sapiens*) out into the solar system, beyond the Earth's atmosphere? Thus far, only a handful of human beings have voyaged into space. All of the American astronauts have, at least in their professional lives, a classical view of reality, strongly focussed on the hierarchy of technological ideas underlying the vehicles in which they flew. Yet for most of them, the experience of seeing the entire living Earth from a new, spectacular, and dynamic viewpoint had almost mystical and religious force. Russell Schweickart, who flew on the Apollo 9 test flight in Earth orbit in 1969, and took a lengthy "space walk" outside the capsule, has vividly described the changes this experience triggered in him:

> ...you go around every hour and a half, time after time after time...you look out the window as you're going past and there's the Mediterranean area and Greece and Rome and North Africa and the Sinai, the whole area, and you realize that in one glance...what you're seeing is what was the whole history of man for years — the cradle of civilization...
>
> ...you go around down across North Africa and out over the Indian Ocean and look up at that great subcontinent of India pointed down toward you ... you've never realized how big that is before.
>
> ...you do it again and again and again...And the next thing you recognize in yourself, is you're identifying with North Africa. You look forward to that, you anticipate it, and there it is. The whole process begins to shift of what it is you identify with. When you go around it in an hour and a half, you begin to recognize that your identity is with that whole thing. And that makes a change.
>
> ...you think about what you're experiencing and why. Do you deserve this? This fantastic experience? Have you earned this in some way? Are you separated out to be touched by God to have some special experience that other men cannot have? You know the answer to that is "No." There's nothing special you've done that deserves that, that earned that. It's not a special thing for you. You know very well at that moment, and it comes through to you so powerfully, that you're the sensing element for man.
>
> You look down and see the surface of that globe that you've lived on all this time and you know all those people down there. They are like you, they are you, and somehow you represent them when you are up there — a

Doomsday Has Been Cancelled

sensing element, that point out on the end, and that's a humbling feeling. It's a feeling that you have a responsibility. It's not for yourself.

The eye that does not see does no justice to the body. That's why it's there, that's why you're out there, and somehow you recognize that you're a piece of this total life. You're out on that forefront and you have to bring that back somehow and that becomes a rather special responsibility. It tells you something about your relationship with this thing we call life, and so that's a change, that's something new.

...there's a difference in that world now...in that relationship between you and that planet, and you and all those other forms of life on that planet, because you've had that kind of experience. It's a difference and it's so precious...all through this I've used the word "*you*" because it's not me, it's not [any one of the other astronauts] it's you, it's us, it's we, it's life. [Life has] had that experience, and it's not just *my* problem to integrate, it's not my challenge to integrate, my joy to integrate — it's yours, it's everybody's.[1]

Living in a space community, whether near or far from Earth, people will be intensely aware of their dependence and connectedness to other lifeforms, to the technological systems used, to the social institutions by which they live, to the Sun, the Moon, and the asteroids, and to the Earth itself, where life and consciousness originated. This intense consciousness of interdependence, of identity with Gaia, will be constantly reinforced by the modest scale of the new worlds. On the Earth, these connections — even in simple agrarian societies — are often so large in scale as to be invisible in daily life.

Such changes in consciousness would certainly be expected among emigrants newly arriving in space. The first time people fly among clouds, especially in a small airplane, their perception of clouds is drastically and permanently altered. Clouds are no longer flat, two-dimensional patterns painted on a hemispherical blue sky; they become three-dimensional objects, with structure and internal movement. The ascent into space for the first time will likewise alter personal perceptions of the atmosphere, the biosphere, and the planet Earth forever. The extension of life into outer space, combined with the prolongation of human lifespans, will have impacts on consciousness which will be greater still.

Here on Earth, various places of natural beauty attract afficionados, who prefer spring in Yosemite, or autumn in the Grand Tetons, or the winter rains in the Kalahari Desert. In space, long-lived people, who will have had multiple opportunities to revisit many of the spectacular natural wonders of the solar system, will come to develop their own favorite places and seasons: perihelion passage in the tail of Halley's Comet; the polar

[1]Russell L. Schweickart, remarks at the Lindisfarne Association, Box 1395, Southhampton, N.Y. 11968, in 1974. Reprinted in *CoEvolution Quarterly*, Summer 1975, p. 42–45.

twilight regions of Mercury, where the Sun can be seen to rise slowly in the East, sink back below the horizon, and rise again before traversing the sky during the long, Mercurial day; springtime near the Martian icecaps, where the icecaps retreat each day, and advance again at night, only to be pushed back relentlessly a bit farther the next day. Our identification with Nature will extend outward, encompassing more and more of Creation.

Perhaps before too long, we shall finally establish contact with another civilization in the Galaxy. Cornell University's Professor Frank Drake, a radio astronomer who has been deeply involved in the search for intelligence elsewhere in the universe, has pointed out that the first advanced civilizations we find are likely to be immortals or, at any rate, to have extremely long lifespans. One of the variables determining the chances of contacting another civilization is the length of time an advanced civilization will survive at a level high enough to generate strong radio signals. Long-lived individuals, it might be expected, would tend to have more enduring civilizations.

The expansion into the solar system on a large scale is almost inevitable within the next few decades. Should the anticipated longevity breakthrough also occur in the next few decades, many of you reading this book will live to experience these things yourselves.

However long we live, neither we nor our descendants will forget the new, conscious identification with the Earth, the Sun, and the entire solar system. Until the naturalistic philosophy of Rousseau, the writings of the English Lake poets, especially Wordsworth and Byron, and the paintings of Friederich, Constable, and Turner, very few Westerners had ever considered mountain scenery to be of intrinsic value. Mountains were obstacles along the road, to be crossed or forgotten, never to be enjoyed for their beauty.[2] Today millions voyage every year to the Swiss Alps, the North American Rockies, the Peruvian Andes, to stand in awe at the majestic forms and living textures of forests and meadows, eagles and bears, and picas and glaciers. The new consciousness of solar citizens, imbued with a sense of identity with Gaia and her offspring, will have become part and parcel of the human experience. *Homo sapiens* may evolve into one or more new species, but our offspring will remember their mother, the Earth, as long as sentience survives.

[2]Kenneth Clark, *Civilization: A Personal View*, (New York: Harper and Row, 1969),Chapter 11, "The Worship of Nature."

Edge-On Galaxy, NGC 4565.

36. ...And They All Lived Happily Ever After

I have presented a small selection of ideas and developments, emerging all around us, which offer hope for a more humane and positive future. Countless other new potentialities are being uncovered each day, in laboratories and homes, in universities and villages, around the world, wherever people cooperate, to put knowledge to use in response to perceptions of Quality. Many of these quantum leaps which I have omitted or overlooked will turn out, in hindsight, to be so important that the viewpoints I have given here will seem hopelessly conservative. Doomsday is not just around the corner; doomsday has, in fact, been cancelled.

We are prone to look at the dark side of things, to overlook or devalue good news, and a climate of gloom has flourished in recent decades in the more affluent parts of the Western world. The skepticism which properly underlies the scientific method may have contributed to this bias. Every new hypothesis, every new theory invented to explain certain phenomena, must be sharply and critically examined to find weaknesses and inadequacies; it is the failures of a scientific theory which lead us most surely to new and deeper knowledge and understanding. Our difficulties in groping with the present and the future arise when we apply skepticism, with too much vigor and eagerness, to every proposed solution, without applying equal skepticism to every newly proclaimed problem.

Conventional wisdom in recent years has asserted that the Earth cannot tolerate even one more doubling of the human population and that our very survival demands prompt draconian measures. A reasonable skeptic would ask, "What is the evidence that we cannot accomodate another doubling of population in the next forty years here on Earth? What is the evidence to show that population is likely to double in the next forty years? How reliable are the sources of data used in making such projections? Are massive global programs necessary if we are to feed everyone? Or can local market mechanisms provide the increased food production needed, as they always have in the past?"

Other historical accidents in our thinking and attitudes have also contributed to the climate of despair and helplessness, and I have touched on several of these in earlier chapters. Perhaps all of these reflect our basic human nature. In the fairy tales we tell our children, the hero or heroine struggles gallantly against immense adversities, and in the end, overcomes one or more major obstacles to achieve some worthy goal. The doomsday prophets of our times have likewise painted very vivid and terrifying of the dragons and perils we face within our lifetime.

But all the fairy tales end with the phrase "...and they all lived happily ever after," because it is far more dificult to describe a happy, comfortable period of life without sounding naive, utopian, and boring. Whether or not the fairy tales can describe a happy and contented state of affairs, as convincingly as they describe the trials and tribulations, the simple fact is that many people do experience lives of comfort, personal satisfaction, and progressive self-actualization. The experience is difficult to describe — it can only be lived and accepted.

It is very easy to construct elaborate and believable scenarios for the collapse of the present socioeconomic system. To describe, step by step, how the present system can evolve into something better, is far more difficult. Perhaps it is no accident that the teachings of the major religions and the great mystics throughout history have generally been taciturn about Heaven or Nirvana, although they have often been very explicit and detailed about Hell.

I have made the case that we are not entering an age of scarcity and increased regimentation, but rather that we stand on the threshold of a more humane and positive future. I must reject any suggestion that this is merely another exercise in inventing utopias. I do not expect any medical breakthrough to produce a serum which will cure us of the capacity to do evil to one another, as well as help each other to do good. I do not expect that we will be able in the future to choose and pursue our goals free of anguish, frustration, disenchantment, or ambivalence. In the pursuit of whatever goals we may choose, we will have some successes and we will have some failures; we will abandon some goals before we have any inkling of success or failure, just as we have always done. Having attained or abandoned one goal, we will soon move on to invent and pursue new goals. A humane and positive future is thus a process of being and becoming; it is not a utopian endpoint into which society will evolve once and for all, but rather a continuing journey we can all undertake. The journey itself can be satisfying and enjoyable if we bring a spirit of playfulness to the effort, even if we have no tangible and final destination. In this sense, we can live happily ever after.

In the times of the pharoahs, Moses and the children of Israel set out on a journey to reach the Promised Land. But Moses and his entire generation were condemned to wander in the desert until they died, never setting foot inside the land promised to Abraham. This is clearly explained in the Midrash, a collection of early Hebrew commentaries on the scriptures, as follows:

"You doubted me," God tells the lawgiver, "But I forgave you that doubt.

...And They All Lived Happily Ever After

You doubted your own self and failed to believe in your own powers as a leader, and I forgave that also. But you lost faith in these people and doubted the divine possibilities of human nature. The loss of faith makes it impossible for you to enter the Promised Land."[1]

With faith in the possibility of a humane and positive future, we can move forward in joy and hope to build the kind of future we desire for ourselves and our children.

[1]Levi Olan, "The Nature of Man," in A.E. Millgram, ed., *Great Jewish Ideas*, (Washington, D.C.: B'nai B'rith Department of Adult Jewish Education, 1964).

VI.
The Future Makers

Echo Satellite trail in the Milky Way.

37. The Journey of a Thousand Miles

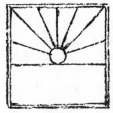 It is impossible to provide a complete guide to every new breakthrough, to every new possibility now emerging, but the sampling I have given should be sufficient to show that doomsday is not our fate. Instead of a future of ever dwindling options, it seems that we can choose, ever more freely, the kind of lifestyle we prefer, and that more and more of the world's population will have these choices as well.

Rampant proliferation of diverse goals and value systems, however, could be dangerous, leading to a repetition of the fragmentation and chaos into which the nations of the world were thrown when their hubris inspired them to build the great tower of Babel. The stability of society requires some underlying unity of purpose or intent. The necessary unity, it seems to me, lies in the common pursuit of excellence—*aretê*—and this notion has appeared repeatedly in the preceding chapters for precisely this reason. Although each of us has a very different idea of Quality, the fabric of human society and of the worlds we shall inhabit, will hold fast as long as we each remain faithful to our respective visions of Quality. Without attention to *aretê*, a space colony will fail as surely as a back-to-the-land commune.

The deliberate pursuit of excellence can bridge the apparent chasms between artist and scientist, humanist and technologist, the Romantic mind and the Classic mind. Such objects as crescent wrenches, microscopes, and radio telescopes have no meaning without some knowledge of the classical ideas they embody; yet if the people who fashioned these technological tools kept sight of *aretê* in their work, these objects could have an aesthetic quality which would make them appeal to the most romantic mind. Quality tools make not only good craftsmanship possible, but they also make a subtle but insistent appeal to reach for greater excellence. Conversely, an excellent painting, a moving symphony, a poem, or a sculpture that demands touching, has an elegance of form and a symmetry of parts and functional relationships which the most Classical mind can grasp, analyze, and appreciate.

Although underlying unity is essential, any attempt to impose it on a system of diverse elements runs the risk of failing to see the individual elements as unique and valuable — because of their differences. The result is, not unity, but a constraining and brutalizing uniformity which is blind to the uniqueness and wonder of specific moments in time, particular places, or individual living creatures. Fortunately, our physical survival does not require everyone to march in lockstep to the cadence of the majority or to the beat of a vociferous elite. The pursuit of excellence, in all its diversity, paradoxically provides a unifying force—precisely because it requires attention to the details of each event or thing—in a way which preserves and enhances what is unique, valuable, and beautiful about each moment, place, and person.[1]

The conscious effort to achieve excellence does not demand utopian perfection in everything we do. Because *aretè* commands attention to the whole, it recognizes that important values may be sacrificed if we place too much effort on a single detail; it recognizes when good enough is sufficient. We can eliminate a great deal of waste and inefficiency in our daily lives, in industrial projects, and in governmental programs if we recognize that, if something is not worth doing well, it probably shouldn't be done at all.

How can we go about implementing our visions of a humane and positive future? We need, first, to have a keen sense of what our values are; from there we can take the steps of inventing the goals each of us wants to pursue, leading to the design of specific projects we undertake to reach those goals.

Some of the most ironic and poignant works of literature deal with people who strive long and hard to attain some chosen goal, only to discover, when they have succeeded, that their goals have turned to dry ashes in the mouth. If we dedicate our efforts and resources to a consciously chosen goal, the risks of reaching the goal are high. Thus it is wise to be sure to know what we really value and desire. Careful introspection is an essential prerequisite for each of us to discover our values and to invent our goals. This search is perhaps done most effectively in conversation with close friends. I want to offer a few starting points for this kind of soul-searching.

What constitutes quality of life for you? Although everyone can immediately list a large number of things which interfere with their enjoyment of life, surprisingly few have given this matter conscious thought. One recent, popular song portrays an elderly southern gentleman describing his personal vision of quality of life in a very concise form:

> Ain't but three things in this world worth a solitary dime:
> Old dogs and children, and watermelon wine.[2]

For most of us a definition of quality of life would probably be less concise; for many, it would be nostalgic in content.

Having explored your own values in this way and identified some of the goals you wish to reach, a map of the territory is also necessary to arm

[1]E.F. Schumacher, "The Difference Between Unity and Uniformity," *CoEvolution Quarterly*, Fall 1975, pp. 52-59.
[2]Tom T. Hall, "Watermelon Wine," Mercury Records, 1975.

yourself with greater confidence. What is your image of time; as a flowing river whose embankments and course through the future have already been determined? Or is time more like a living, growing tree, with new branches and possibilities emerging in surprising places, a tree whose direction and shape of growth can be guided by pruning or grafting, a tree whose growing tips are the present moment, with the future as yet only latent in the existing branches and buds?

How do you feel about the future? Is it threatening, full of dismay and disappointment? Or is it joyous, playful, and hopeful? For many, the future inspires feelings of ambivalence:

> But I dream, and because I dream, I severely condemn, fear, and salute the future. It is the salute of a gladiator ringed by the indifference of the watching stars. Man himself is the sole arbiter of his own defeats and victories.[3]

Do you tend to view the present as a continuation of the past? Or do you view it as the beginning of the future? Alternatively, do you think of it as a unique and perennial watershed between what is and what might be, the loom on which dreams are spun and woven into reality? The creation of the future always happens in the present moment, which is itself transformed into the future of our dreams—or of our nightmares. The difference depends crucially on our constant awareness of the quality of our efforts and on our fidelity to our visions of what Quality means to us.

What elements of your present life-style are directly destructive to the good life for you? How could you change or alter these elements so that they make a positive contribution to your life? Are you really satisfied with your present job or profession? Could you make your job more satisfying and fulfilling, perhaps by deliberate efforts to inject excellence into your work? Would a different position, or an altogether different field of work, be more satisfying for you? One year of forty-hour workweeks adds up to about two thousand hours a year on the job. Multiplying those hours by the number of years you expect to continue working before retirement is just too many hours to waste in unpleasant or distasteful pursuits, whether or not longevity is dramatically increased in your lifetime.[4]

What ideas or concepts discussed in this book really appeal to you? Which ideas do you find unsettling or even repugnant? What can you learn about your own values and about yourself from the emotional reactions

[3]Loren Eisely, *The Invisible Pyramid*, (New York: Charles Scribner's Sons, 1970), p. 2.
[4]Richard N. Bolles, *What Color is Your Parachute? A Practical Manual for Job Seekers and Career Changers*, (Berkeley: Ten Speed Press, 1976). Presents a sensitive and pragmatic program to explore just what kind of work you would really like to do, and shows how to go about finding or, better yet, creating such a job. Had I not run across this manual, the present book might never have come to be.

these ideas have produced in you? To the extent that each of these developments would change the general social and economic context in the future, how could you make use of them in furthering of your own notion of quality of life?

In recent years, much has been made of "impact assessment" of new projects, programs, or even technologies. Properly considered, impact assessment is an integral part of the design process; it should not be viewed as a definitive judgment about whether or not a particular project is, or is not, a "good" thing. Impact assessment must begin from a clear statement of the values which motivated the specific goals of the project. The likely consequences of carrying out a particular design must be considered as thoroughly and imaginatively as possible, identifying both the positive contributions of the project to our intended goals, and the undesirable side effects which are contrary to our values and goals. The design must be modified to reduce the adverse impacts and enhance the positive benefits. The process is reiterated until an acceptable balance is reached, or until it becomes clear that the entire approach is unworkable.

None of the developments I have discussed in this book are complete or frozen in final form; both the design and the impact assessment for these ideas and new systems are still in a state of rapid conceptual evolution. To the extent that some of these developments will influence your own lifestyle ten or thirty or a hundred years from now, it is in your interest to become involved in the impact assessment process, whether or not you have technical expertise or knowledge of the design process. This type of constructive effort, it seems to me, should form the central core of public debate about new ideas and developments.

How do you feel about recycling your own newspapers, glass, steel cans, and aluminum cans? Since we face no intrinsic shortages of the mineral raw materials, recycling glass and metals is not a matter of long term economical survival but rather a question of environmental aesthetics. How do you feel about the aesthetics of the present waste disposal systems? How do you feel about the aesthetics of present forest management systems? Do the aesthetics of these industries matter?

How do you feel about the technological devices and systems in your life? Does the thought of repairing your own dripping faucet intimidate you; or would you feel comfortable and competent to overhaul your own car engine? Day to day competence in living in the modern world does not require all of us to be master automobile mechanics, electricians, plumbers, carpenters, and computer programmers. What does seem to be necessary, however, is a degree of understanding the basic concepts and ideas on which our technologies are based. These ideas and concepts must be understood experientially as well as intellectually. Understanding can be gained by doing at least some of the small jobs for yourself: fixing a leaky faucet;

filling your own gas tank and checking the oil level in the engine and the air pressure in the tires; replacing the filters in your air conditioner and furnace. Doing these things provides a sense of mastery over the technology on which we depend. The mental work of designing space habitats, overhauling the engines of a jet airplane, repairing a faulty computer, or carrying out a comprehensive physical examination of a patient is no different in kind from the thinking required to do these everyday tasks.

Farming and gardening are among the most future-oriented human activities. While the tangible rewards which motivate the gardener usually lie in the future, excellence in present efforts is an important additional benefit. How would you feel about growing some of your own food? Would it be an onerous task for you, or an enjoyable and creative pastime? If you live in a small apartment, have you considered growing some vegetables, flowers, or even dwarf fruit trees in planters? Have you considered the use of fruiting shrubs and trees in your landscaping instead of the more conventional ornamentals which bear no fruit?

The reinforcing effects of our physical posture and facial expressions, on our own moods and those of people around us, is widely recognized. A depressed and insecure person proclaims these feelings to the world by a sagging, beaten down posture; that very posture makes it more difficult to regain confidence and cheerfulness. Similarly, our attitudes toward the future are revealed in the colors and styles of the clothing we wear, in the ways we decorate our homes and workplaces. Dull, drab colors sap confidence.

Do your wardrobe and your decor reflect your attitudes and feelings about the present and the future? Do they inspire you, your family, your fellow workers, and your visitors to hope, or do they reinforce despair and depression? Even if you doubt that the future will be bright, you can help to make it positive and joyful by adding touches of brightness. The overall effect of your clothing and surroundings can be changed dramatically with a few inexpensive touches and accessories, if these are selected with attention to *arete*.

Social and political action is important in creating a humane and positive future. Constructive support for those developments which appeal to your personal sense of quality of life will be far more fruitful than spending your entire life, combatting and opposing developments which appeal to others, but do not appeal to you. Lifelong advocacy of a positive goal does not erode and destroy the spirit, even if attainment of the goal is frustrated; lifelong opposition extracts a heavy toll indeed. *Real injustices and evils must be opposed, but the focus should remain constructive.* Organizations which emphasize community development and personal rehabilitation are more effective, in the long run, than groups dedicated to ferreting out the evildoers responsible for the mess. Do the charities which you support include positive

215

social goals as well as negative goals? How do you feel about the relative proportions you give to educational and research foundations, to social rehabilitation work, to wilderness and wildlife preservation, to famine relief, to institutional and legislative reform?

Would you consider working in a space colony for a few years? Would you consider emigrating there permanently, with occasional vacation or business trips back to Earth? What features of life in space appeal to you? What features do you find distasteful? Many of the features described earlier in the book may yet turn out differently; others may vary tremendously from one colony to the next. If your children were to emigrate, under what circumstances would you go to visit them?

If the breakthrough in longevity results, would that change your attitudes toward the future? How would it affect your own life plans? Would you take longevity therapies? If you had a steady source of income from capital investments, would you continue to work in your present occupation? What other fields would you like to work in? Would you consider going back to school for a few years to learn a new profession?

Numerous books about the future have been published in the last ten or twenty years. Many of these are distinctly pessimistic in tone; a few verge on euphoria. All of these can be useful points of departure for lateral thinking about the future. While you read the more pessimistic books, I would suggest that you keep two questions in mind:

- What are the hidden assumptions which make the conclusions so pessimistic?
- Is the issue which the author considers to be a major problem really a problem at all?

When we read about proposed solutions to problems or about newly initiated programs to solve specific problems, we are accustomed to looking for flaws and trying to identify all the reasons the solution won't succeed. A far more constructive approach is to ask:

- Is the proposed solution consistent with my notions of quality of life? If not, how could the solution be altered to make it consistent?
- Whether or not I like the proposed solution, what other solutions might be possible?

After all, if one solution has been found, it is almost certain that other solutions can also be invented. Finding more solutions increases our options and provides greater security and flexibility for all of us.

Our elected officials and their appointees play important roles in shaping the future. Yet the word "future" is almost never heard in political campaigns. The rhetoric of most candidates seems to suggest that two years from today or four years or six years from today, the world will be essentially unchanged. Campaign promises seem to be based on an eternal today with only slight adjustments to be made, correcting the few things we recognize as inconvenient, unpleasant, or wrong about the present system.

What are the views of your own elected officials about the future? Do they consider it their role to create the future, to maintain the present forever, or to defend the past? Do they consider it their proper role to implement the goals chosen by the electorate they represent? Do they believe it is their job to select goals for the people, for their own good, or do they attempt to stimulate discussion about what the values of the electorate are and what goals would implement those values? Such questions, it seems to me, should be addressed by every elected or appointed governmental official and by every candidate for office. We, as voters, would be wise to demand answers.

What do you think you might be doing, and how do you imagine you will be living, ten years, twenty years, fifty years from today? What do you think the shape of society will be? What shape do you want it to be? What effects do you think some of the newer developments I have discussed will have on society, on your family, on you? What about other developments you have learned about from other sources? A common error many people make in thinking about the future is to imagine revolutionary and dramatic changes in the fabric of society, economics, and technology, and to imagine simultaneously that their own lives will somehow remain insulated and immune from all of these changes — that they will be doing the same job in the same way, commuting to work by the same means of transportation, wearing the same kinds of clothing, enjoying the same entertainments. Our schools teach our children nothing about the future and little enough about the present.[5]

How many children do you want? Whether or not you want to have children of your own, are you able to enjoy the company of children? Have you kept the natural playfulness of children? While it is certainly true that children can be incredibly cruel (largely because of a lack of sufficient maturity to see another person's viewpoint), children are a reliable test of our values: if you are troubled about the basic morality of some new development, imagine describing it thoroughly in terms which a five or six year old could comprehend. Having described it completely, would you feel ashamed or proud of what you told him or her?

In the final analysis, everything depends on what individual human beings do and on how well they do them. The journey of a thousand miles, the Chinese proverb tells us, begins with a single step. Each of us must take

[5] Alvin Toffler, ed., *Learning for Tomorrow: The Role of the Future in Education*, (New York: Random House, 1974).

that first step toward a humane and positive future by our own individual decisions to pursue our personal visions of Quality, with constant striving for excellence in our efforts to transform those visions into reality.

So the thing to do when working on a motorcycle, as in any other task, is to cultivate the peace of mind which does not separate one's self from one's surroundings. When that is done successfully then everything else follows naturally. Peace of mind produces right values, right values produce right thoughts. Right thoughts produce right actions and right actions produce work which will be a material reflection for others to see of the serenity at the center of it all . . . .

I think that if we are going to reform the world, and make it a better place to live in, the way we do it is not with talk about relationships of a political nature, which are inevitably dualistic, full of subjects and objects and their relationship to one another; or with programs full of things for other people to do. I think that kind of approach starts it at the end and presumes the end is the beginning. Programs of a political nature are important *end products* of social quality that can be effective only if the underlying structure of social values is right. The social values are right only if the individual values are right. The place to improve the world is first in one's own heart and head and hands, and then work outward from there . . . .

this is how any further improvement of the world will be done: by individuals making Quality decisions and that's all.[6]

---

[6]Robert M. Pirsig, *Zen and the Art of Motorcycle Maintenance: An Inquiry Into Values*, (New York: Bantam Books, 1974), pp. 290-1, p. 352.

38. Unanswered Questions

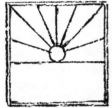Throughout this book I have emphasized possible solutions rather than problems. All too often the conventional wisdom of an era has asserted the impossibility of solving current topical difficulties, or has imagined that problems of the day were of crisis proportions, in places where no problem existed at all as seen in retrospect. It is undeniable that problems requiring solutions can be found throughout the globe. Some of these problems pose real obstacles for multitudes of people in their attempts to achieve what they consider to be higher quality of life. Here I want to touch briefly on some of the problems and questions which seem to merit particular attention and effort; to mention a few tantalizing possibilities, now emerging, which I have not discussed previously in this book; and to make some observations on research itself.

First and foremost, people need the material means of sustenance: food, water, clothing, shelter, and fuel. In the Third World an important contribution to greater stability and certainty in the supply of these essentials would be the development of orderly markets for the distribution of farm products throughout each region. Large price fluctuations from season to season are especially injurious to the small farmer who will continue to be the backbone of agricultural production for some time to come. Such fluctuations are especially disruptive when rents, taxes, and costs for raw materials and equipment rise gradually, but inexorably. It is precisely this problem in the United States, during the years following the Civil War, which led to the creation of the commodity futures market which served to smooth out sharp fluctuations in farm incomes. The development of continent-spanning railroads, with nationwide and worldwide markets for staple crops, provided additional stability and security. The types of institutions which would be appropriate to the needs of any particular Third World country must be examined on a case-by-case basis. The role of an international food bank, as has been proposed by many to minimize the human misery resulting from crop failures in any large region, needs careful study as well.

A far more sensitive political issue is that of land reform—without social disruption. Widespread ownership of land is as important in an agrarian economy as is widespread ownership of capital in an industrial economy. Devising institutional changes which would permit and encourage the transfer of large landholdings, owned by absentee landlords, to the indigenous rural population, especially the unlanded and the unemployed, is a major challenge to our ingenuity. Such programs must rely on expanded credit arrangements which presupposes stable income from season to season.Tackling both these problems together is more likely to provide satisfactory solutions and rapid results at an early date.

The economic interdependence of the global village can increase the security of any single district against the ravages of drought, famine, or the exhaustion of local sources of critical natural resources. Yet interdependence has its perils as well; such risks have been the subject of some of the doomsday literature. We have seen a brief war in the Middle East produce long queues for gasoline in the United States. We have seen a decrease in the anchovetta catch off the Pacific coast of Southern America produce rapid escalation in the price of beef and soybeans in Japan. It is not difficult to foresee that an economic crash in a Westen European nation could have major economic and political repercussions in the United States, Japan, Australia, and the Soviet Union.

Finding the means of increasing the resiliency of the interdependent, global economic system, especially in the industrialized nations (none of which is self-sufficient for its basic raw materials) is of vital importance. The first step is identifying the particularly sensitive points in the system (such as the anchovetta fisheries), followed by creative thinking about possible alternative elements which would be able to take over in times of crisis. The multinational corporations, often blamed for many of the problems of the world, may in fact turn out to be a valuable and effective tool for greater resiliency. Space industries in the next few decades may also assume major importance in enhancing global resiliency.

At the present time complex negotiations are underway to draft new international treaties governing economic use of the ocean's natural resources, including metal nodules on the deep ocean floors or oil deposits far out on the continental shelves. Until recent technological developments made use of the deep sea economically feasible, legal questions about the ownership and use of the ocean had been ignored. The situation in outer space is similar, although one major treaty on peaceful uses of outer space was signed by both the United States and the Soviet Union in 1967, before anyone anticipated really extensive economic development of the resources of the solar system. Innovative approaches to international law, which transcend the logic of Westphalia, are needed, both for space and for the oceans — very soon.

The world economic system is based no longer on natural resources but on human knowledge. Present economic theories, founded on notions of scarcity, are already inadequate for the purposes of making decisions on public policy. These theories will be hopeless for dealing with the economy, as capital machinery becomes less and less expensive. New formulations of economic theory are urgently needed, if we are to deal successfully with some of the thorny, new issues. Can an economic value, for example, be assigned to knowledge (the only commodity which increases when it is shared among more people)? What significance, if any, would the concept of trade balance have for a nation or a space colony which imports large quantities of food, energy, or raw materials, but exports only information?[1]

Increasingly, society is undertaking larger and larger scale projects, many of which require large monetary investments before anything of direct economic value can be produced. Solar Power Satellites are one such undertaking; how can they be financed? Several new alternatives have been proposed which could work satisfactorily for other long term projects as well.[2]

As strange and marvelous as some of the developments I have discussed here may seem to you, several other developments on the horizon may have still more profound effects on the shape of the future. These have been omitted due to insufficient space and time, and because their development as yet appears to be very primitive.

Biofeedback techniques offer a deeper understanding of the functioning of the nervous system as well as early practical applications for the treatment of hypertension, asthma, and chronic pain. Perhaps they may also assume major importance in the treatment of such dread diseases as cancer, for which stress appears to be a significant causative factor. Exploration of biofeedback techniques may lead to important new ideas about the relation between mind and body.

Psychic and paranormal phenomena, should their existence be convincingly demonstrated beyond mere coincidence, and communication with other terrestrial species, notably dolphins and chimpanzees, may have profound consequences for our phil and metaphysical views of reality. Warthogs appear ugly to most people; do dolphins consider us attractive in appearance? Would it matter to us what they thought of us?

A major breakthrough in artificial intelligence, considered likely in the next few decades by many of the leading workers in the field, would likewise expand our philosophy, and deepen our understanding of such difficult concepts as consciousness, intelligence, language, and perhaps personality. If a device can be built and programmed in such a way that it begins to learn from its environment, generating and testing new hypotheses about the world around it, our notions of consciousness and intelligence would surely

---

[1]Peter F. Drucker, *The Age of Discontinuity: Guidelines to Our Changing Society*, (New York: Harper and Row, 1968). Discusses the impact new knowledge has already had on the economic system, and outlines some of the difficult issues new economic theory must treat.

[2]Christian O. Basler, "Space Industrialization, the Challenge to Private Enterprise Capitalism" in Richard A. Van Patten, Paul Siegler and E.V.B. Stearns, eds., *The Industrialization of Space*, Vol. 36.

undergo a Copernican revolution. In the wake of artificial intelligence, we would soon have intelligent robots, stimulating further overhaul of economic theory.

Since computers that can "recognize" speech and produce recognizable speech from a keypunched text already exist, it would not be long before simultaneous, idiomatically correct, computer translation between any two human languages became a reality. An intelligent computer could become a "native" speaker of any language by "listening" to tape recordings of dozens or hundreds of natives to learn the language in the same self-correcting way in which human children now learn their mother tongues.

The possible synergisms of space technology and ocean technology have not yet been examined, except in the most superficial fashion as yet. A floating city, positioned near the equator, would be an ideal launch and retrieval site for an advanced space transportation system. Noise effects would not disturb the environment. The city could be registered as a vessel under the flag of a stable country, avoiding the economic risks of building a launch complex in a potentially unstable equatorial country. Internal law would protect the city from physical attack, which would constitute piracy. Recovery of raw materials, returned as foamed metal lifting bodies, would be facilitated. Such a city could raise its own food with a combination of hydroponic farming and mariculture, using waste heat from industrial processing to help marine growth. Power from space could be used for electrolysis of water, to provide liquid oxygen and liquid hydrogen for chemical rockets, and for export to countries moving toward a hydrogen fuel economy.

All of these developments presuppose the continual creation of new knowledge and the invention of new metaphors for the future. We are doomed to an age of scarcity only if we allow new knowledge, and cooperative efforts to use our knowledge, to become scarce through neglect of research. The knowledge on which the modern world is based did not fall from heaven like manna. It can only be created by diligent and intentional efforts.

When Christopher Columbus requested funding from King Ferdinand and Queen Isabella of Spain, for an oceanic expedition to find a new trade route to Cathay, he was asked to justify the expenditure to learned committees on three occasions. The rewards which actually resulted from Columbus's discovery of the New World were completely unpredictable and unforeseen. New crops such as potatoes, yams, beans, and corn and a new domestic animal, the turkey, revolutionized agriculture throughout Europe. The economic benefits to agriculture alone were far more important and long lasting than all the Inca gold which engorged the coffers of Spain for nearly a century.

Yet, all too often today, proposals for the funding of basic research are

222

required to justify that research in economic terms. "Just exactly what will be the results of your research, Professor? What will your findings be and what will they imply?" Until a significant expenditure of time and effort has been invested in a genuinely innovative idea, it is very difficult to describe it in a way which can be understood from the viewpoint of established theoretical frameworks. For this reason, many innovations come from unsupported, "bootleg" research. How much more might be possible with less skepticism of innovative ideas? The list of unanswered questions in the air is enormous; they represent for me a major source of hope for the more humane and positive future we desire.

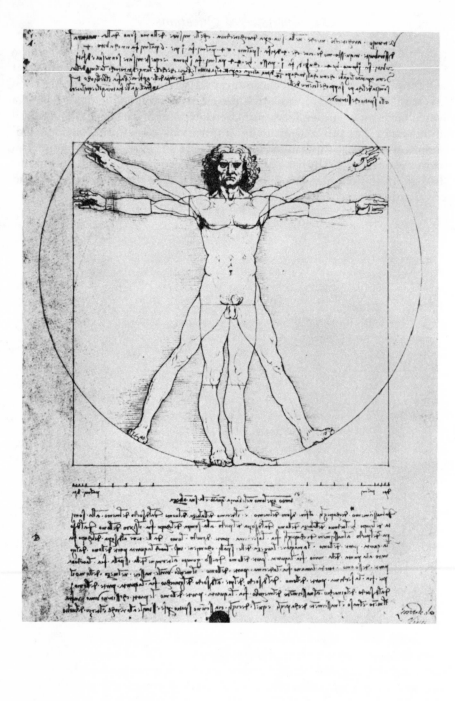

39. The Present Positive

Of all the marvelous inventions of the human mind, perhaps no other idea has been as enigmatic as the concept of time. Julian Jaynes has argued that the "spatialization of time" is essential to modern human consciousness.[1] Our everyday experience convinces us that we live immersed in time. We interpret our memories, extending back to childhood, as a sequence of processes of change, linked by our awareness of a self which maintains its identity through our lifetime. We can imagine the Sun rising tomorrow morning and we can visualize, in general terms, what we will experience as we get up, get dressed, eat breakfast, and do our work tomorrow. The past in our personal memories, and the future in our imaginations, seems to behave according to certain laws and patterns which we attribute to the operation of an external and objective time.

For the physicist time is a mathematical parameter which is chosen in such a way as to make the motion, or process under study, appear to be simple. Very simple kinds of motion, such as a tiny particle in free-flight, in a vacuum, far away from all other bodies, suggest the use of a time parameter in terms of which the motion is uniform, and Newton's first law of motion seems to be reduced to a tautology. But it is not a tautology, because once the time parameter has been defined in terms of the simple motion of a free, test particle, as I just described it, Newton predicts that other free particles of differing sizes, compositions, speeds, and directions of motion will also move uniformly with respect to the same definition of time.

We have come to define time, and to claim we have measured it, by observing the position of arrows on the face of a machine whose only purpose seems to be to consume energy in making those arrows rotate around and around and around monotonously. Certainly these clocks are indispensable for coordinating the activities of people in different places, engaged in a variety of activities. But have we really measured time? Are the past and the future real?

In the final analysis, only the present moment is real. We seem to have been provided with a continuing supply of "now's" as long as this mortal frame can draw breath. Yet the present instant is neither completely subjective nor completely objective. Like Quality it lies in the preintellectual

[1]Julian Jaynes, *The Origin of Consciousness in the Breakdown of the Bicameral Mind*, (Boston: Houghton Mifflin Company, 1976).

experiencing of our environment and of ourselves. It is in the present instant that being, becoming, remembering, imagining, loving, learning, and doing all have their existence and their significance.

This book has discussed the avenues available to us to build a humane and postive future. When will we arrive in that future? Since only the present moment is "real," this book has really been about the present. What is perhaps different about the present epoch in history is the degree to which, in contrast with earlier periods, we are free and able to create whatever kind of future we desire for ourselves and for our children. We cannot shirk responsibility to ourselves for creating that future; to do so leaves the future to be chosen for us by default. Now is the time for each of us to take up the task of creating the present positive, the dawn of the humane and positive futures toward which our values urge us.

"The age of nations is past," Teilhard de Chardin wrote before the beginning of the space age. "If mankind is not to perish, we must build the earth." This program can succeed only if we accept the richness of the open world we inhabit, if we discard the miserly and misanthropic assumptions of the zero-sum game, and if we guide our steps by the only reliable compass each of us knows — our own sense of *aretè*. These are the foundation stones. Each of us can begin to build our contributions, here and now, in the present moment; we need not wait until human nature has been totally perfected, until every last trace of the capacity to do evil has been eradicated from every human being. It is entirely possible that we may totally fail in our efforts; the risk makes the challenge of creating the world we seek real and important.

Despite the imperfections of the world, abundant reason for hope and confidence surrounds us. The indicators of hope can be found all around us if we care to use our knowledge with others who share our visions. Instead of blindly seeking answers to difficult questions, we should occasionally pause, to ask ourselves whether we have formulated the right questions.

The limitless bounty and the marvelous intricacies of the universe lie before us — waiting for us to discover them — to savor their beauty and mystery. Working with the rest of nature, guided by Quality, we can create endless possibilities of wonder and joy in an ever playful future. Occasionally we may become disheartened, temporarily unable to delight in ourselves, in each other, or in the rest of nature.

Even in dark moments we can join Hamlet in his melancholy, acknowledge the goodness of creation, and the miracle of consciousness incarnate in humanity:

> this goodly frame the earth . . .
> this most excellent canopy, the air . . .
> this brave o'erhanging firmament,
> this majestical roof fretted with golden fire . . . .

226

The Present Positive

What a piece of work is a man,
how noble in reason, how infinite in faculties;
in form and moving how express and admirable,
in action how like an angel, in apprehension how like a god:
the beauty of the world, the paragon of animals!

We are the Future Makers. Doomsday has been cancelled; the humane and positive future is ours to make.

J. Peter Vajk, Ph.D., is a physicist, futurist, author and lecturer. He received an A.B. in Physics from Cornell University in 1963 and a Ph.D. in Physics from Princeton University in 1968. Soon after receiving his doctorate, he accepted a position with the Theoretical Physics Division of Lawrence Livermore Laboratory in California to pursue research in Astrophysics and Cosmology.

While at Livermore, Dr. Vajk began to develop his commitment to the concepts of space industrialization and colonization. In his 1975 landmark paper, "The Impact of Space Colonization on World Dynamics," he investigated the effects of a vigorous space colonization program on future civilizations.

Early in 1976, Dr. Vajk joined Science Applications, Inc. (SAI) where he was a major contributor to a study entitled "Space Industrialization: 1980-2010" for the National Aeronautics and Space Administration's Marshall Space Flight Center. He also participated in a 1977 NASA study of manufacturing possibilities in space using non-terrestrial materials and was the principal investigator for a 1978 Department of Energy study researching alternative financing and management of a Solar Power Satellite program.

In addition to the 1978 release of *Doomsday Has Been Cancelled*, Dr. Vajk continues to publish technical papers and popular articles and to lecture extensively before college and professional audiences on the positive prospects of our venture into space for the long-range future of humanity.

Bibliography

Abelson, Philip H., ed. *Energy: Use, Conservation, and Supply*. Washington, D.C., American Association for the Advancement of Science, 1975.

_____. *Food: Politics, Economics, Nutrition, and Research*. Washington, D.C., American Association for the Advancement of Science, 1976.

Abelson, Philip H. and Hammond, Allen L., eds. *Materials: Renewable and Nonrenewable Resources*. Washington, D.C., American Association for the Advancement of Science, 1976.

Avis, Warren E. *Shared Participation*. Garden City, Doubleday, 1973.

Bahr, Howard M.; Chadwick, Bruce A.; and Thomas, Darwin L., eds. *Population, Resources, and the Future: Non-Malthusian Perspectives*. Provo, Brigham Young University Press, 1972.

Barnett, Harold J. and Morse, Chandler. *Scarcity and Growth: The Economics of Natural Resource Availability*. Baltimore, Resources for the Future and Johns Hopkins University Press, 1963.

Bernal, J.D. *The World, the Flesh, and the Devil*. Bloomington, Indiana University Press, 1969.

Berne, Eric. *Games People Play*. New York, Grove Press, 1964.

Berry, Adrian. *The Next Ten Thousand Years: A Vision of Man's Future in the Universe*. New York, E.P. Dutton, 1974; New York, New American Library, 1975.

Bicchieri, M.G., ed. *Hunters and Gatherers Today: A Socioeconomic Study of Eleven Such Cultures in the Twentieth Century*. New York, Holt Rinehart and Winston, 1972.

Bolles, Richard Nelson. *What Color is Your Parachute? A Practical Manual for Job Hunters and Career Changers*. Berkeley, Ten Speed Press, 1977.

Bracewell, Ronald N. *The Galactic Club: Intelligent Life in Outer Space*. San Francisco, W.H. Freeman, 1974, 1975.

Brand, Stewart, ed. *The Whole Earth Catalog: Access to Tools*. New York, POINT and Penguin Books, 1971, 1975.

_____. *The Whole Earth Epilog: Access to Tools*. New York, POINT and Penguin Books, 1974.

_____. *Space Colonies*. New York, POINT and Penguin Books, 1977.

Bronowski, Jacob. *Science and Human Values*. New York, Harper & Row, 1972.

_____. *The Ascent of Man*. Boston, Little Brown, 1974.

Bry, Adelaide. *est: Sixty Hours That Transform Your Life*. New York, Harper & Row, 1976.

Capra, Fritjof. *The Tao of Physics*. Berkeley, Shambhala Publications, 1975; New York, Bantam Books, 1977.

Carson, Rachael L. *Silent Spring*. Boston, Houghton Mifflin, 1962; New York, Fawcett World Library, 1973, 1977.

Chase, Allen. *The Legacy of Malthus: The Social Costs of the New Scientific Racism*. New York, Alfred A. Knopf, 1977.

Clark, Kenneth. *Civilization: A Personal View*. New York, Harper & Row, 1970.

Clarke, Arthur C. *Profiles of the Future: An Inquiry Into the Limits of the Possible*. New York, Harper & Row, 1973; New York, Popular Library, 1977.

_____. *Rendezvous with Rama*. New York, Harcourt Brace Jovanovich, 1973; New York, Ballantine Books, 1976.

Collins, Michael. *Carrying the Fire: An Astronaut's Journeys*. New York, Farrar, Strauss, and Giroux, 1974; New York, Ballantine Books, 1975.

Cole, H.S.D.; Freeman, Christopher; Jahoda, Marie; and Pavitt, K.L.R., eds. *Models of Doom: A Critique of the Limits to Growth*, New York, Universe Books, 1973.

Commoner, Barry. *The Closing Circle*. New York, Alfred A. Knopf, 1971; New York, Bantam, 1972.

_____. *The Poverty of Power*. New York, Alfred A. Knopf, 1976; New York, Bantam, 1977.

Cooke, Alistair. *Alistair Cooke's America*. New York, Alfred A. Knopf, 1973.

Cooper, Henry S.F., Jr. *A House in Space*. New York, Holt Rinehart and Winston, 1976.

Criswell, David R., ed. *Lunar Utilization: Special Session of the Seventh Annual Lunar Science Conference*. Houston, Lunar Science Institute, 1976.

Daly, Herman E., ed. *Toward a Steady State Economy*. San Francisco, W.H. Freeman, 1973.

Darden, Lloyd. *The Earth in the Looking Glass*. Garden City, Anchor Press, 1974.

Drucker, Peter F. *The Future of Industrial Man*. New York, New American Library.

_____. *The Effective Executive*. New York, Harper & Row, 1966, 1967.

_____. *The Age of Discontinuity: Guidelines to Our Changing Society*. New York, Harper & Row, 1969.

Dubos, René. *So Human an Animal*. New York, Charles Scribner's Sons, 1968.

_____. *A God Within*. New York, Charles Scribner's Sons, 1973.

_____. *Of Human Diversity*. Worcester, Clark University Press, 1974.

Erhlich, Paul R. *The Population Bomb*. New York, Ballantine Books, 1968, 1971.

Erhlich, Paul R. and Anne H. *The End of Affluence: A Blueprint for Your Future*. New York, Ballantine Books, 1974.

_____. *Population, Resources, and Environment: Issues in Human Ecology*. San Francisco, W.H. Freeman, 1972.

Eiseley, Loren. *The Immense Journey*. New York, Random House, 1957.

_____. *The Unexpected Universe*. New York, Harcourt Brace Jovanovich, 1972.

_____. *The Invisible Pyramid*. New York, Charles Scribner's Sons, 1972.

Esfandiary, F.M. *Optimism One: The Emerging Radicalism*. New York, W.W. Norton, 1970.

_____. *Up-Wingers*. New York, John Day, 1973; New York, Popular Library, 1977.

_____. *Telespheres*. New York, Popular Library, 1977.

Falk, Richard A. *A Study of Future Worlds*. New York, Macmillan, 1975.

Fallaci, Oriana. *If the Sun Dies*. New York, Atheneum, 1965.

Feinberg, Gerald. *The Prometheus Project*. Garden City, Doubleday, 1968.

Firth, Raymond. *Primitive Polynesian Economy*. New York, W.W. Norton, 1975.

Forrester, Jay W. *World Dynamics*. Cambridge, Wright-Allen Press, 1971, 1973.

Fuller, R. Buckminster. *Utopia or Oblivion: The Prospects for Humanity*. New York, Bantam Books, 1969.

_____. *Operating Manual for Spaceship Earth*. New York, Touchstone Books, 1970; New York, E.P. Dutton, 1977.

_____. *Untitled Epic Poem on the History of Industrialization*. New York, Touchstone Books, 1971.

_____. *Synergetics: Adventures in the Geometry of Thinking*. New York, Macmillan, 1971.

Georgescu-Roegen, Nicholas. *The Entropy Law and the Economic Process*. Cambridge, Harvard University Press, 1971, 1975.

_____. *Energy and Economic Myths*. New York, Pergamon Press, 1977.

Goldsmith, Edward; Allen, Robert; Allaby, Michael; Davoll, John; and Lawrence, Sam. *Blueprint for Survival*. Boston, Houghton Mifflin, 1972.

Gordon, Thomas. *PET: Parent Effectiveness Training*. New York, Peter H. Wyden, 1970.

Grey, Jerry, ed. *Space Manufacturing Facilities (Space Colonies)*. New York, American Institute of Aeronautics and Astronautics; Vol. I, 1977; Vol. 2, 1978.

Handlin, Oscar and Mary F. *The Wealth of the American People: A Hisotry of American Affluence*. New York, McGraw-Hill, 1975.

Harris, Thomas. *I'm OK – You're OK*. New York, Harper & Row, 1967.

Heilbroner, Robert L. *An Inquiry Into the Human Prospect*. New York, W.W. Norton, 1974.

Heppenheimer, T.A. *Colonies in Space*. Harrisburg, Stackpole Books, 1977; New York, Bantam Books, 1978.

Hoffer, Eric. *The Ordeal of Change*. New York, Harper & Row, 1963.

_____. *The Temper of Our Time*. New York, Harper & Row, 1967.

_____. *First Things, Last Things*. New York, Harper & Row, 1971.

_____. *Reflections on the Human Condition*. New York, Harper & Row, 1973.

Hubbard, Barbara Marx. *The Hunger of Eve: A Woman's Odyssey Into the Future*. Harrisburg, Stackpole Books, 1976.

Huddle, Norie; Reich, Michael; with Stiskin, Nahum. *Island of Dreams: Environmental Crisis in Japan*. New York, Autumn Press, 1975.

Illich, Ivan D. *Celebration of Awareness: A Call for Institutional Awareness*. Garden City, Doubleday, 1971.

James, Muriel and Jongeward, Dorothy. *Born to Win: Transactional Analysis with Gestalt Experiments*. Reading, Addison-Wesley Publishing, 1971.

Jantsch, Erich. *Design for Evolution: Self-Organization and Planning in the Life of Human Systems*. New York, George Braziller, 1975.

Jaynes, Julian. *The Origin of Consciousness in the Breakdown of the Bicameral Mind*. Boston, Houghton Mifflin, 1976.

Jeavons, John. *How to Grow More Vegetables Than You Ever Thought Possible on Less Land Than You Can Imagine*. Palo Alto, Ecology Action of the Midpeninsula, 1974.

Johnson, Richard D. and Holbrow, Charles, eds. *Space Settlements: A Design Study*. Washington, D.C., U.S. Government Printing Office, 1977.

Jonas, Hans. *The Gnostic Religion: The Message of the Alien God and the Beginnings of Christianity*. Boston, Beacon Press, 1963.

Kahn, Herman; Brown, William; and Martel, Leon. *The Next 200 Years: A Scenario for America and for the World*. New York, William Morrow, 1976.

Kelso, Louis O. and Adler, Mortimer, J. *The Capitalist Manifesto*. Westport, Greenwood Press, 1958, 1975.

_____. *The New Capitalists*. Westport, Greenwood Press, 1961, 1975.

Kelso, Louis O. and Hetter, Patricia. *How to Turn Eighty Million Workers Into Capitalists on Borrowed Money*. New York, Random House, 1967.

Kiley, John Cantwell. *Self-Rescue*. New York, McGraw-Hill, 1977.

Land, George T.L. *Grow or Die: The Unifying Principle of Transformation*. New York, Dell Publishing, 1974.

Lappé, Frances Moore and Collins, Joseph. *Food First! Beyond the Myth of Scarcity*. Boston, Houghton Mifflin, 1977.

Laszlo, Ervin. *A Strategy for the Future: The Systems Approach to World Order*. New York, George Braziller, 1974.

_____. *Goals for Mankind: A Report to the Club of Rome on the New Horizons of Global Community*. New York, E.P. Dutton, 1977.

Leonard, George B. *The Transformation: A Guide to the Inevitable Changes in Humankind*. New York, Delacorte Press, 1972.

Lewis, C.S. *Out of the Silent Planet; Perelandra; That Hideous Strength*. A trilogy. New York, Macmillan, 1958.

Lilly, John C. *Simulations of God: The Science of Belief*. New York, Simon and Schuster, 1975; New York, Bantam Books, 1976.

Lindbergh, Anne Morrow. *Earth Shine*. New York, Harcourt Brace Jovanovich, 1969, 1970.

Lindbergh, Charles A. *We*. New York, Putnam's Sons, 1927.

Maddox, John. *The Doomsday Syndrome*. New York, McGraw-Hill, 1972.

Malthus, Thomas Robert. *On Population*. Edited and Introduced by Gertrude Himmelfarb. New York, Modern Library, 1960.

Maslow, Abraham H. *Motivation and Personality*. New York, Harper & Row, 1954, 1970.

_____. *Toward a Psychology of Being*. 2nd ed. New York, Van Nostrand Reinhold, 1968.

McDivitt, James F. and Manners, Gerald. *Minerals and Men: An Exploration of the World of Minerals*. Baltimore, Resources for the Future and Johns Hopkins University Press, 1965, 1974.

McHale, John. *The Ecological Context*. New York, George Braziller, 1970.

McHarg, Ian L. *Design with Nature*. Garden City, Natural History Press, 1971.

Meadows, Dennis L. and Donnela H.; Randers, Jorgen; and Behrens, William W. III. *Dynamics of Growth in a Finite World*. Cambridge, Wright-Allen Press, 1973.

_____. *The Limits to Growth*. New York, Universe Books, 1972.

Meininger, Jut. *Success Through Transactional Analysis*. New York, Grosset & Dunlap, 1973.

Mesarovic, Mihajlo and Pestel, Eduard. *Mankind at the Turning Point: The Second Report to the Club of Rome*. New York, E.P. Dutton and Reader's Digest Press, 1974.

Moore, Patrick. *The Next Fifty Years in Space*. New York, Taplinger Publishing, 1976.

Murray, Bruce C. *Navigating the Future*. New York, Harper & Row, 1975.

Niven, Larry. *Ringworld*. New York, Ballantine Books, 1975.

Niven, Larry and Pournelle, Jerrry. *The Mote in God's Eye*. New York, Simon and Schuster, 1974; New York, Pocket Books, 1975.

_____. *Lucifer's Hammer*. New York, Playboy Press, 1977.

O'Leary, Brian T. *The Making of an Ex-Astronaut*. Boston, Houghton Mifflin, 1970.

O'Neill, Gerard K. *The High Frontier: Human Colonies in Space*. New York, William Morrow, 1977; New York, Bantam Books, 1978.

Ophuls, William, ed. *Ecology and the Politics of Scarcity: Prologue to a Political Theory of Steady State*. San Francisco, W.H. Freeman, 1977.

Osborn, Fairfield. *Our Plundered Planet*. Boston, Little Brown, 1948.

Park, Charles F., Jr. *Earthbound: Minerals, Energy, and Man's Future*. San Francisco, Freeman Cooper, 1975.

Pearce, Joseph Chilton. *The Crack in the Cosmic Egg*. New York, Julian Press, 1971; New York, Pocket Books, 1972.

_____. *Exploring the Crack in the Cosmic Egg: Split Minds and Meta-Realities*. New York, Julian Press, 1974; New York, Pocket Books, 1975.

Peter, Laurence J. *The Peter Prescription: How to Make Things Go Right*. New York, William Morrow, 1972.

Peter, Laurence J. and Hull, Raymond. *The Peter Principle: Why Things Always Go Wrong*. New York, William Morrow, 1969.

Pirsig, Robert M. *Zen and the Art of Motorcycle Maintenance: An Inquiry Into Values*. New York, William Morrow, 1974; New York, Bantam Books, 1974.

Platt, John R. *The Step to Man*. New York, John Wiley and Sons, 1966.

Pournelle, Jerry. *High Justice*. New York, Pocket Books, 1977.

Powell, John. *The Secret of Staying in Love*. Niles, Argus Communications, 1974.

_____. *Why Am I Afraid to Tell You Who I Am?* Niles, Argus Communications, 1975.

Priestley, John B. *Man and Time*. Garden City, Doubleday, 1964.

Reining, Priscilla and Tinker, Irene, eds. *Population: Dynamics, Ethics, and Policy*. Washington, D.C., American Association for the Advancement of Science, 1975.

Rosenfeld, Albert. *Prolongevity*. New York, Alfred A. Knopf, 1976.

Sagan, Carl. *The Cosmic Connection: An Extraterrestrial Perspective*. Garden City, Doubleday, 1973; New York, Dell, 1975.

_____. *The Dragons of Eden*. New York, Random House, 1977.

Salkeld, Robert. *War and Space*. Englewood Cliffs, Prentice-Hall, 1970.

Satir, Virginia. *Peoplemaking*. Palo Alto, Science and Behavior Books, 1972.

Schumacher, E.F. *Small is Beautiful: Economics As If People Mattered*. New York, Harper & Row, 1973.

Schurr, Sam H., ed. *Energy, Economic Growth, and the Environment*. Baltimore, Resources for the Future and Johns Hopkins University Press, 1972.

Sheehy, Gail. *Passages: Predictable Crises of Adult Life*. New York, E.P. Dutton, 1974, 1976.

Smith, Adam. *An Inquiry Into the Nature & Causes of the Wealth of Nations*. Edited by Edwin Cannan. Chicago, University of Chicago Press, 1977.

Soleri, Paolo. *The Bridge Between Matter and Spirit is Matter Becoming Spirit*. Garden City, Anchor Books, 1973.

Stavrianos, L.S. *The Promise of the Coming Dark Age*. San Francisco, W.H. Freeman, 1976.

Stine, G. Harry. *The Third Industrial Revolution*. New York, G.P. Putnam's Sons, 1975.

Stout, Ruth. *How to Have a Green Thumb Without an Aching Back: A New Method of Mulch Gardening*. New York, Galahad Books, 1965, 1968; New York, Cornerstone Library, 1973, 1976.

Taylor, Ted B. and Humpstone, Charles C. *The Restoration of Earth*. New York, Harper & Row, 1973.

Teilhard de Chardin, Pierre. *The Phenomenon of Man*. New York, Harper and Brothers, 1959.

_____. *Human Energy*. New York, Harcourt Brace Jovanovich, 1969.

_____. *Activation of Energy*. New York, Harcourt Brace Jovanovich, 1971.

_____. *Christianity and Evolution*. New York, Harcourt Brace Jovanovich, 1971.

_____. *Hymn of the Universe*. New York, Harper & Row, 1969.

_____. *On Suffering*. New York, Harper & Row, 1975.

_____. *Building the Earth*. New York, Avon Books, 1969.

Theobald, Robert. *Futures Conditional*. Indianapolis, Bobbs-Merril, 1972.

Thomas, Lewis. *The Lives of a Cell: Notes of a Biology Watcher*. New York, Viking Press, 1974; New York, Bantam Books, 1975.

Thompson, William Irwin. *Passages About Earth: An Exploration of the New Planetary Culture*. New York, Harper & Row, 1973, 1974.

Tinbergen, Jan; Dolman, Anthony J.; and Van Ettinger, Jan, eds. *Reshaping the International Order: A Report to the Club of Rome*. New York, E.P. Dutton, 1976.

Toffler, Alvin. *Future Shock*. New York, Random House, 1970.

————. *The Eco-Spasm Report*. New York, Bantam Books, 1975.

————, ed. *Learning for Tomorrow: The Role of the Future in Education*. New York, Random House, 1974; New York, Vintage Books, 1974.

Tuccille, Jerome. *Here Comes Immortality*. New York, Stein and Day, 1973.

Vacca, Roberto. *The Coming Dark Age*. Garden City, Doubleday, 1974.

Van Patten, Richard A.; Siegler, Paul; and Stearns, E.V.B., eds. *The Industrialization of Space*. Vol. 36. San Diego, Advances in the Astronautical Sciences, American Astronautical Society, 1978.

Wagar, W. Warren. *Building the City of Man: Outlines of a World Civilization*. San Francisco, W.H. Freeman, 1971.

Wahlroos, Sven. *Family Communications: A Guide to Emotional Health*. New York, Macmillan, 1974.

Ward, Barbara. *The Home of Man*. New York, W.W. Norton, 1976.

Watt, Kenneth E.F. *The Titanic Effect*.

Webb, James E. *Space Age Management: The Large Scale Approach*. New York, McGraw-Hill, 1969.

Wescott, Roger T. *The Divine Animal: An Exploration of Human Potentiality*. New York, Funk and Wagnalls, 1969.

Wood, Barry. *The Magnificent Frolic*. Philadelphia, Westminster Press, 1970.

JOURNALS FOR CURRENT AWARENESS

American Scientist (bimonthly), Sigma Xi, The Scientific Research Society of North America, 345 Whitney Avenue, New Haven, Connecticut 06511. $15 per year.

CoEvolution Quarterly (quarterly), POINT, P.O. Box 428, Sausalito, California 94965. $12 per year.

Human Nature (monthly), 757 Third Avenue, New York, N.Y. 10001. $15 per year.

The Journal of the New Alchemists (annually), The New Alchemy Institute, P.O. Box 432, Woods Hole, Massachusetts 02543. $20 per year.

L-5 News (monthly), L-5 Society, Inc., 1620 North Park Avenue, Tucson, Arizona 85719. $20 per year ($15 for students).

Organic Gardening (monthly), Rodale Press, Inc., 33 East Minor Street, Emmaus, Pennsylvania 18049. $9 per year.

Science (weekly), American Association for the Advancement of Science, 1515 Massachusetts Ave. NW, Washington, D.C. 20005. $31 per year ($21 for students).

Scientific American (monthly), 415 Madison Avenue, New York, N.Y. 10017. $18 per year.

Smithsonian (monthly), Smithsonian Associates, 900 Jefferson Drive, Washington D.C. 20560. $12 per year.

Index

Age of Substitutability, 83-84
Aging: causes of, 190; cross-linking in, 192-193; genetic mechanisms of, 190-193; Hayflick limit and, 191; hormone role in, 191-192; oxygen atoms in, 192-193; quality of life and, 194; therapy of, 193
Agriculture: in space colonies, 143; technology in, 73-77
Albedo, 116
Animals: breeding of, 76; disease control and food production, 77
Apollo program, 109-110
Arms race, 54-55
Asteroids: mining in, 165; raw materials on, 131-132, 135
Atmosphere: composition of, 31-32; in weather forecasting, 115-116

Barnett, Harold, 50
Biodynamic/French intensive method, 75, 77
Biofeedback, 221
Biosphere, 31; balances in, 59, 61; boundaries of, 45; evolution of, 33-35; extent of, 32-33; pollution of, 71; size of, 64
Bjorksten, Johan, 193
By-products: of industrial processes, 101-104

Carrying capacity, 63-65
Chemical energy, 166
Climax forest, 65
Closed system, 44
Coal: environmental concerns with, 82; mine wastes of, 84
Collins, J., 70-71
Communication: by computers, 222; feelings and, 185-187; improved technology of, 97. See also Communication satellites
Communication satellites: capacity of, 116-117; economic value of, 112; military uses of, 158
Computers: communication by, 222; economic growth predicted by, 51-52; improved efficiency of, 96-97
Consciousness: evolution of, 37, 183-184
Conservation: danger of, 59; energy policy and, 93
Cooperation: as root of economic wealth, 49, 52
Copper shortage, 79-80

Cousteau, Jacques-Yves, 168
Cross-linking: of genes, 192-193

Death: causes of, 190; genetic mechanisms of, 190-193; importance to civilization, 189
de Chardin, Teilhard, 226
DECO, 192
Deforestation, 152-153
Denckla, W. Donner, 192
DNA: recombinant, 161-162
Doomsday prophecies, 25-28; arms race, 54-55; consequences of economic development, 152-153; deforestation, 152-153; depletion of nonrenewable resources, 43, 50-52, 54-55, 79; despair, 11; energy crisis, 88; environmental despoilation, 25, 71; famine, 25, 68; food production, 26-28, 67-68, 70; imperfection of human nature, 173-175, 183; increased longevity, 193-194; land scarcity, 50, 54-55; Malthus views, 25-28; militarization in space, 157; nuclear holocaust, 25, 149-150; population, 25-28, 63-65, 205; recombinant DNA experimentation, 161-162; social inequities, 182; social instability, 211; socioeconomic collapse, 206; suffering, 12-13; technology as evil, 15; terrestrial chauvinism, 109; waste disposal problem, 103; zero-sum games, 53-55
Drake, Frank, 203
Dubos, René, 60

Earth: atmosphere of, 31-32; balances on, 59-61; carrying capacity of, 63-65; creation of, 33; extent of, 31; geomagnetic field of, 32; mass inconstancy of, 32. See also Biosphere
Ecology, 59
Economic issues: Employee Stock Ownership Plans, 198; financing Solar Power Satellites, 221; in food production, 219-220; knowledge and, 220-221; labor role, 197; land reform, 219-220; money, 196; in Polynesia, 195-196; roots of wealth, 49-52; in space colonies, 149, 151; in space manufacture, 119-121; taxes, 198-199
Ecosystem, 65
Efficiency: of energy conversion, 91-93; in industrial processing, 101-104; in utilization of matter, 95-99

235